T0373857

REDRAFTING CONSTITUTIONS IN DEMOCRATIC REGIMES

Growing public discontent with the performance and quality of many contemporary democracies makes them vulnerable to popular pressures to profoundly transform or replace their constitutions. However, there is little systematic academic discussion on the legal and political challenges that these events pose to democratic principles and practices. This book, a collaborative effort by legal scholars and political scientists, analyzes these challenges from an interdisciplinary and comparative perspective. It fills a theoretical vacuum by examining the possibility that constitutions might be replaced within a democratic regime, while exploring the conditions under which these processes are more compatible or less compatible with democratic principles. It also calls attention to the real-world political importance of the phenomenon, because recent episodes of constitutional redrafting in countries including Kenya, Poland, Venezuela, and Hungary suggest that some aspects of these processes may be associated with either the improvement or the gradual erosion of democracy.

GABRIEL L. NEGRETTO is Associate Professor, Pontificia Universidad Católica de Chile. Specializing in comparative constitutional politics, institutional change, and democratization, he is the author of *Making Constitutions: Presidents, Parties, and Institutional Choice in Latin America* (2013). Negretto has been a consultant to various international organizations and has held visiting appointments at several universities in the United States, Europe, and Latin America.

COMPARATIVE CONSTITUTIONAL LAW AND POLICY

Series Editors

Tom Ginsburg *University of Chicago*
Zachary Elkins *University of Texas at Austin*
Ran Hirschl *University of Toronto*

Comparative constitutional law is an intellectually vibrant field that encompasses an increasingly broad array of approaches and methodologies. This series collects analytically innovative and empirically grounded work from scholars of comparative constitutionalism across academic disciplines. Books in the series include theoretically informed studies of single constitutional jurisdictions, comparative studies of constitutional law and institutions, and edited collections of original essays that respond to challenging theoretical and empirical questions in the field.

Books in the Series

Redrafting Constitutions in Democratic Regimes

THEORETICAL AND COMPARATIVE PERSPECTIVES

Edited by

GABRIEL L. NEGRETTO

Pontificia Universidad Católica de Chile

CAMBRIDGE
UNIVERSITY PRESS

CAMBRIDGE
UNIVERSITY PRESS

University Printing House, Cambridge CB2 8BS, United Kingdom

One Liberty Plaza, 20th Floor, New York, NY 10006, USA

477 Williamstown Road, Port Melbourne, VIC 3207, Australia

314-321, 3rd Floor, Plot 3, Splendor Forum, Jasola District Centre, New Delhi - 110025, India

103 Penang Road, #05-06/07, Visioncrest Commercial, Singapore 238467

Cambridge University Press is part of the University of Cambridge.

It furthers the University's mission by disseminating knowledge in the pursuit of
education, learning and research at the highest international levels of excellence.

www.cambridge.org
Information on this title: www.cambridge.org/9781108813778
DOI: 10.1017/9781108885287

© Gabriel L. Negretto 2020

First published 2020
First paperback edition 2022

A catalogue record for this publication is available from the British Library

ISBN 978-1-108-83984-6 Hardback
ISBN 978-1-108-81377-8 Paperback

In memory of Ana María Bejarano

Contents

Tables

Contributors

Ana María Bejarano (†) was Associate Professor of Political Science, University of Toronto.

Joel I. Colón-Ríos is Professor of Law, Victoria University of Wellington.

Tom Ginsburg is Leo Spitz Professor of International Law and Professor of Political Science, University of Chicago.

Thorvaldur Gylfason is Professor of Economics, University of Iceland.

David Landau is Mason Ladd Professor of Law and Associate Dean for International Programs, Florida State University.

Christina Murray is Professor of Constitutional and Human Rights Law, University of Cape Town.

Gabriel L. Negretto is Professor of Political Science, Instituto de Ciencia Política, Pontificia Universidad Católica de Chile.

William Partlett is Associate Professor of Law, Melbourne Law School.

Renata Segura is Deputy Director for Latin America and the Caribbean, International Crisis Group.

Solongo Wandan was Assistant Professor of Political Science at the University of Oklahoma and currently works as Advisor in Energy and Climate Policy.

Acknowledgments

This book grew out of a panel I organized for the American Political Science Association Meeting in September 2015 in San Francisco entitled "Constitution Making in Democratic Constitutional Orders." This event was followed by an international conference on the same topic held in August 2016 at the Centro de Investigación y Docencia Económicas (CIDE) in Mexico City. I would like to thank Joel Colón-Ríos, Todd Eisenstadt, Zachary Elkins, Juan F. González-Bertomeu, Thorvaldur Gylfason, David Landau, William Partlett, Xisca Pou, Andrea Pozas-Loyo, Julio Ríos-Figueroa, and Solongo Wandan for their important initial contributions to this project. I would also like to extend my appreciation for the financial support that CIDE provided for the conference as well as the personal encouragement of its Director General, Sergio López Ayllón. Jorge Olmos Camarillo provided research assistance and Cirenia Hernández Romero invaluable logistic support. Finally, I wish to thank the editors of the *International Journal of Constitutional Law*, who published material from Chapter 5 in Volume 18, Issue 1, 2020.

New Constitutions in Democratic Regimes

Gabriel L. Negretto

Democracies may from time to time need a radical overhaul of existing constitutional structures to overcome a political crisis, improve governability, increase popular control and influence over collective decisions, or modernize their basic institutions. Yet most democratic constitutions lack explicit provisions regulating their own replacement, following the traditional view in constitutional theory that new constitutions are created outside the law, at the founding moments of a political order. In the face of this legal vacuum, government and opposition may acknowledge the necessity of reform, negotiate the content of revisions, and reach an agreement on politically inclusive rules to govern the process. The lack of replacement clauses, however, may end up blocking a change desired by citizens, exacerbating political conflict, or facilitating partisan manipulation of the process. These outcomes might degrade instead of improving the quality of democracy or, in the worst case, even compromise the continuity of the regime.

This volume is a collaborative effort by legal scholars and political scientists to address the juridical problems and political challenges involved in the replacement of constitutions within a democratic regime from an interdisciplinary and comparative perspective. In particular, it provides a conceptual map and a comparative framework of analysis to understand the different alternatives available to channel these processes, the consistency of these alternatives with the principles of democracy and constitutionalism, and the possible conditions that determine whether a constitutional replacement may result in the strengthening or weakening of democracy.

There is a vast body of literature on the exceptional creation of new constitutions at times of deep political change, as well as on the more frequent and ordinary amendment of democratic constitutions. There are also works that consider constitutional replacements and amendments as alternatives within a broader notion of "constitutional change," without distinguishing among the various environments in which these transformations can take place.[1] Constitutional scholars and political scientists, however, have traditionally paid little attention to the possibility that constitutions might be replaced within a democratic regime, thus neglecting the special features of these processes and the challenges they pose to democratic principles and democratic practices. This study thus seeks to fill a theoretical vacuum in the comparative analysis of constitution making. It also aims to call attention to the real-world political importance of the phenomenon. Democratic constitutional replacements are significant political events because many democracies today face pressures to revise their basic institutions, and recent episodes of constitutional redrafting in places as far apart as Kenya and Poland, or Venezuela and Hungary offer lessons about the factors that may lead to the success or failure of these experiences from the point of view of deepening the liberal and other dimensions of democracy.

The volume is divided into general issues and case studies. Part I discusses the conceptual problems involved in the idea of constitution making through law, the design of replacement clauses, the role of the judiciary, and the impact of direct citizen participation and elite cooperation during constitutional rewrites on democratization. Part II provides the analysis of particular episodes of democratic constitution making in Latin America, Western Europe, Eastern Europe, Africa, and Asia, highlighting the different paths to and outcomes of constitutional replacement in democratic orders. This introductory chapter discusses the phenomenon of constitutional redrafting in democratic orders around the world and the contributions each chapter in the book makes to an understanding of the factors leading to the adoption of new constitutions in the context of free and fair elections, the procedural and political features of these episodes, and the relationship between constitutional replacements in democratic regimes, democratic theory, and democratization.

I CONSTITUTIONAL REPLACEMENTS UNDER DEMOCRATIC INSTITUTIONS

Research on constitutional origins in political and legal theory has often focused on the adoption of the first democratic constitution that emerged after a disruptive political event, such as the creation of a new state after independence, a revolution, or a regime transition. Most of these cases fall into what Klein and Sajó (2012) call "ex nihilo" models of constitutional creation, in which a new constitutional text symbolizes the displacement of old political and legal structures. Constitutional replacements can also, however, occur in the context of preexisting democratic

---

[1] A recent, non-exhaustive list of works on these topics includes Miller (2010); Oliver and Fusaro (2011); Contiades (2013); Arato (2016); Choudhry and Ginsburg (2016); Landau and Lerner (2019); and Albert (2019).

institutions. Historically, these changes have not been as frequent as those that have taken place during the creation of a new state, a revolution, or a regime transition, but as we will see, they are sufficiently numerous to warrant scholarly attention.[2] In addition, given citizens' growing dissatisfaction with the performance and quality of contemporary democracies across various countries and regions, it is likely that this phenomenon will increase in the future, particularly (but not only) where representative institutions are relatively new and fragile.

In order to distinguish cases of new constitutions adopted within a democratic regime from cases of constitution making in other political environments, we first need to determine when a country that experienced non-democratic forms of government in the past becomes democratic. According to a widely accepted definition in political science, a transition to democracy begins with the dissolution of an authoritarian regime and ends with the first free (without proscription of any political party) and fair (without open state intervention in favor of the government party) general elections in a country.[3] This does not mean, of course, that at the end of the transition a democratic regime is consolidated in the sense that an authoritarian reversal is no longer possible or highly unlikely because all relevant actors have internalized the rules of democratic behavior.[4] It only implies that the method of selection of governments has changed and that a democracy has been established in the minimal, electoral sense of the term. This is the basic concept of democracy used in this introduction and throughout this book before assessing other relevant dimensions such as effective institutional constraints on executive power and civil liberties.[5]

Although this definition suggests that an electoral democracy exists when the first competitive election is held, it is reasonable to consider that an intra-democratic constitutional replacement takes place when a new constitution is adopted some time after the founding election. Although a different cutoff point could be established, a five-year time span seems a reasonable one for the purpose of qualitative comparative analysis. At this point, at least one competitively elected government has usually completed its term and representative legislative and executive institutions have clearly replaced the institutions of the authoritarian regime. Also, among both new and old democracies, a period of five years provides a sufficient

---

[2] For a recent analysis of intra-democratic constitutional replacements in Latin America, see Corrales (2018).

[3] See Boix, Miller, and Rosato (2010), whose coding of democratic years based on the existence of free and fair elections I have followed for the purpose of determining the inauguration and duration of democracies in all countries of the world from 1900 to 2015.

[4] For a distinction between democratic transition and democratic consolidation, see O'Donnell and Schmitter (1986) and Mainwaring, O'Donnell, and Valenzuela (1992).

[5] On the idea that a regime must first meet the conditions of free and fair elections to be a democracy before considering its liberal, participatory, or other dimensions, see Coppedge and Gerring et al. (2011).

and yet manageable time frame to compare political conditions before and after a new constitution is enacted.[6]

We also need to identify the nature of constitutional change so that we can differentiate between wholesale replacements and amendments. For the purposes of this analysis, a constitution was considered to be new when its drafters claimed it was new (usually by stipulating the abrogation of the previous constitution and all its amendments at the end of the text) and when state institutions and official sources in the country acknowledged the text as such (Negretto 2012; 2017b).[7] In doubtful cases, country sources on the evolution and history of constitutions were consulted.

Following these criteria, a total of twenty-five new constitutions have been adopted in independent democratic states from 1900 to 2015. Table 1.1 lists these cases and their geographic locations.[8] Based on this sample, this section will discuss the possible factors that have led to intra-democratic constitutional replacements around the world.

The political and legal contexts where democratic constitutional replacements took place have been widely diverse. Sometimes these episodes derived from decisions made during the early years of a transition to democracy and were temporally close to this process; at other times, they were the consequence of unexpected events that occurred after many decades of stable democratic government. New constitutions were adopted in rich as well as in poor states, and in both more heterogeneous and less heterogeneous societies.

Reconstructing the precise factors that led to rewriting the constitution in each case would require a detailed historical analysis. Yet one can infer the general reasons that activated these processes from the contexts in which they emerged and the content of the transformations incorporated into the new constitutional texts. In particular, four factors seem relevant to explaining most cases: democratization of basic institutions, political crises, balance-of-power shifts, and the obsolescence or inconsistency of preexisting constitutional rules. Although one of these

[6] In order to expand the number of cases of democratic constitutional replacements for a statistical analysis of the political impact of elite cooperation and citizen participation in these processes, in Chapter 5 Negretto includes all constitutions adopted in or after the third year since a free and fair election was held while keeping a five-year time frame to compare political conditions before and after the new constitution is adopted.

[7] Conceptually, this definition has a political and positive component that departs from the perspective according to which constitutional replacements only occur when revisions are made without claiming to follow the procedure established in the preexisting constitution, which is the criterion adopted by the *Comparative Constitutions Project* (see Elkins, Ginsburg, and Melton 2009, 55). In practice, however, the global database I have built around the definition used in this chapter is largely consistent with the new constitutions included in the CCP.

[8] The cases have been selected from a larger database of constitution making across the world that will be released in the future as the *Comparative Constitution Making Database*. This database contains observations on 135 new constitutions created between 1900 and 2015 that remained in force during years of free and fair elections for the largest portion of their lives. For a preliminary analysis of its content, see Negretto (2017b).

TABLE 1.1 *Constitutional replacements in democratic regimes, 1900–2015*

Country[a]	Year	Region	Sub-region	Reason for replacement
DENMARK	1915	Europe	Western	Democratization
DENMARK	1953	Europe	Western	Democratization
FINLAND	2000	Europe	Western	Modernization/ Democratization
FRANCE	1958	Europe	Western	Political crisis
GREECE	1952	Europe	Western	Democratization
ICELAND	1944	Europe	Western	Independence/ Democratization
IRELAND	1937	Europe	Western	Balance-of-power shift / Democratization
SWEDEN	1974	Europe	Western	Democratization/ Modernization
SWITZERLAND	1999	Europe	Western	Modernization
HUNGARY	2011	Europe	Eastern	Balance-of-power shift
POLAND	1997	Europe	Eastern	Democratization
UKRAINE	1996	Europe	Eastern	Democratization/State-building
KENYA	2010	Africa	Sub-Saharan	Democratization/Political crisis
THAILAND	1997	Asia	East	Democratization
SRI LANKA	1972	Asia	South	Balance-of-power shift
NEPAL	2015	Asia	South	Democratization
BOLIVIA	2009	Latin America	Andean	Political crisis/Balance-of-power shift
COLOMBIA	1991	Latin America	Andean	Political crisis
ECUADOR	1998	Latin America	Andean	Political crisis
ECUADOR	2008	Latin America	Andean	Balance-of-power shift
URUGUAY	1952	Latin America	South	Democratization
URUGUAY	1967	Latin America	South	Democratization
VENEZUELA	1999	Latin America	Andean	Balance-of-power shift
DOMINICAN REPUBLIC	2010	Caribbean	South	Democratization
TRIN. &TOB.	1976	Caribbean	South	Political crisis/ Democratization

[a] Independent states with populations of more than 300,000 that adopted a new constitution between 1900 and 2015 after at least five years since the first free and fair election in the country.
Source: Author, based on Negretto (2017b); Boix, Miller, and Rosato (2010), and various country sources

possible causes tends to predominate in any given case, they are obviously not mutually exclusive. For instance, the inability or unwillingness of successive governments to implement long-demanded democratic reforms may lead to social unrest, which in turn may induce a political crisis that makes necessary the adoption of a new constitution.

The need to implement significant changes in the basic structures of the state or the political regime, usually to further democratization, is a common reason to replace the constitution in force in a democratic regime.[9] Whereas a minor adjustment of existing constitutional rules can be solved by amending or reinterpreting them, politically significant changes, even if few in number, often require signaling the transformation by means of a wholesale replacement of the existing constitution. Such is the case of constitutional transformations that seek to deepen democracy by expanding opportunities for indirect and direct citizen input, oversight, and participation in policy making; and by enhancing the accountability of elected representatives to the people. Various cases included in the sample shown in Table 1.1 illustrate these goals.

The 1915 Danish Constitutional Act was meant to broaden democracy by extending suffrage to women and servants, and by reducing the voting age from 30 to 25. It also replaced the single-member district plurality electoral system for the lower house by a proportional one, and incorporated the popular referendum as the last stage for ratification of constitutional revisions in the future. Similarly, the 1953 Danish constitution abolished the upper house of parliament, strengthened human rights, and legalized executive accountability to the parliament (Krunke 2013). In 1974, Sweden also replaced the 1809 Instrument of Government to reduce the powers of the monarchy and formalize the parliamentary democracy that had evolved in the country over time (Congleton 2003).

Democratization is also a common reason for constitutional replacement among new democracies that need to complete unfinished tasks of the transition process. As discussed by Negretto and Wandan in Chapter 7, in 1997 Poland finally replaced the 1952 constitution by one that regulated the multi-party democracy that had existed in the country since 1989. It also fixed the rules that would regulate the premier–presidential constitutional regime created at that time. Thailand replaced the 1991 interim constitution in 1997, and as Ginsburg points out in Chapter 8, the new constitution was meant to resume the democratization process initiated in 1983 after it had been interrupted by a coup in 1991. Among its main goals, the new constitution sought to improve the rule of law, government transparency, and electoral accountability (see Klein 1998).

Political crises are another important factor leading to constitutional replacements in a democratic regime. Constitutions organize electoral competition, enable representatives to provide public goods, and maintain citizen support for a political regime. When constitutions fail to perform these tasks, politicians are likely to have an incentive to replace them, usually under popular pressure for reform. The Algerian crisis in France and the widespread perception of lack of government

[9] To be sure, due to its strong legitimating effects democratization is often invoked as the main reason for replacements and is usually related to the content of at least some revisions even when other factors played a more important role in the decision to adopt a new constitution.

effectiveness under the 1946 constitution led to its replacement in 1958 (Foyer 1988). As Christina Murray argues in Chapter 9, an extremely close and disputed presidential election in Kenya in 2007 led to an escalation of political and ethnic violence that required a new constitution as part of a peace agreement.[10] A severe state and regime crisis in Colombia during the late 1980s, discussed by Bejarano and Segura in Chapter 6, created a popular demand for the constituent assembly that replaced the 1886 constitution in 1991. In Ecuador, the irregular ousting of president Bucaram in 1997 unleashed a political crisis that culminated in the replacement of the constitution a year later (see Negretto 2013).

Not all democratic constitutional replacements, however, occurred as a result of the need to implement major structural changes or in response to dramatic political events. Constitutional change may also take place when existing institutions no longer serve the interests of those with the power to change them, or when the losers under a particular set of rules organize a successful reform coalition. This form of constitutional change usually follows significant shifts in party competition, such as when established parties collapse or decline and new parties and leaders emerge, or when a preexisting party obtains an unusual electoral advantage. Transformations in the partisan context may also go hand in hand with changes in the programmatic or ideological content of public policies.

Although the adoption of a new constitution in Hungary had been debated in the country since 1989, central aspects of when and how this would take place were left undefined. For this reason, it could be argued, as Negretto and Wandan do in Chapter 7, that the 2011 constitution was a by-product of the success of a center-right coalition, Fidesz, in the 2010 parliamentary elections (see also Bánkuti, Halmai, and Scheppele 2012; Kornai 2015). Sri Lanka also replaced its 1947 constitution in 1972 as a consequence of the victory of the leftist United Front (see Jayawickrama 2012). As shown by Bejarano and Segura in Chapter 6, the 1998–1999 constitution-making process in Venezuela was to a large extent the effect of a dramatic shift in popular support from established parties to a new political movement advocating radical reform. Similarly, the 2008 Ecuadorean constitution was part of a government party strategy to redistribute power in its favor after winning the presidency without achieving majority support in the legislature (see Brewer Carías 2007; Negretto 2015; 2016).

Democracies may also replace their constitutions simply to modernize, clarify or unify constitutional norms. A constitution regulates political interactions by stabilizing expectations about the behavior of state actors and citizens. When the constitutional text (perhaps due to the accumulation of multiple unconnected amendments or the existence of separate norms of constitutional status) becomes

[10] See also Final Report of the Committee of Experts on Constitutional Review, October 11, 2010, pp. 21–22. http://mlgi.org.za/resources/local-government-database/by-country/kenya/commission-reports/CoE_final_report.pdf.

inconsistent, then this crucial task cannot be performed. Switzerland enacted a new constitution in 1999 to update provisions related to its government structure and expand fundamental rights (Biaggini 2011). Finland also adopted a new constitution in 2000 to legalize existing practices of parliamentary democracy, rewrite certain provisions, and unify various acts of constitutional status in a single text (Suksi 2011).

The main factor that triggers a democratic constitutional replacement has an obvious impact on the level of political conflict about the crafting of a new constitution. The stakes are usually low when the sole or main purpose of a new constitution is simply to update or clarify the previous text, or formalize preexisting constitutional conventions. By contrast, the stakes tend to be high when constitutions are replaced in the midst of a political crisis and social upheaval or when the process derived from a sudden shift in the distribution of power among political actors and the agenda of reform aims at changing important institutional structures. The level of political conflict, in turn, would determine whether the process is activated and a new constitution approved, its procedural and political features, and whether it compromises the future stability or quality of the democratic regime. For instance, it is noticeable that when constitutional replacements are clearly associated with a redistribution of partisan power on behalf of a particular political group, the process itself or its short-term effects tend to undermine democratic institutions.

II PROCEDURAL AND POLITICAL FEATURES

Four features stand out in the analysis of the origins of constitutions adopted within a democratic regime: the rules that regulate the process, the nature of the constitution-making body, the degree of pluralism in political representation and decision-making, and the level of direct citizen involvement. These features reveal substantial cross-national variation, and this variation is greater if one considers the actual impact of various rules and mechanisms and their interaction with the widely different political and social contexts where these processes have taken place. At the same time, some general trends are discernible. As Table 1.2 shows, in most cases constitution making in democratic orders has followed the principles of legal continuity, parliamentary constitution making, plural political representation and decision-making, and direct citizen participation, particularly in the form of ratification referendums.

According to traditional constitutional theory, new constitutions can only be a creation of the people, whose power is not supposed to be subject to legal regulation (see Kalyvas 2005; Loughlin 2007). This concept, as Colon-Rios argues in Chapter 2, is questionable on theoretical grounds because the exercise of popular power can and should be constrained by procedural rules, particularly in a context where the constitution in force has a democratic origin or, if initially adopted under an authoritarian regime, was reformed to fit democratic conditions. Yet one obstacle to this strategy is that most constitutions lack an explicit process for their

TABLE 1.2 *Features of constitution making in democratic regimes, 1900–2015*

Country	Year	Legal continuity	Constituent legislature	Pluralistic representation & decision making	Public consultation/ submissions[a]	Popular referendum[b]
DENMARK	1915	YES	YES	YES	NO	YES
DENMARK	1953	YES	YES	YES	NO	YES
FINLAND	2000	YES	YES	YES	NO	NO
FRANCE	1958	YES	NO	NO	NO	YES
GREECE	1952	NO	YES	YES	NO	YES
ICELAND	1944	YES	YES	YES	NO	YES
IRELAND	1937	YES	YES	NO	NO	YES
SWEDEN	1974	YES	YES	YES	NO	NO
SWITZERLAND	1999	YES	YES	YES	YES	YES
HUNGARY	2011	YES	YES	NO	YES	NO
POLAND	1997	YES	YES	YES	YES	YES
UKRAINE	1996	YES	YES	YES	NO	NO
KENYA	2010	YES	YES	YES	YES	YES
THAILAND	1997	YES	YES	YES	YES	NO
SRI LANKA	1972	NO	YES	NO	YES	NO
NEPAL	2015	YES	YES	YES	YES	NO
BOLIVIA	2009	YES	NO	YES	YES	YES
COLOMBIA	1991	NO	NO	YES	YES	YES
ECUADOR	1998	YES	NO	YES	NO	YES
ECUADOR	2008	NO	NO	NO	YES	YES
URUGUAY	1952	YES	YES	YES	NO	YES
URUGUAY	1967	YES	YES	YES	NO	YES
VENEZUELA	1999	NO	NO	NO	YES	YES
DOMINICAN REPUBLIC	2010	YES	YES	YES	YES	NO
TRIN. &TOB.	1976	YES	YES	NO	NO	NO
TOTAL	25	20 (0.80)	19 (0.76)	18 (0.72)	12 (0.48)	16 (0.64)

[a] Citizen involvement in the formulation of reform proposals during drafting.
[b] Citizen voting on reform proposals either before or after the writing of the new text.
Source: Author, based on various country sources

replacement. Even though some countries do not distinguish between amending and repealing an existing constitution or constitutional act, the adoption of a new constitution at critical moments may require a special procedure to signal the political importance of the event. This explains why only 44 of 135 constitutions adopted between 1900 and 2015 and in force during years of free and fair elections were made following a preexisting procedure.[11] How do political actors deal with this problem?

In the sample used in this introductory chapter, in only five of the twenty-one countries that experienced democratic constitutional replacements from 1900 to 2015 (Denmark, Finland, Sweden, Switzerland, and Uruguay) was there a legal tradition in which the constitution in force at the time explicitly authorized its own replacement. In these cases, it was possible to channel the process legally from the very beginning. This situation inherently holds several advantages, particularly when the initial regulation built a plurality of checks into the process so that no institution or actor could manipulate it for its own benefit. Preexisting regulations of this kind may not only reduce political conflict about the possibility of replacement but also prevent the creation of ad hoc procedural rules that reflect the relative bargaining power of partisan actors at a particular juncture. As Landau discusses in Chapter 4, constitutional courts often face difficult choices when they are asked to intervene to assess the constitutional validity of central aspects of a constitution-making process. The existence of a constitutional roadmap may facilitate at least some court decisions in these cases and make them more acceptable to the various political actors involved.

There is variation in the actual set of regulations that constitutions may provide to authorize the replacement of the existing constitutional text. In some of them, the constitution in force enables the legislature to amend or repeal an existing constitution or constitutional act. Just as in 1915 Denmark adopted a new constitution based on the revision procedures established in the 1866 constitution, in 1953 it adopted another constitution following the terms of the 1915 Constitutional Act (see Krunke 2013). In 1974, the Swedish parliament replaced the 1809 instrument of government following a procedure established in Articles 81 and 82 of the latter document (Congleton 2003). Similarly, in 2000 the Finnish parliament approved a new constitution following the procedure established in Section 67 of the 1928 Constitutional Act (Suksi 2011). In all these cases, the procedure required as a check on preexisting legislative majorities a new parliamentary election before the legislature could approve the desired constitutional changes and, in the case of Denmark 1953, also ratification of the reform in a popular referendum.

A similar method has been used in constitutions that enable the legislature or a special body to adopt partial or total reforms. In Uruguay, the 1952 and 1967 constitutions were enacted based on a preexisting procedure that authorized the

---

[11] Data from the *Comparative Constitution Making Database*. See n. 8.

legislature to propose and pass total reforms subject to ratification in a referendum (see Negretto 2016).[12] In other cases, the constitution established two different procedures for adopting partial or total reforms, but delegated these tasks to the same body. This is the case of the 1874 Swiss constitution, which underwent several partial revisions approved by parliament and ratified in popular referendums, but which also established a special procedure of "total reform" (*"Totalrevision"*) that was used to pass a new constitution in 1999, with previous approval in parliament and ratification by referendum (see Biaggini 2011).[13]

In the absence of preexisting regulation, however, several strategies have been implemented to preserve legal continuity. The most straightforward option has been amending the existing amendment procedure to include the possibility of replacement and regulate basic aspects of this alternative in the constitution. This course of action was followed in the making of Iceland's 1944 constitution, France's 1958 constitution, Bolivia's 2009 constitution, Thailand's 1997 constitution, and Kenya's 2010 constitution (see Foyer 1988, 15; Sucharitkul 1998; Brandt et al. 2011; Böhrt Irahola 2013).

In spite of its apparent simplicity, amending amendment rules might not be sufficient or appropriate to give legal foundations to some incremental processes of constitution making. Such is the case when the adoption of the final constitution demands a sequence of steps to build consensus among the major social and political actors about the process or the content of reforms, and the old constitution is inadequate to regulate the transition (see Jackson 2008). One solution in these circumstances is the creation of an interim constitution, which works as a provisional structure of government and may include provisions about the process or time frame to pass the final constitutional document (see Zulueta-Fülscher 2015). This strategy, usually inherited from the negotiated transition that inaugurated the democratic regime, was followed in the cases of Poland and Ukraine (see Wolczuk 2007; Garlicki and Garlicka 2010).

One final way of preserving some legal continuity, illustrated by the case of Ecuador between 1997 and 1998, is to regulate the process by means of an institutional agreement between the executive and the legislature. After the irregular impeachment of Ecuadorian president, Abdalá Bucaram, the new interim president, in agreement with Congress, convened a referendum asking for authorization to elect a constituent assembly (see Negretto 2013). As a result of the popular support

---

[12] The 1942 constitution derived from an initiative made by two-fifths of the whole legislature, the 1952 constitution from agreement between the main parliamentary parties, and the 1967 constitution from a text proposed by the Colorado and Nacional parties and passed by the legislature.

[13] Several Latin American constitutions initially made without following preexisting procedures have now incorporated a distinction between amending and replacing the constitution, delegating the latter task to a special body. Such is the case of the 1991 constitution of Colombia, the 1999 constitution of Venezuela, and the 2008 constitution of Ecuador. See Negretto (2017a) and Colon-Ríos (2012).

obtained in the referendum, Congress passed a transitory constitutional provision to regulate the election and tasks of the constituent assembly.

As a result of these options, most cases of democratic constitution making in the world have provided for some form of continuity between the old and new legality, though only a few had a framework for regulating the process before the decision to replace the existing constitution was made. Specifically, legal continuity of some form was observed in twenty (80 percent) of the twenty-five episodes of democratic constitution making between 1900 and 2015. To be sure, this continuity was not always created without conflict and sometimes it was even unclear whether legality was really preserved.[14] Against this background, however, it is important to consider the relatively fewer cases where the new constitution was adopted in open violation of existing legality.

A legal break was observed in the cases of Greece (1952), Sri Lanka (1972), Colombia (1991), Ecuador (2008), and Venezuela (1999). Even in this situation, however, cases differed depending on whether the break was negotiated among multiple political actors or imposed by one political group. Colombia offers a model of negotiated rupture, because in spite of bypassing the constitution and the existing legislature, the process was regulated by a multi-party agreement (see Bejarano and Segura 2013; Negretto 2013). Also in Greece, although the existing amendment process was neither followed nor reformed to make a replacement possible, no single party had control over the parliament that adopted the new constitution in December 1951 (Contiades and Tassopolus (2013), 154). Sri Lanka, Venezuela, and Ecuador (2008), however, are all cases of radical and unilateral legal breaks (see Viciano Pastor and Martínez Dalmau 2001; Brewer Carías 2007; Jayawickrama 2012; Wray Reyes 2013). As William Partlett points out in Chapter 3 of this volume, disregard for legal forms can facilitate the replacement of constitutions against entrenched interests that benefit from the status quo. At the same time, however, it can also make it possible for a majority faction to capture the process and shift it in an authoritarian direction.[15] This is exactly what happened in the cases of non-consensual legal breaks, where legislative and judicial constraints over the executive and the effective protection of constitutional rights invariably declined after the enactment of the new constitution.[16]

---

[14] See, for instance, the controversy about the legality of the making of Hungary's 2011 constitution. www.iconnectblog.com/2011/04/arato-on-constitution-making-in-hungary-and-the-45-rule.

[15] As Partlett points out, a similar outcome could occur in the presence of a replacement procedure if this was exclusively designed to benefit government majorities. On the partisan use of seemingly democratic constitution-making procedures, see also Partlett (2012) and Landau (2013).

[16] According the liberal democracy index of V-DEM (a compound measure of institutional constraints over the executive and protection of constitutional rights), the difference between the five-year period before and after the enactment of the new constitution was −0.35 in Venezuela, −0.15 in Ecuador (2008), and −0.06 in Sri Lanka. See Coppedge et al. (2016).

An elected convention specially commissioned to write a constitution is usually considered the ideal representative body in a democratic process of constitution making because it is supposed to reflect citizens' preferences accurately and prevent the influence of constituted powers on the design of a new legal order (see Elster 2006; 2013).[17] This view can be questioned on several grounds. As I have argued elsewhere, the superiority of conventions over constituent legislatures, regardless of the selection method, composition, or decision-making procedures of each body, has no solid theoretical or empirical support. Special conventions also create the risk of partisan capture of the process when, as is often the case, they are elected and delegates are exclusively or primarily party representatives (see Negretto 2018).[18]

As a matter of practice, constituent conventions (at least in their pure form) are rarely used to draft a new constitution, and constitution makers seem particularly reluctant to use them in democratic settings.[19] A visible trend in these environments has been the election of different forms of "constituent" legislatures as instances where the new constitutional text was drafted, approved, or both. Among the twenty-five democratic constitution-making episodes referred to before, twenty-four used a deliberative collective body to draft or vote on the new text. However, in only five of those cases – all located in Latin America – was a constituent convention the approval body of the new constitution. The rest were all legislatures that acted as constituent bodies.

Although the vast majority of constitution-making bodies were assemblies that doubled as constituent bodies and ordinary legislatures, their source of authority varied. Variation among constituent legislatures depends on whether they were authorized to adopt a new constitution by a popular election, by a political decision, or by the existing constitution (see Elster 2006; Negretto 2016; 2018). Sometimes constituent legislatures were able to invoke more than one source of authority to adopt a new constitution. In seventeen of the nineteen cases in which a constituent legislature was used, the constitution or a norm of constitutional status authorized the legislature to turn into a constituent body. In seven of those cases, the legislature that approved the constitution was also voted on in a special election. By contrast, both the 1952 Greek constitution and the 1972 constitution of Sri Lanka were adopted by a legislature not initially authorized by a constitutional provision or a

---

[17] Strictly speaking, constituent assemblies can be either constituent conventions or constituent legislatures. The former are assemblies specially commissioned to write a constitution and dissolve afterwards and the latter assemblies that continue as ordinary legislatures after enacting a new constitution (see Elster 2006; Negretto 2018). Throughout this book, however, the terms constituent convention, convention, or constituent assembly (as opposed to constituent legislature) are most of the time used interchangeably.

[18] See also Ginsburg, Elkins, and Blount (2009).

[19] According to Negretto (2017b), from 1900 to 2015 only 38 out of 124 deliberative bodies created to adopt a new constitution may be classified as constituent conventions.

popular vote that would enable the assembly to assume a constituent function (see Wickramaratne 2010; Contiades and Tassopolus 2011).[20]

The geographic distribution of constituent bodies seems to support the idea that their nature is closely related to the type of political system and to inherited legal traditions. Most cases of parliamentary constitution making took place in Europe under parliamentary regimes, while all cases of special conventions were in Latin America under presidential systems. Yet there are presidential systems with constituent legislatures (Kenya, for instance) and in the Latin American context the use of constituent legislatures has historically been the rule, not the exception (see Negretto 2016).

Regardless of the political system and inherited traditions, expediency, opposition by the existing legislature to the creation of a different assembly with constituent powers, and, most importantly, the fear of jurisdictional and political conflicts between a special convention and the ordinary legislature explain the frequent use of constituent legislatures in democratic constitutional replacements. Nevertheless, some political junctures make resorting to constituent legislatures impossible or highly inconvenient. Such is the case when legislators are so discredited in the eyes of the people that neither the existing parliament nor any other future parliament would seem adequate for the task of writing a new constitution. Due to the generally low levels of public trust in legislatures, this situation has been common in recent constitution-making processes in Latin America.[21] As discussed by Gylfason in Chapter 10, however, this is also the reason why a special convention was called in Iceland in 2010 after traditional parties and the parliament lost public credibility following the 2008–2009 financial crisis.

Another key aspect of democratic constitutional replacements is the degree of pluralism among political representatives during the writing of the new text. In theory, this depends on the mechanism to select delegates to the constitution-making body and the threshold of votes required to adopt the constitution. However, it is the interaction between these rules and the actual outcomes they bring about in particular environments that really matters for determining the extent of political pluralism in constitution writing. As Negretto argues in Chapter 5, in order to determine how inclusive or exclusive a constitution-making process is, one must consider both the actual number of independent political groups that win representation in the constituent body and the decision-making rule that establishes the threshold of votes necessary to approve the new constitutional text. According to this view, a constitution-making process is pluralistic and induces cooperation among

---

[20] If one follows the position that the parliament elected in Hungary in 2010 adopted a new constitution in 2011 in violation of existing constitutional provisions, this can also be considered a case of a "self-authorized" constituent legislature. See n. 14.

[21] As of the time of this writing (November 2019), a new constitution-making process is underway in Chile and in part due to the low level of legitimacy of the existing legislature, the new constitution will be drafted by a special convention.

representative elites when an agreement between at least two independently elected political parties or groups is necessary to pass the constitution according to the decision rule. Following this definition, in eighteen of the twenty-five cases (72 percent), a plurality of organized political interests and views had influence over the approval of the new constitution.

All the constitutions included in the sample, except the 1958 French constitution (the single case of executive constitution making), were made by elected assemblies. In these cases, the electoral system determines, on average, the number of parties that compete and win seats in the constitution-making body. A proportional electoral system (PR) was used in thirteen cases, a majority formula in eight, and a mixed one in three. The fact that in eleven of the eighteen episodes where we observe plural representation a PR formula was used to elect reformers indicates that this election method has a positive impact on the dispersion of decision-making power at the time of designing the new constitution. By contrast, in some of the cases that used a majoritarian electoral system (Ukraine, Kenya, Thailand, Sri Lanka, Ecuador [1998], Venezuela, and Trinidad and Tobago), these rules were responsible for the disproportionate control they gave to a particular political group.

In the 1970 election of the parliament that would adopt a new constitution in Sri Lanka (then Ceylon), the existing plurality system provided the Sri Lanka Freedom Party 60 percent of the seats with just 38 percent of the vote. In Venezuela, a personalized voting system that worked in practice as a plurality formula provided Polo Patriótico with 92 percent of constituent assembly seats with 66 percent of the vote (see Neuman and McCoy 2001). In Hungary, the mixed system used in the 2010 parliamentary elections had a large majoritarian bias because a party could add seats won in the plurality and PR districts, and only 58 seats in an assembly of 386 seats were reserved to compensate for the disproportionality created in the first tier (see Benoit 1996). This is one reason why Fidesz won 68 percent of the seats with slightly over 50 percent of the vote.

Extra-institutional factors may, however, alter the expected effects of electoral rules. Some of these factors are a sudden decline in popular support for one of the established parties, the emergence of new political forces, or abstention by some parties from participating in the election. In the 1971 parliamentary election in Trinidad and Tobago, the People's National Movement ended up controlling 100 percent of the seats not because of the electoral system (which was majoritarian) but because the opposition parties decided to boycott the election. On the other hand, in the 1996 parliamentary election in Thailand the fragmentation of voter preferences gave no party a majority in spite of the fact that members of parliament were elected using a plurality block vote system in multi-member districts.

The number of parties that win representation is crucial, but the decision rule also accounts for how many of them are finally included in the drafting or approval of the constitution. Contrary to what one would expect, qualified majority decision rules are not common for the adoption of new constitutions across the world.

Only 33 of 124 constitution-making bodies created between 1900 and 2015 required a qualified majority to pass the constitution (see Negretto 2017b). In democratic orders, however, stringent decision rules are more frequent and were used in half of the cases where the constituent body was elected. It is interesting to note that when qualified majorities are used, the constitution-making body tends to be a constituent legislature. Among constituent conventions, only the 2006–2007 Bolivian assembly had to pass the constitution by two-thirds of the present members.[22] In the absence of a qualified majority threshold, the most common decision rule across all types of constitution-making bodies is absolute majority rule; that is, more than 50 percent of the whole membership of the body.[23]

An additional feature of democratic constitution making, which must be distinguished from representative channels, is the direct involvement of citizens in the process. Broadly speaking, citizens may participate in constitution making either through the election of representatives who will propose or decide on the content of revisions or by proposing or deciding those revisions themselves. However, this generic use of the term "participation" creates confusion about the meaning and potential impact of citizen input in constitution making. Most of the time, representatives are either rank-and-file party members who follow orders from the leaders of the organization or individuals who themselves occupy a position of authority in the party.[24] From this perspective, even if delegates to a constituent body are selected in a free and fair election it makes more sense to consider them as part of the political elite than to identify their decisions as those that ordinary citizens would make themselves.

In a recent important work, Eisenstadt et al. (2017, 30) consider that a constitution-making process is "popular" rather than "elite-led" when at the convening stage (the most important part of this process, in their view) there is "systematic civil society input or strong transparency or specially elected drafters freely and fairly elected." This view is problematic because it does not discriminate between direct and indirect citizen involvement. Although it is not clear when civil society input is systematic or how strong transparency is measured, these indicators supposedly refer to instances of direct citizen involvement (public consultation processes, for

---

[22] One could argue that Bolivia is a partial exception, however, because the rules governing the constituent assembly required the vote of two-thirds of the delegates present at the session, not counted over the total membership. This threshold is thus more demanding than absolute majority rule (that is, more than 50 percent of the members of the body) only if there are no absentees at the voting session.

[23] I have not found among episodes of constitution making in democratic orders a case of approval of the new text by simple majority, that is, by the vote of a majority of the members present and voting.

[24] A "citizen" assembly, where all or most of its members are randomly selected citizens, or an assembly whose members are elected on a non-partisan basis, will of course be made of representatives that do not belong to the political elite. Yet these types of assemblies are uncommon; in practice, they have not yet been used to adopt a whole new constitution or have failed to enact one, as in the case of Iceland. See Negretto (2017b).

instance) before decisions are made about the content of the new constitution. By contrast, measuring when a constituent body is elected in a free and fair electoral contest is relatively straightforward, yet it only implies that the constitution was crafted by representative elites, not that citizens had control over the process.[25]

In practice, there are several cases of constitutions, such as those of Sweden in 1974 and Finland in 2000, which were drafted by constituent bodies specially elected in free and fair elections but in which the process did not include any instance of direct citizen involvement either before, during, or after the new text was deliberated, negotiated, and voted on by members of the assembly. For this reason, to compare and measure concepts in a precise way, popular participation should be restricted to instances of direct citizen involvement, which can take place before or during the drafting process, in the form of public consultations and proposal submissions, or before and after the adoption of the new text, in the form of voting in referendums (see Negretto 2019).

Public consultation may refer to deliberate efforts to truly engage citizens in debates about the constitution through public meetings, participatory workshops or digital means, or to the more formal and window-dressing practices of simply broadcasting deliberations and inviting comments from the public. An example of the first type of consultation was the participation program implemented in Colombia in 1990–1991 (see Bejarano and Segura 2013). Also genuine was the innovative process though which citizens in Iceland participated in the drafting of a new constitutional text and submitted comments on the work of the 2010–2011 constitutional assembly (see Meuwese 2013; Gylfason and Meuwese 2016). A more opportunistic form of consultation was seen in Hungary, where public debate was conducted through a website that invited everyone to make her or his opinion heard (see Dani 2013).

Proposal submissions took place in Colombia, Poland, Bolivia, Ecuador (2008), and Kenya. One case in which this form of participation seemed to be significant was Kenya, where within eight months of being established, the Committee of Experts responsible for preparing the draft constitution had collected a total of 26,451 memoranda and presentations from members of the public (see Murray, Chapter 9, and Committee of Experts Report 2010). Within the twenty-five cases of democratic constitution making, direct citizen participation took place before or during the drafting process in the form of public consultations or proposal submissions in twelve (48 percent) cases.

[25] In a new article, Eisenstadt and Maboudi (2019) attempt to distinguish individual participation from group inclusion in constitution making. However, they still conflate the notion of representation with direct participation (or participation proper). In particular, they maintain a measure of participation that includes both the direct election of the constitution-making body (which is a representative mechanism) and the ratification referendum (which is a mechanism of participation).

One of the main criticisms of public consultations and proposal submissions alike is that they may work as information-gathering mechanisms without visible consequences in terms of the final decisions made by representatives (Blount 2011). It is not clear in what way the preferences expressed by citizens in participatory forums or in concrete reform proposals have an impact on the content of the final text. Popular demands channeled through these forms of citizen involvement are inevitably filtered and it is often difficult to make representatives accountable for substitutions, omissions, and distortions. For this reason, the ability of citizens to have direct influence over the adoption of a constitution or particular provisions in democratic constitution making usually takes the form of a referendum.

Popular referendums can take place at the beginning, to provide authorization for the process, as in Ecuador in 1997 and in Colombia in 1990, to enable the election of a special convention that was not regulated by the existing constitutional framework.[26] Initial referendums can also be used to decide on substantive issues that become binding for reformers. In September 1946, Greek voters supported the maintenance of the monarchy and that decision was later incorporated into the 1952 constitution. A referendum of this type was also held in 1997 in Ecuador to consult voters about a series of electoral reforms to be later adopted by the constituent assembly. The most common referendum, however, is held at the end of the process to ratify or reject the constitutional text.[27] Popular referendums were used to ratify constitutions in Denmark (1953), Ireland (1937), Sri Lanka (1972), Bolivia (2009), and Uruguay (1952, 1967). In most cases, referendums are used either at the beginning or at the end of the process. Only in Venezuela (1999) and Ecuador (2008) were referendums held at both points in time. In all, authorization or ratification referendums were observed in sixteen (64 percent) of the twenty-five cases of democratic constitution making included in the sample.

Since information on the reform proposals is typically limited and public debate on their merits is usually superficial, popular participation through referendums is obviously questionable on normative grounds (Lenowitz 2015). Nonetheless, in competitive environments, referendums may have an important influence on the outcome. A referendum held at the beginning of the process could create an "upstream" constraint on the institutions that reformers will adopt, while a ratification referendum may work as a "downstream" constraint on the reform alternatives that representatives can chose from.[28] Whether this constraint works in reality may

[26] To the best of my knowledge, however, there are no cases in which citizens have been asked to authorize a constitutional replacement and at the same time decide on the type of constitution-making body that should draft the new constitution. Political representatives usually established the latter beforehand. The recently activated constitution-making process in Chile may be an exception in this regard.

[27] The use of ratification referendums is part of a relatively recent and growing trend around the world that takes place under both democratic and authoritarian conditions. See Elkins, Ginsburg, and Blount (2008), and Ginsburg, Elkins, and Blount (2009).

[28] On the concept of "upstream" and "downstream" constraints in constitution making, see Elster (1995; 2013).

be related to the number of actors with control over the activation of the referendum and the framing of the proposal submitted to popular vote (see Tierney 2012). The more concentrated the control over these instances in the hands of one institution or political group, the more likely the referendum could be subject to manipulation, as were the cases in Venezuela and in Ecuador (2008).

It is important to note that among the cases under consideration there is no significant correlation between the use of mechanisms of direct citizen involvement during constitution making (either in the form of consultations and proposal submissions or voting in referendums) and plurality of representation and decision-making. This provides support to the argument that we need to differentiate representative channels from mechanisms of direct citizen participation. In addition, and although in some cases we do observe the use of public consultations or proposal submissions along with voting in referendums, there is no significant correlation, either, between these forms of direct citizen involvement, suggesting that one should also distinguish them for the purpose of assessing the nature and potential effects of participatory constitution making.

III CONSTITUTIONAL REPLACEMENTS, DEMOCRACY, AND CONSTITUTIONALISM

The works collected in this volume focus on some of the main issues involved in the replacement of constitutions within an existing electoral democracy, such as the role of precedent institutions, the design of replacement procedures, the impact of judicial interventions, and the interaction between representation and participation. The cases selected for comparative analysis show the various ways in which reformers addressed these issues in relevant episodes of constitution making in democratic regimes across different regions of the world and the potential consequences of their decisions.

The contributors share a common concern with the relationship between constitutional change, democracy, and constitutionalism. Some authors adopted a normative perspective to analyze the extent to which the various alternative ways to replace a constitution in a democratic environment are compatible with democratic principles, whereas others took a more empirical approach to assess how the options actually implemented might have in fact affected democratization. This variety of perspectives is justified to understand the different dimensions of constitution making in democratic regimes.

The design of an ideal democratic constitution-making process faces the problem that there are competing normative principles and conceptions of democracy, so that while certain features of the process may satisfy one view of democracy they contradict another (see Arato 1995; Fishkin 2011). As discussed in the chapters by Colon-Rios, Partlett, and Negretto, whereas some perspectives conceptualize democratic constitution making as a radical legal break with the existing order carried out by sovereign conventions that express the will of a mobilized mass of citizens, others portray it as a lawful transformation implemented by parliaments or non-sovereign conventions with limited or no direct citizen involvement. These opposite visions about procedures reflect a deeper disagreement about a participatory or liberal understanding of democracy. For this reason, a discussion of different democratic principles, the specific circumstances where they should apply to constitution making, and how it is possible to reach a balance among them is necessary for a theoretically grounded normative analysis of democratic constitutional replacements.

From a social science perspective, it is clear, as various authors in this volume point out, that the (usually short-lived) events that characterize constitutional origins cannot alter the long-term impact that structural variables such as state capacity, socioeconomic development, and ethnic or other social divisions have over the quality and performance of a democratic regime. At the same time, however, certain features of constitution making may work as an intervening variable that helps to explain relatively different political outcomes under similar preexisting conditions, particularly in the short term (see Linz and Stepan 1996). Furthering democratization has been a common motive for replacing the constitution in force in a democratic regime in countries initially sharing a number of relevant social, political, and economic conditions. However, the result of these processes does not always meet initial expectations.

Table 1.3 shows the short-term political impact of democratic constitutional replacements using the Liberal Democracy Index of the *Varieties of Democracy Project* (V-DEM) and the Polity index of democratization of the *Polity IV Project*, comparing the average scores five years before and five years after the enactment of the new constitution.[29] The first index captures the extent to which constitutionally protected civil liberties, strong rule of law, an independent judiciary, and effective checks and balances limit the exercise of executive power. It ranges from 0 to 1 and takes into account whether the regime already qualifies as an electoral democracy. The second index measures relative levels of democratization in a scale that goes from −10 (pure dictatorship) to 10 (complete democracy). It intends to capture the degree of competition in the election of representatives, which is a key feature of electoral democracy, and the extent of institutional constraints over executive power, which is one of the components of liberal democracy. The indices are thus not strictly identical although they both attempt to capture central aspects of the contemporary notion of democracy.

The comparison shows that while the liberal dimension of democracy improved in nine cases, it declined in nine, and remained at the same level in six. Using the aggregate index of Polity IV, in turn, democratization improved in seven cases; in nine the impact was neutral, and in eight it was negative. To be sure, these associations do not imply a causal connection between the procedural or political

---

[29] See Coppedge et al. (2016), and Marshall, Gurr, and Jaggers (2019).

TABLE 1.3 *Constitutional replacements and democracy after enactment, 1900–2015*

		Impact on democratization	
Country	Enactment year	Liberal democracy[a]	Polity IV[b]
DENMARK	1915	Positive	Positive
DENMARK	1953	Positive	Neutral
FINLAND	2000	Neutral	Neutral
FRANCE	1958	Negative	Negative
GREECE	1952	Positive	Negative
ICELAND	1944	Positive	Neutral
IRELAND	1937	Negative	Negative
SWEDEN	1974	Positive	Neutral
SWITZERLAND	1999	Neutral	Neutral
HUNGARY	2011	Negative	Neutral
POLAND	1997	Neutral	Positive
UKRAINE	1996	Negative	Positive
KENYA	2010	Positive	Positive
THAILAND	1997	Positive	Neutral
SRI LANKA	1972	Negative	Positive
NEPAL	2015	NA	NA
BOLIVIA	2009	Negative	Negative
COLOMBIA	1991	Positive	Positive
ECUADOR	1998	Neutral	Negative
ECUADOR	2008	Negative	Negative
URUGUAY	1952	Neutral	Positive
URUGUAY	1967	Negative	Negative
VENEZUELA	1999	Negative	Negative
DOMINICAN REPUBLIC	2010	Neutral	Neutral
TRIN. &TOB.	1976	Positive	Neutral

[a] Difference between the average score of the V-DEM Liberal Democracy index of democratization (0–1) in the country five years before and five years after enactment of the new constitution (neutral if absolute difference < 0.00).

[b] Difference between the average score of the Polity IV index of democratization (−10 to 10) in the country five years before and five years after enactment of the new constitution (neutral if no difference between ex ante and ex post average scores).

conditions under which the new constitution was enacted and levels of democracy after promulgation. Moreover, we know that in some cases events external to the origins of the new constitution explain subsequent developments, such as the 2000 coup in Ecuador shortly after the adoption of its 1998 constitution (see Lucero 2001). Yet the wide variations observed in the difference between democracy levels before and after constitutional replacements across countries within the same region (such as Colombia and Venezuela) or at a comparable level of economic development (such as Hungary and Poland) strongly suggest the need for further exploration of the possible impact that constitutional origins had on these outcomes.

This volume makes several contributions to the normative and empirical debate about intra-democratic constitutional replacements. Some authors discuss the importance of preexisting provisions to regulate constitutional replacements. The traditional constituent power doctrine, which continues to be influential to this day, emphasizes the need or desirability of legal discontinuity in constitution making based on the idea that the old legal system cannot regulate the process because it has been abolished or is deemed illegitimate (see Kay 1987; 2011). This is of course true in the context of a revolutionary overthrow or a transition to democracy where the authoritarian regime has suddenly collapsed. However, things are different in a democratic regime, where the existing legal order may have been legitimately established or adapted to fit the conditions of free and fair elections and representative institutions over time. In this context, a bridge between the old and the new legality is normatively and politically desirable.

In Chapter 2, Colon-Ríos argues that even from the point of view of the constituent power of the people as the only legitimate source of democratic constitutions, a distinction should be made between substantive and procedural limits on this power. Imposing substantive limits on the provisions a new constitution should have may be incompatible with a democratic theory of the constituent power because the people themselves or their representatives should have no restrictions to decide the content of the new text. Yet procedural constraints established beforehand to channel citizen preferences and decisions might facilitate rather than impede democratic constitution making. From this perspective, he argues, it is perfectly consistent with democratic principles to have a constitution that prescribes specific procedures to carry out the popular will in a constitutional replacement, such as the election of an independent constituent assembly or ratification of the text by means of a popular referendum.

William Partlett, in turn, argues that the regulation of democratic constitutional replacements – just like democracy in general – should avoid the tyranny of both minorities and majorities. In his view, these processes face the Scylla of minorities that may use ordinary legislatures and constitutional courts to block changes that endanger their interests and the Charybdis of factional majorities that attempt to use special conventions and referendums to unilaterally reshape the constitutional order in a self-interested manner. To strike a balance between these two hazards, Partlett proposes that a framework for democratic constitution making should establish rules that promote popular input to the process as well as consensual decision-making among political representatives. From this perspective, such a balance can be achieved by either constituent legislatures deciding by qualified majority and whose work is ratified by popular referendums or by special conventions with only limited proposing powers.

Decisions on whether democratic constitutional replacements should be subject to preexisting rules or whether these rules should be complemented in a particular direction derive from opposing conceptions of constitution making.

These conceptions also affect the type of intervention that judges may make in the process of providing for or improving the legal foundations of new constitutions. As Landau discusses in Chapter 4, constitutional judges may play different roles depending on whether they resort to the theory of constituent power to channel a process not allowed by existing rules, whether they adhere to legality in order to block the process, or whether they shape certain features of the process by using existing sub-constitutional rules. As he warns, none of these functions is universally desirable and their effects would depend on context. In some environments, blocking constitutional change may effectively prevent democratic backsliding; in others, however, it may ossify and potentially debilitate a democratic order in need of change.

One important issue for debate in the design of a desirable constitution-making process in a democratic regime is the role that ordinary citizens and political elites should have in it. A widespread view in constitutional theory proposes that direct citizen participation in constitution writing enhances the sense of collective ownership over the new text, promotes a democratic institutional design, and facilitates its enforcement. Other scholars, particularly political scientists, have made claims about the importance of elite constitutional agreements for the creation and implementation of institutions that limit the stakes of power in a liberal democracy. In Chapter 5, Negretto presents arguments and provides evidence in support of the position that only cooperation among a plurality of elected political representatives at the constitution-making stage is likely to make institutional constraints on executive power and civil liberties effective after the enactment of the new constitution, at least in the short term. This analysis does not contradict the idea that participatory constitution making is desirable on normative grounds and often politically necessary. It strongly suggests, however, that no form of direct citizen involvement in the process is likely, by itself, to improve liberal democracy after a new constitution is in force.

The case studies included in the second part of this volume enrich both normative and empirical perspectives by discussing the lessons that emerge from concrete episodes of constitution making in democratic regimes. Whether these episodes of constitutional replacement took place a few or many years after the founding democratic election, in all cases the political regime at the beginning of the process qualified as an electoral democracy. The political outcomes, however, were widely different.

Using evidence from Colombia and Venezuela, in Chapter 6 Bejarano and Segura provide a nice complement to Negretto's analysis. According to these authors, participatory constitutional replacements may lead to the expansion of rights and mechanisms of participation in ongoing governance, allowing for the inclusion of new actors, interests and demands. Yet they do not always result in an institutional architecture that favors the level of competition, opposition dissent, and accountability that are necessary to preserve and improve a democratic regime. The latter only happens, the authors propose, when power is distributed evenly among the various forces present in the constitution-making body, leading to a centripetal dynamic of negotiation and bargaining that results in a balanced, power-sharing constitutional text. Bejarano and Segura's argument is supported by the contrasting outcomes in terms of democratization observed in the negotiated and consensual Colombian constitution-making process and in the unilateral and executive-led process in Venezuela.

The comparison between the cases of Colombia and Venezuela also highlights the importance of Partlett's proposal on the need to strike a balance between the use of mechanisms of direct citizen participation in constitution making to bypass the veto power of status quo minorities and the possibility that a partisan majority may manipulate those mechanisms for self-serving purposes. Whereas in Colombia a popular referendum was used to activate the process and make the election of a special convention possible, the election and decision-making rules of this body were designed to induce collaboration and cooperation among the different parties. In Venezuela, by contrast, the incumbent party used popular participation during the process to marginalize the opposition and impose its preferred institutions.

Negretto and Wandan's comparative analysis of democratic constitutional replacements in Hungary and Poland in Chapter 7 shows the importance that coalitional politics and opposition strategies have for understanding the level of concentration or diffusion of political power during the constitution-making process. As they argue, whereas in Poland the Democratic Left Alliance (SLD) and the Polish People's (or Peasants') Party (PSL) formed a super-majoritarian coalition government after the 1993 election, they did not act as a single unified force willing and able to control the process, as the also super-majoritarian Fidesz-KDNP coalition in Hungary did following the 2010 election. The SLD and PSL were initially voted in as separate political forces; they faced an effective extra-parliamentary opposition, and acted under the constraints of a series of previous agreements in which basic aspects of the new constitution and the process were decided consensually. As a result, although in both cases the incumbent government had formal control over the decision rule, it was only in Hungary that the constitution was imposed with limited or no negotiation, thus creating the basis for the erosion of representative institutions in that country.

Negretto and Wandan also emphasize how the quality and impact of direct citizen involvement on constitutional rewrites is itself dependent on the degree of inclusion and pluralism achieved at the elite level. In particular, they show that while participatory practices were implemented in both Poland and Hungary, it was only in the former that a greater degree of cooperation between incumbent and opposition elites made possible the implementation of genuine and consequential participatory practices during the making of the new constitution. In other words, without inclusion and cooperation at the elite level, participatory constitution making tends to be used, as in Hungary, as a window-dressing mechanism that only seeks to legitimate unilateral government decisions.

The adoption of Thailand's 1997 constitution could be considered a model of perfect balance between consensual politics at the elite level and the direct involvement of ordinary citizens. It also exemplifies the virtues of legal continuity and collaboration among different institutions with limited powers in the drafting and voting of a new text. As Ginsburg notes in Chapter 8, however, the case of Thailand also illustrates how vulnerable a successful constitutional agreement can be to the vagaries of electoral competition. In 2001, a few years after the new constitution was implemented, an electorally successful populist leader and a recently created party upset the incipient achievements of Thai democracy. Between 2001 and 2006, Thaksin Shinawatra used his electorally dominant position to stack, intimidate and influence various independent institutions, including the Senate. These actions, in addition to a high-profile corruption case that directly involved Shinawatra, led to a level of social and political polarization that eventually ended in a military coup that abrogated the constitution and cancelled the upcoming elections.

The origins and effects of Kenya's 2010 constitution also show how the evolution of post-constitutional politics is an important element in understanding the democratic legacy of new constitutions. As Murray argues in Chapter 9, the unprecedented ethnic violence that took place after the 2007 election led to a conscious decision to adopt a new constitution by means of elite consensus while meeting the public's or, at least, organized civil society's expectation of participation. As the memories of the 2007 conflict were still fresh and the balance of forces that participated in the initial agreement remained stable, the 2013 election was relatively peaceful and its outcome respected in spite of the fact that the opposition lost against the incumbent party, contrary to its expectations. By 2017, however, violence emerged once more, the incumbent party won a new election in the midst of allegations of wrongdoing, and the opposition refused to stand in a court-ordered rerun. This, in addition to other signs of democratic erosion, such as continuing corruption and state abuse, has cast doubts over the future of Kenyan democracy.

Gylfason's chapter is the only contribution to this volume that analyzes a constitution-making process that thus far has failed to produce a new constitution in spite of the fact that the text was unanimously adopted by a democratic constitutional assembly and approved by a two-thirds majority of votes in a popular referendum. It is also the only case in which a constituent assembly composed of elected nonpartisan candidates effectively sidelined party elites at the start. His study is, however, a reminder of how the net result of popular participation depends on the constraints and conditions that political elites face when they decide on the creation of a new constitution. Although leaders from the main political parties accepted that a highly participatory constitution-making process be opened up under strong social pressures for political reform as a result of the 2008–2009 economic crisis, they blocked the process after the crisis was over and they were able to regain political control. Although by most standards democracy in Iceland is still very strong, Gylfason argues that this may be a case in which betraying the popular mandate for a new constitution could backfire in the future and lead to democratic decline.

From this point of view, the Icelandic case presents an interesting counterpoint to the cases of Venezuela and Ecuador (2008), where a dominant political group manipulated direct participation by the public to hide the exclusionary and non-consensual nature of the process. In Iceland, genuinely autonomous citizen participation in constitution making took place and had a real impact on the content of the new text, but the outcome of this participation was finally blocked by self-interested political elites. This shows that the balance between consensual forms of agreement among political elites and the active and direct involvement of citizens during democratic constitution making is indeed difficult to achieve, in part because political elites are never willing to give up control over the design of a new constitution.

Taken as a whole, the works collected in this volume make several substantive contributions to the future conceptual and empirical analysis of constitutional replacements in the context of representative institutions and their potential impact on democratization. These contributions can be summarized in five points: the importance of a preexisting legal framework that regulates the process, the need to design this process keeping a balance between overcoming the blocking power of entrenched minorities and avoiding the risk of factional majorities, the contingent but consequential effects of judicial intervention, the central role of inclusive agreements among a plurality of representative elites to assess the overall quality of the process and its impact on democratization, and the vulnerability of those agreements to balance-of-power shifts and ex post opportunism. As portrayed in the different scenarios and cases reviewed in this book, democratic constitutional replacement may enhance and deepen democratization or give way to a gradual but sure process of democratic backsliding. Whether and how a constitution is replaced in a democratic context may determine to a large extent which of these outcomes we observe in reality.

REFERENCES

Albert, Richard. 2019. *Constitutional Amendments: Making, Breaking, and Changing Constitutions.* Oxford: Oxford University Press.

Arato, Andrew. 1995. "Forms of Constitution Making and Theories of Democracy." *Cardozo Law Review* 17(2): 191–232.

2016. *Post Sovereign Constitution Making: Learning and Legitimacy.* Oxford: Oxford University Press.

Bánkuti, Mikós, Gabor Halmai, and Kim Lane Scheppele. 2012. "Hungary's Illiberal Turn: Disabling the Constitution." *Journal of Democracy* 3(23): 138–146.

Bejarano, Ana Maria, and Renata Segura. 2013. "Asambleas Constituyentes y Democracia: Una Lectura Crítica del Nuevo Constitucionalismo en la Región Andina." *Colombia Internacional,* 79: 19–48.

Benoit, Ken. 1996. "Hungary's Two-Vote Electoral System." *Journal of Representative Democracy* 33(4): 162–170.

Biaggini, Giovanni. 2011. "Switzerland" in *How Constitutions Change*. Dawn Oliver and Carlo Fusaro (eds.) Oxford: Hart Publishing, 303–328.

Blount, Justine. 2011. "Participation in Constitutional Design" in *Comparative Constitutional Law*. Rosalind Dixon and Tom Ginsburg (eds.) Cheltenham: Edward Elgar, 38–56.

Böhrt Irahola, Carlos. 2013. "El Proceso Constituyente Boliviano" in *Los Procesos Constituyentes Boliviano y Ecuatoriano: Analisis Comparativo y Prospectiva*. Carlos Böhrt Irahola and Norman Wray Reyes (eds.) Stockholm: IDEA International, 9–153.

Brandt, Michelle, Jill Cotrell, Yash Ghai, and Anthony Regan. 2011. *Constitution-Making and Reform: Option for the Process*. Geneva: Interpeace.

Brewer Carías, Allan. 2007. "El inicio del proceso constituyente en Ecuador en 2007 y las lecciones de la experiencia Venezolana de 1999." *Iuris Dictio* 7(11): 71–94.

Carles Boix, Michael Miller, and Sebastian Rosato. 2010. "A Complete Dataset of Political Regimes, 1800–2007." *Comparative Political Studies* 46(12): 1523–1554.

Choudhry, Sujit, and Tom Ginsburg (eds.) 2016. *Constitution Making*. Northampton: Elgar.

Colon-Ríos, Joel. 2012. *Weak Constitutionalism: Democratic Legitimacy and the Question of Constituent Power*. New York: Routledge.

Congleton, Roger D. 2003. *Improving Democracy through Constitutional Reform: Some Swedish Lessons*. Boston: Kluwer Academic Publishers.

Contiades, Xenophon (ed.) 2013. *Engineering Constitutional Change: A Comparative Perspective on Europe, Canada and the USA*. Oxon: Routledge.

Contiades, Xenophon, and Ioannis Tassopoulos. 2013. "Constitutional Change in Greece" in *Engineering Constitutional Change: A Comparative Perspective on Europe, Canada and the USA*. Xenophon Contiades (ed.) Oxon: Routledge, 151–177.

Coppedge, Michael, John Gerring, et al. 2011. "Conceptualizing and Measuring Democracy: A New Approach." *Perspective on Politics* 9(2): 247–267.

Coppedge, Michael, et al. 2016. V-Dem Country-Year Dataset v6. *Varieties of Democracy (V-Dem) Project*.

Corrales, Javier. 2018. *Fixing Democracy: Why Constitutional Change Often Fails to Enhance Democracy in Latin America*. Oxford: Oxford University Press.

Dani, Marco. 2013. "The 'Partisan Constitution' and the Corrosion of European Constitutional Culture." *LSE 'Europe in Question' Discussion Paper Series* No. 68/2013. London: London School of Economics and Political Science.

Eisenstadt, Todd, A. Carl LeVan, and Tofigh Maboudi. 2015. "When Talk Trumps Text: The Democratizing Effects of Deliberation during Constitution-Making, 1974–2011." *American Political Science Review* 103(3): 592–612.

2017. *Constituents before Assembly: Participation, Deliberation, and Representation in the Crafting of New Constitutions*. Cambridge: Cambridge University Press.

Eisenstadt, Todd A., and Tofigh Maboudi. 2019. "Being There Is Half the Battle: Group Inclusion, Constitution Writing, and Democracy." *Comparative Political Studies* 52 (13–14): 2135–2170.

Elkins, Zachary, Tom Ginsburg, and Justine Blount. 2008. "The Citizen As Founder: Public Participation in Constitutional Approval." *Temple Law Review* 81(2): 361–382.

Elkins, Zachary, Tom Ginsburg, and James Melton. 2009. *The Endurance of National Constitutions*. New York: Cambridge University Press.

Elster, Jon. 1995. "Forces and Mechanisms in Constitution-Making." *Duke Law Review* 45: 364–396.

Elster, Jon. 2006. "Legislatures As Constituent Assemblies" in *The Least Examined Branch. The Role of Legislatures in the Constitutional State*. Richard W. Bauman and Tsvi Kahana (eds.) Cambridge: Cambridge University Press, 181–197.

2013. *Securities against Misrule: Juries, Assemblies, Elections*. Cambridge: Cambridge University Press.

Fishkin, James. 2011. "Deliberative Democracy and Constitutions." *Social Philosophy and Policy* 28(1): 242–260.

Foyer, Jean. 1988. "The Drafting of the French Constitution of 1958" in *Constitution Makers on Constitution Making*. Robert A. Goldwin and Art Kaufman (eds.) Washington, DC: American Enterprise Institute for Public Research, 4–46.

Garlicki, Lech, and Zofia A. Garlicka. 2010. "Constitution Making, Peace Building, and National Reconciliation. The experience of Poland" in *Framing the State in Times of Transition: Case Studies in Constitution Making*. Laurel E. Miller (ed.) Washington, DC: United States Institute of Peace, 391–416.

Ginsburg, Tom, Zachary Elkins, and Justine Blount. 2009. "Does the Process of Constitution-Making Matter?" *American Review of Law and Society* 5: 201–223.

Gylfason, Thorvaldur, and Anne C. M. Meuwese. 2016. "Digital Tools and the Derailment of Iceland's New Constitution." CESifo Working Paper Series 5997, CESifo Group Munich.

Jackson, Vicky C. 2008. "What's in a Name? Reflections on Timing, Naming, and Constitution Making." *William & Mary Law Review* 49(4): 1249–1305.

Jayawickrama, Nihal. 2012. "Reflections on the Making and Content of the 1972 Constitution: An Insider's Perspective" in *The Sri Lankan Republic at 40: Reflections on Constitutional History, Theory and Practice*. Asanga Welikala (ed.) Colombo: The Centre for Policy Alternatives (CPA), and the Friedrich Naumann Stiftung für die Freiheit (FNF), 44–124.

Kalyvas, Andreas. 2005. "Popular Sovereignty, Democracy, and the Constituent Power." *Constellations* 12(2): 223–244.

Kay, Richard. 1987. "The Illegality of the Constitution." *Constitutional Commentary* 4(1): 57–80.

2011. "Constituent Authority." *American Journal of Comparative Law* 59(3): 715–762.

Klein, Claude, and András Sajó. 2012. "Constitution-Making: Process and Substance" in *The Oxford Handbook of Comparative Constitutional Law*. Michael Rosenfeld and András Sajó (eds.) Oxford: Oxford University Press, 419–441

Klein, James. 1998. "The Constitution of the Kingdom of Thailand, 1997: A Blueprint for Participatory Democracy." The Asia Foundation Working Paper Series: 1–50.

Kornai, János. 2015. "Hungary's U-Turn: Retreating from Democracy." *Journal of Democracy* 26(3): 34–48.

Krunke, Helen. 2013. "Formal and Informal Methods of Constitutional Change in Denmark" in *Engineering Constitutional Change: A Comparative Perspective on Europe, Canada and the USA*. Xenophon Contiades (ed.) Oxon: Routledge, 73–92.

Landau, David. 2013. "Abusive Constitutionalism." *UC Davis Law Review* 47(1): 189–260.

Landau, David, and Hanna Lerner. 2019. *Comparative Constitution Making*. Northampton: Elgar.

Lenowitz, Jerry. 2015. "A Trust That Cannot Be Delegated: The Invention of Ratification Referenda." *American Political Science Review* 109(4): 803–816.

Linz, Juan, and Alfred Stepan. 1996. *Problems of Democratic Transition and Consolidation: Southern Europe, South America, and Post-Communist Europe*. Baltimore: John Hopkins University Press.

Loughlin, Martin. 2007. "Constituent Power Subverted: From English Constitutional Argument to British Constitutional Practice" in *The Paradox of Constitutionalism: Constituent*

Power and Constitutional Form. Martin Loughlin and Neil Walker (eds.) Oxford: Oxford University Press, 27–48.

Lucero, Jose Antonio. 2001. "Crisis and Contention in Ecuador." *Journal of Democracy* 12(2): 59–73.

Mainwaring, Scott, Guillermo O'Donnell, and Samuel Valenzuela. 1992. *Issues in Democratic Consolidation: New South American Democracies in Comparative Perspective*. South Bend: University of Notre Dame Press.

Marshall, Monty G., Ted R. Gurr, and Keith Jaggers. 2019. *Polity IV Project: Political Regime Characteristics and Transitions, 1800–2008*.

Meuwese, Anne. 2013. "Popular Constitution Making: The Case of Iceland" in *The Social and Political Foundations of Constitutions*. Denis J. Galligan and Mila Versteeg (eds.) Cambridge: Cambridge University Press, 469–496.

Miller, Lauren E. 2010. "Designing Constitution-Making Processes: Lessons from the Past, Questions for the Future" in *Framing the State in Times of Transition*. Lauren E. Miller (ed.) Washington, DC: US Institute of Peace, 601–666.

Negretto, Gabriel. 2012. "Replacing and Amending Constitutions. The Logic of Constitutional Change in Latin America." *Law and Society Review* 46(4): 749–779.

2013. *Making Constitutions: Presidents, Parties, and Institutional Choice in Latin America*. Cambridge: Cambridge University Press.

2015. "Procesos Constituyentes y Refundación Democrática: El Caso de Chile en Perspectiva Comparada." *Revista de Ciencia Política* 31(1): 201–215.

2016. "Constitution Making in Democratic Constitutional Orders. The Challenge of Citizen Participation" in *Let the People Rule? Direct Democracy in the Twenty-First Century*. Saskia P. Ruth-Lovell, Yanina Welp, and Laurence Whitehead (eds.) Essex: ECPR Press, 21–40.

2017a. "Constitution Making and Constitutionalism in Latin America: The Role of Procedural Rules" in *Comparative Constitutional Law in Latin America*. Tom Ginsburg and Rosalind Dixon (eds.) Northampton: Elgar, 17–56.

2017b. "Constitution Making in Comparative Perspective" in *Oxford Research Encyclopedia of Politics*. William R. Thompson (ed.) Oxford: Oxford University Press.

2018. "Democratic Constitution-Making Bodies: The Perils of a Partisan Convention." *International Journal of Constitutional Law* 16(1): 254–279.

2019. "Review Essay 'Democratization through Constitutional Change.'" *Latin American Politics and Society* 61(3): 154–160.

Neuman, Laura, and Jennifer McCoy. 2001. *Observing Political Change in Venezuela: The Bolivarian Constitution and 2000 Elections*. Atlanta: The Carter Center.

O'Donnell, Guillermo, and Philippe Schmitter. 1986. *Transitions from Authoritarian Rule: Tentative Conclusions about Uncertain Democracies*. Baltimore: John Hopkins University Press.

Oliver, Dawn, and Carlo Fusaro (eds.) 2011. *How Constitutions Change: A Comparative Study*. Oxford: Hart Publishing.

Parlett, William. 2012. "The Dangers of Popular Constitution-Making." *Brooklyn Journal of International Law* 8: 193–238.

Sucharitkul, Sompong. 1998. "Thailand: Constitutional Developments since Amendment No. 5 of 10 February 1995 to the Constitution of 9 December 1991." *Publications. Paper* 565: 1–13.

Suksi, Markku. 2011. "Finland" in *How Constitutions Change: A Comparative Study*. Dawn Oliver and Carlo Fusaro (eds.) Oxford: Hart Publishing, 87–114.

Tierney, Stephen. 2012. *Constitutional Referendums: The Theory and Practice of Republican Deliberation*. Oxford: Oxford University Press.

Viciano Pastor, Roberto, and Rubén Martínez Dalmau. 2001. *Cambio Político y Proceso Constituyente en Venezuela (1998–2000)*. Valencia: Tiranto Lo Blanch.

Wickramaratne, Jayampathy. 2010. "1972 in Retrospect" in *Sirimavo: Honouring the World's First Woman Prime Minister*. T. Jayatilaka (ed.) Colombo: The Bandaranaike Museum Committee, 63–77.

Wolczuk, Kataryna. 2007. "Ukraine: Tormented Constitution-Making" in *Democratic Consolidation in Eastern Europe, Volume I Institutional Engineering*. Jan Zielonka (ed.) Oxford: Oxford University Press, 241–268.

Wray Reyes, Norman. 2013. "El Proceso Constituyente Ecuatoriano" in *Los Procesos Constituyentes Boliviano y Ecuatoriano: Analisis Comparativo y Prospectiva*. Carlos Böhrt Irahola and Norman Wray Reyes (eds.) Stockholm:IDEA, 155–276.

Zulueta-Fülscher, Kimana. 2015. *Interim Constitutions: Peacekeeping and Democracy-Building Tools*. Stockholm: International IDEA. www.constitutionnet.org/files/interim-constitutions-peacekeeping-and-democracy-building-tools-pdf.pdf.

PART I

Conceptual, Normative, and Empirical Issues

2

Constitution Making through Law

Joel I. Colón-Ríos

The validity of a rule that presents itself as an ordinary law depends, first, on whether it has been adopted according to the correct procedures. A rule that is created in violation of the procedures that are recognized, in a particular society, as necessary and sufficient for bringing into existence ordinary laws, is not a law at all. But that does not apply, at least not in the same way, to constitutions. The constitution of Colombia or the constitution of the United States, for example, were each adopted through legally irregular and previously untried procedures, and yet their validity can hardly be put into question. The reason for this phenomenon seems to be that, unlike ordinary laws, constitutions are seen as emanating directly from "the will of the people," a constituent will that cannot be subject to any form of positive law. Nevertheless, there are also successful constitutions, such as those of Canada and South Africa, which were by and large adopted through previously established rules of change. Does the absence of a legal rupture, the failure to put into practice the idea of a legally unrestrained popular sovereignty, necessarily mean that an exercise of constituent power has not taken place? Can constituent power be exercised through law? These are questions that indirectly challenge one of the features normally attributed to constituent power: its unmediated and uncontrollable nature.

As seen in Chapter 1, the adoption of a new constitution does not only take place after revolutions or after transitions from different forms of authoritarianism to constitutional democracy. Constitutional democracies often engage in acts of constitutional renewal, and most constitutions lack a process of constitutional replacement separate from the ordinary amendment rule. This is entirely consistent, and indeed reflects, the prevailing conception of constituent power: a constitution-making force not subject to legal regulation. Accordingly, a process of constitutional replacement in a constitutional democracy could either take place through the ordinary amendment procedure (which typically places the amending power in the ordinary institutions of government), or through a more participatory, but extralegal, process. In the first case, a new constitution would be produced but its legitimacy would be in question: the eighteenth-century idea that constitutions should be adopted by "the people" and not by government has become almost axiomatic. In the second case, as Partlett argues in Chapter 3, there is the possibility that a political act uncontrolled by any previously established procedures puts at risk the very stability and democratic character of the regime in question. Since none of these scenarios are desirable, the result might be a decision to maintain the constitutional status quo at the price of not making the necessary constitutional changes.

This chapter revisits the theory of constituent power and argues that, when properly understood, constituent power is not inconsistent with legal regulation. Constitutional replacement in constitutional democracies, from this perspective, can take place through legally recognized procedures that, in some contexts, may be understood as facilitating the exercise of constituent authority. The chapter proceeds in the following way. Section I introduces two competing approaches to constituent power, one defended by Rousseau and the other by Sieyès. Rousseau, it will be seen, insisted on the periodic, direct, and legally regulated exercise of the constituent power of the people. Sieyès, on the contrary, ruled out the possibility of a direct exercise of constituent power in a modern society and rejected the idea that the law should attempt to facilitate such an exercise. A true constitution-making act, for Sieyès, was always of an extralegal nature. Section II begins with a brief examination of works by Carl Friedrich and Ernst Böckenförde, which, to an important extent, are representative of the traditional Sieyesian approach. For these authors, it would be futile to try to domesticate constituent power, a power that necessarily belongs outside the legal terrain. There is, however, an alternative approach to constituent power, exemplified in the works of Raymond Carré de Malberg and Georges Vedel, which brings it closer to the legal system.

Under that second (partially Rousseauean) approach, constituent power is freed from all substantive limits of a legal nature, but it is made subject to legally enforceable *procedural* limits. In other words, after a constitutional order is in place, the original constituent power of the people is left behind, and a "pacified" constituent power capable of producing any constitutional content through specified procedures is born. The implication of this conception is that extralegal constitution-making activities, regardless of how popular or participatory, would be incapable of producing law. In other words, the people would no longer be "sovereign." Section III shows that, consistent with this second approach, since the eighteenth century, a handful of national constitutions have attempted to regulate constitutional replacement. For these constitutions, however, the nature of the constitution-making process mattered. They did not merely establish amendment procedures that could be used to replace the constitution, but – as Rousseau's periodic assemblies – sought to reproduce the main characteristics of a popular constitution-making episode. That is to say, procedures that were highly participatory for the standards of the time. Finally, Section IV considers whether a procedurally limited constituent power can retain the radical democratic qualities that serve as the foundation of legitimate constitutional orders.

I ROUSSEAU AND SIEYÈS ON THE CREATION OF NEW CONSTITUTIONS

Rousseau is not generally seen as a theorist of constituent power and, at least at first sight, there are good reasons for that. It is true that his distrust of political representation and support for popular sovereignty is consistent with the idea of the constituent power of the people; through his work, he defended the people's direct and exclusive law-making faculty (and that, at the very least, must include laws of a constitutional nature). From those ideas, it seems to follow that Rousseau is a proponent of direct democracy, and in such a form of government there is no place for a concept that presupposes, above all, a separation between those who exercise a delegated authority (e.g., legislators), and those who possess an original constitution-making power (the people). As in an absolute monarchy or a system of parliamentary sovereignty, in a legal order in which all laws must be directly made by the people, such a separation is absent: the constituent and the legislative body are one and the same. Nevertheless, Rousseau did defend a distinction between the "legislative" and the "executive" power, one that has a very close affinity (and to a large extent corresponds) to the distinction between constituent and constituted power. This is why Carlos Sánchez Viamonte, the Argentinian jurist, maintained that what Rousseau called "legislative power," we call today "constituent power" (Sánchez Viamonte 1952, 196).

The idea, which I cannot develop at length here, is that the role of the legislative power (which always remained in the hands of the sovereign people) was only to create certain types of rules. That is to say, Rousseau used the term "law" to refer to rules of a constitutional nature (Colón-Ríos 2016). In the *Social Contract*, he thus wrote that "laws are, properly speaking, only the conditions of civil association." He also stated that his only concern in that book were those rules that "determine the structure of government," and placed special emphasis on the people's role in creating the "constitution of the State by giving its sanction to a body of law" (Rousseau 1973, 211, 216, 259). The executive power, in contrast, was to be exercised by government and had the role of creating rules that implemented the constitution. Naturally, those rules (which Rousseau called "decrees" but today we would simply call "statutes"), had to be consistent with the body of law that comprised the constitution of the state. The legislative power could only be exercised by the people directly, but the executive power could be put in the hands of a representative body: "It is clear that, in the exercise of the legislative power, the people cannot be represented; but in that of the executive power, which is only the force that is applied to give the law effect, it can and should be represented" (Rousseau 1973, 264).[1]

Just as in contemporary societies the constituent people are usually seen as having the right to create any constitution it wants; Rousseau's legislative power involved the ability of creating any body of laws (laws whose content could not be limited by the positive legal system). "There neither is nor can be," Rousseau famously wrote, "any kind of fundamental law binding on the body of the people, not even the social contract itself" (Rousseau 1973, 193). Rousseau's views about the role of constituent power in actual constitutional practice were radical for his time: he not only thought that the constitution-making (or legislative) power is to be exercised by the entire people, but it had to take place at set periods of time determined by law (and, as we will see shortly) through procedures regulated by the established body of law. The possibility of periodic constitutional replacement was a necessary condition for the legitimacy of a juridical order, without it, the people could not be seen as a self-governing people. Being "not enough for the assembled people to have once fixed the constitution of the State," he maintained that "besides the extraordinary assemblies unforeseen circumstances may demand, there must be fixed periodical assemblies which cannot be abrogated or prorogued, so that on the proper day the people is legitimately called together by law, without the need of any formal summoning" (Rousseau 1973, 259).

Both extraordinary and periodic assemblies could only be convened legally: only a public meeting that complies with the forms established in the constitutional framework could be taken as authorized to pronounce the people's voice. Rousseau's sovereign could create any constitutional content, but not every assembly could claim to be sovereign. In this respect, one can say that, although the people were not subject to any substantive limits found in positive law, it could only act according to certain *procedures* recognized by law (Rousseau 1973, 259).[2] There is no clear indication of how frequently Rousseau thought periodic assemblies should be convened. Even if it does not provide conclusive evidence of his views, it is worth noting that in his native Geneva it was once agreed that the General Council

---

[1] In this sense, the claim that Rousseau proposed direct democracy as a form of government is plainly false. For him, direct interventions by the people were only necessary during instances in which the form of government itself was altered. As he noted in the *Social Contract*: "If we take the term in the strict sense, there has never been a real democracy, and there never will be. It is against the natural order for the many to govern and the few to be governed" (Rousseau 1973, 238–239). "It is unimaginable," he wrote, "that the people should remain continually assembled to devote their time to public affairs, and it is clear they cannot set up commissions for that purpose without the form of administration being changed. . . . Were there a people of gods, their government would be democratic. So perfect a government is not for men" (Rousseau 1973, 238–239).

[2] Periodic assemblies would be "authorized by their date alone," but any other "assembly of the people not summoned by the magistrates appointed for that purpose, and in accordance with the prescribed forms, should be regarded as unlawful" (Rousseau 1973, 259).

(where all citizens sat) would meet every five years (the General Council was also convened in times of crisis) (Rosenblatt 1997, 109).

These assemblies were designed, as it were, to reproduce the two acts that take place when government is instituted for the first time. Not surprisingly, they would always put to the people two different propositions: "The first is: 'Does it please the Sovereign to preserve the present form of government?' The second is: 'Does it please the people to leave its administration in the hands of those who are actually in charge of it?'" (Rousseau 1973, 269). Of course, in most states (and certainly in contemporary ones), the idea of convening an assembly of all the people presents an important practical difficulty. Aware of this problem, Rousseau proposed two possible solutions. First, different groups of citizens could assemble in the relevant locality or region (e.g., town, city) (Rousseau 1973, 260). Under this approach, multiple primary assemblies (that is, assemblies open to all citizens residing in a particular locality) would participate in the exercise of the legislative (constituent) power by expressing their views on the two questions mentioned above. The votes of all the citizens participating in these assemblies, it seems, would be taken as the declaration of the general will, that is, as an indication of the type of constitution that would serve the common good in that particular society.

The second solution was addressed to states so large that even multiple assemblies would not be enough to allow for the direct participation of all citizens. In those states, the people had no choice but to exercise their constituent power with the assistance of a "representative" body. As he noted in *Considerations on the Government of Poland*: "One of the greatest disadvantages of large states, the one which above all makes liberty most difficult to preserve in them, is that the legislative power cannot manifest itself directly, and can act only by delegation" (Rousseau 1772, 16). But in order for that situation not to amount to a form of slavery, it was necessary for delegates to be strictly bound by the instructions of their constituents (Rousseau 1772, 16). Rousseau thus referred to "the negligence, the carelessness and, I would even venture to say, the stupidity of the English nation, which, after having armed its deputies with such supreme power, has added no brake to regulate the use they may make of that power through the seven years of their mandate" (Rousseau 1772, 16). The fact that the English Parliament could adopt ordinary statutes was not problematic; the problem was that that entity could change the country's constitution without the intervention of the people.[3]

In contrast to Rousseau, Sieyès looked at constitutional replacement as a purely extralegal phenomenon. He thought that Rousseau's approach would make the

---

[3] This is, in fact, the meaning of Rousseau's famous statement: "Every law the people has not ratified in person is null and void – is, in fact, not a law. The people of England regards itself as free; but it is grossly mistaken; it is free only during the election of members of parliament. As soon as they are elected, slavery overtakes it, and it is nothing" (Rousseau 1973, 263). The problem was not that the English Parliament was passing ordinary statutes without the direct participation of the citizenry, but that it also passed "laws."

stability of any constitution impossible, and therefore that the law should only allow for partial revisions. A constitution could very well contain an amendment rule authorizing a legislative supermajority (or a special assembly, as the Constitution of 1791 did) to modify its provisions, but such a rule could not be used for the creation of an entirely new constitutional order.[4] Sieyès's preferred approach to constitutional reform, as presented in *Préliminaire de la Constitution*, could lead one to a different conclusion, one that seems consistent with Rousseau's argument for periodic constituent assemblies convened according to law. In that essay, read at the Constitutional Committee in July 1789, Sieyès included a draft declaration of the rights of man and the citizen. Article 32 of that draft, in an apparently Rousseauean/Jeffersonian fashion (Jefferson 1984, 1402), established that "the people always has the right to revise and reform their constitution. It is even desirable to establish fixed intervals, where such revisions considered necessary will take place" (Sieyès 1789, 32).

Sieyès did not offer specific commentary on that provision, and what appeared to be an elaboration of the principle reflected on it had to wait for a speech delivered two years later, when the revolution had already entered a different stage. In that speech ("Second Thermidorian Intervention"), he maintained that a constitution would be imperfect unless it provided for its own conservation through time: a constitution "must be able to assimilate the materials needed for its proper development" and must be susceptible to perfection through periodic revision (Sieyès 2014, 177). That did not mean, however, that a constitution must be subject to the type of "periodic recreation" that extremists such as Rousseau and Jefferson seemed to look forward to (Sieyès 2014, 177). Indeed, in a Madisonian fashion, Sieyès suggested that "once a constitution has been placed on a reliable foundation, it should no longer be exposed to moments of complete renewal," otherwise "it would lose all those sentiments of love and veneration that a free people devote to it" (Sieyès 2014, 177).[5] Ideally, he wrote, the constitution would have "the terrible permanence of the laws governing the universe itself," but since human beings were imperfect, it needed to be open to piecemeal revision. That, however, was not in any way a defense to an approach to constitutional change that rendered "constituent power permanent" (Sieyès 2014, 177).

---

[4]   That is, arguably, the meaning of chapter 7 of the Constitution of 1791, whose text seems to exclude the possibility of "total revisions," only authorizing the reform of individual articles (Carré de Malberg 1948, 1184n6). Note, also, that in an intervention supported by the National Constituent Assembly, Jacques Guillaume Thouret (president of the assembly) argued that since the constitution was fundamentally a good one, founded on the "immutable bases of justice and in the eternal principle of reason," it was unnecessary to provide rules for its replacement (Archives Parlementaires 1791, 186).

[5]   Madison, it is well known, thought that Jefferson's views about constitutional change suggested to the citizenry that their current system of government was somehow defective, depriving the government of "that veneration which time bestows on everything, and without which perhaps the wisest and freest governments would not possess the requisite stability" (*The Federalist Papers*, No. 49).

Quite the opposite: a constituent power that always threatens the constitutional order was no different from having no constitution at all. The constitution should instead be guided by the "principle of unlimited perfectibility, which makes it adaptable to the needs of different eras, rather than a principle of destruction by total revision, which leaves it at the mercy of contingent events" (Sieyès 2014, 177). Sieyès thus rejected the idea of institutionalizing the periodic recreation of the constitutional order, and instead embraced a system in which a "constitutional jury" *(jury constitutionnaire)* was in charge of proposing revisions to the constitutional text. Such revisions, as noted in the previously mentioned draft Article 32, would take place at fixed intervals: "Every ten years, beginning at the end of this century, in 1800, the Constitutional Jury will publish a collection of proposals for improving the constitution." These proposals would be sent to the legislature and disseminated along primary assemblies in the relevant cantons. Primary assemblies would then determine, through a "yes" or "no" vote, whether the legislature should be "invested with constituent power" and thus empowered to act on them (Sieyès 2014, 177). However, not being the true constituent subject, the legislature would not be able to "edit or replace" the relevant proposals. Rather, it would have the authority to "reject some or all of them, but it would have to cite reasons for doing so" (Sieyès 2014, 177).

This approach, to a certain extent, brings Sieyès closer to Rousseau. For both authors, the entire citizenry (even if defined in a way that excludes part of the population, such as women and passive citizens) must be consulted before constituent power is to be exercised. Nevertheless, unlike Rousseau, Sieyès was not prepared to see primary assemblies as the constituent power in action. First, as noted earlier, their power could not be used to adopt an entirely new constitutional order: it was a mere *amending* power. Second, Sieyès made sure that none of the institutions invested with the amending power could claim to be the constituent subject. "Constituent activity," he wrote, should be "divided among the primary assemblies, the Constitutional Jury, and the legislature" (Sieyès 2014, 177). Attributing primary assemblies with the legal faculty of changing the constitution (even if in this substantively and procedurally limited form) would be inconsistent with his conception of representation, but would also be too risky. A constitutional jury, and the approach to constitutional change that it involves, did not mean that an exercise of constituent power that resulted in the adoption of a radically new constitution was rendered impossible. Sieyès, in fact, made clear that, in defending that proposal, he had nothing to say about extralegal "revolutionary upheavals, whose prevention is not the task of our jury" (Sieyès 2014, 171).

II TWO APPROACHES TO CONSTITUENT POWER

Sieyès's and Rousseau's approaches are, to a certain extent, exemplified in the two main ways in which the theory of constituent power has been treated by academics since it was put into practice in the great revolutions of the eighteenth century.

Under the first approach, constituent power's extralegal and uncontrollable character is emphasized. It is presented as a power located outside the dominion of law and therefore incapable of legal regulation. This is the way in which most legal scholars understand it,[6] and partially explains the reason for the relative inattention to the concept in some constitutional circles. Under the second, less influential approach, constituent power is constitutionalized: it is seen as the power of altering or replacing a constitution according to certain prescribed rules. From this perspective, the fact that even the exercise of an ultimate constitution-making power is subject to law tends to be celebrated as one of the greatest achievements of modern constitutionalism: the domestication of an apparently unruly political force. The first approach reflects the traditional Sieyèsian conception; the second has some interesting affinities with Rousseau's views. In this section, I will examine these two conceptions with the objective of showing that the idea of a substantively unlimited constituent power does not necessarily require placing it in an extralegal space.

The first approach is well exemplified in the work of Carl Friedrich. For Friedrich, understanding constituent power correctly requires one to distinguish it from the amendment rules contained in typical constitutional documents. The adoption of formal amendment rules "should not be assumed to [supersede] the constituent power," which always threatens the constitutional order from the outside (Friedrich 1950, 149). The implication is that any attempt to channel constituent power through law would make it subject to substantive limits, which could be explicit or implicit (e.g., limits identified by judges through the application of the doctrine of unconstitutional constitutional amendments). In order to be a true power of constitutional replacement, this view suggests, constituent power must be left outside the domain of law. The idea of constituent power as necessarily extralegal and uncontrollable is also shared by jurists who attribute to it the function of legitimizing the existing constitutional order. Ernst-Wolfgang Böckenförde provides a good contemporary example. For Böckenförde, the mere fact that a constitution has been successfully brought into existence is not sufficient to guarantee its continuing acceptance through time. A constitution can only be legitimate, he argues, if it rests in the (always present) constituent authority of the people. Constituent power is thus seen as an original and rudimentary potency that serves as the source of democratic legitimacy, a power that is "capable of creating, sustaining, and cancelling the constitution" (Böckenförde 2000, 160, 163).

In Böckenförde's view, the question of constituent power is a juridical question because it is directly connected to the legitimacy of the legal order, but constituent power itself, he suggests, is a power that precedes the constitution and remains forever uncontrolled by its rules of change (Böckenförde 2000, 160, 168). It is true, Böckenförde says, that one can attempt to devise procedures that attempt to "channel" constituent power (such as constituent assemblies). It is also correct that the

---

[6] See, for example, Negri (1999), Kalyvas (2008), Wall (2012), and Wenman (2013).

exercise of constituent power is always accompanied by a certain degree of "constitutionality," since it must always end in the production of a constitution (Böckenförde 2000, 169–172, 176). Nevertheless, these potential "limits" are never enough to bring constituent power under the full reins of the constitution it precedes and legitimizes. Constituent power, he maintains echoing Carl Schmitt, is always capable of manifesting itself in unanticipated ways.

Raymond Carré de Malberg, who devoted an entire chapter of his *Contribution à la Théorie Générale de l'Etat* to an analysis of constituent power, provides a good introduction to the second approach (Carré de Malberg 1948, 1161). For Carré de Malberg, there is a clear sense in which the theory of constituent power should not even be the concern of lawyers: when used to explain the creation of a state's first constitution (the constitution that brings a new state into existence), the exercise of constituent power must be understood as purely factual, unable of being governed by legal principles (Carré de Malberg 1948, 1167). The same applies when a new constitution is created as a result of a revolution or a coup d'état, where formal amendment rules are violated and the chain of legality between the old and the new constitutional order is irreparably broken (Carré de Malberg 1948, 1173). In those contexts, it is not preposterous to associate constituent power with unlawfulness, extralegal action, and legally unregulated force. Those exercises of constituent power are clearly outside the scope of the legal system, either because there is no positive law yet in place (as when the primitive constitution of a state is created) or because the existing positive laws have proved unable to stop the destruction of the constitutional order.

Political actions of that sort may very well raise urgent moral issues but, for Carré de Malberg, they do not present any juridical questions to be answered by a lawyer (the most a lawyer can do, he wrote, would be to identify the moment in which a revolutionary constitution becomes valid) (Carré de Malberg 1948, 1168). This is why he criticized the view shared by some of his contemporaries, who saw in the concept of constituent power "the capital problem of public law" (Carré de Malberg 1948, 1161, 1168). There is no role in the science of public law for the consideration of the extraordinary sovereignty of the "great days" (Carré de Malberg 1948, 1209), just as there is no space in it "for a legal theory of *coups d'état*, or of revolution and its effects" (Carré de Malberg 1948, 1173). Despite Carré de Malberg's scathing critique of those who attribute to constituent power a juridical character, he did not think this concept was altogether irrelevant for the student of public law. On the contrary, he maintained that in the context of an already existing constitutional order, one could speak of a "regular and pacific" constituent power: the power to modify the existing constitution (or to replace it with a new one) according to procedures established by law. He called this the "juridical concept" of constituent power (*la notion juridique de pouvoir constituant*), which presupposes the existence of a constitutional order and is procedurally regulated by it (Carré de Malberg 1948, 1175).

Modern constitutions, in fact, frequently reflect this view, which is why they contain carefully designed mechanisms for constitutional change not seen as subject to limits of a substantive nature. The fortunate consequence is that when a constitution is to be amended or replaced, it is neither necessary to resort to the whole body of citizens nor to engage in the exercise of an extralegal power (Carré de Malberg 1948, 1174). In such scenarios, "the intervention of the organs that the constitution – the same constitution that will be amended or replaced – prescribes in advance for the regular and pacific exercise of the constituent power" is sufficient (Carré de Malberg 1948, 1174). Those organs (e.g., a legislative supermajority) are legally authorized to alter or replace the existing constitution as long as they follow the legal procedures that channel their constituent activity (Carré de Malberg 1948, 1173). Generally, academics who advance this approach distinguish, like Carré de Malberg, between a revolutionary (original) constituent power and a legally regulated (or derived) one. Nevertheless, what characterizes this second approach is that both notions of constituent power are seen as capable of producing the same results: the radical transformation or the entire replacement of the constitutional regime. They are instances of the same phenomenon, moments in which the *same* power is exercised even if in different contexts and through different means.

Georges Vedel further exemplifies this view. Vedel operated under the standard distinction between the material and formal conceptions of a constitution. From the material point of view, the constitution is equivalent to the set of rules that establish the form of government and that regulate the relationship between the state and its citizens; it is the expression of the most important norms of the political system. From the formal point of view, a constitution is a legal norm that, unlike ordinary statutes, can only be enacted or modified through special procedures (Vedel 2002, 112). The main consequence of the formal notion of the constitution is that there must be a special (constituent) organ authorized to make use of procedures designed to procure alterations of the constitutional text (Vedel 2002, 114). Of course, if there is no state in place, or if the constitution is being replaced by illegal means, then such organs will not exist yet or they will be ineffective. In such cases, Vedel, like Carré de Malberg, thought that constituent power functioned as an original power (*pouvoir originaire*) not subject to any rules. However, Vedel maintained that constituent power does not only manifest in those extralegal contexts: it also appears whenever a constitutional text is modified or replaced, even if this occurs through organs bound by certain procedural rules (Vedel 2002, 116).

Notwithstanding the above, Vedel perhaps is simply using the term "constituent power" (or more specifically, *pouvoir constituant dérivé*) to describe the activity of ordinary constitutional reform, that is, to refer to the power of amending a constitution in accordance with its own rules. It is true that for Vedel, any amendment to a constitution would count as an exercise of constituent power. In that sense, it might be argued that Vedel is merely an example of the fact that some authors use the term constituent power (or "derived constituent power") to refer to what others would call the "amending power."[7] However, Vedel thinks that the power exercised in revolutionary situations and the one exercised in the context of constitutional reform are identical in the most relevant sense. Both are sovereign powers that cannot be subject to any kind of substantive limit (Vedel 1993, 90). For instance, a clause prohibiting the amendment of certain articles of the constitution (inserted into the document by the original constituent power) cannot bind the derived constituent power. "The constituent [power] of today," he writes, "cannot bind the nation of tomorrow" (Vedel 1993, 117). The idea is that despite being subject to certain procedures, the derived constituent power is a *constituent* power in terms of its effect (Vedel 1992, 179). As Kemal Gözler has maintained, under this view, there is an original and a derived power, but only one constituent function (Gözler 2004, 15).

III THE CONSTITUTIONALIZATION OF CONSTITUENT POWER

What I have identified as the "second" approach to constituent power, it could be insisted, is simply the ordinary power of constitutional reform. A power regulated by law, even if only procedurally, cannot be a constituent power. At first sight, it is difficult to disagree with that objection. As we saw before, Sieyès, who gave constituent power its first major theoretical formulation and distinguished it from the constituted powers of government, placed it outside the legal order, and most contemporary analyses of the concept tend to follow Sieyès in that respect. But there are good reasons for not dismissing the second approach so quickly – to at least consider the possibility that "original" and "derived" constituent power are conceptualizations of the same type of power. As shown earlier, both approaches attribute to – what they call – constituent power (even if qualified by words such as "pacific," "regular," "derived," "constituted," "original," or "primary") the very same substantive ability: that of introducing any content into a constitutional order. That is to say, a constituent organ (which could be, for example, the legislature acting in a special capacity) is a juridical means for exercising the same power that once brought the constitution into existence.

Moreover, both derived and original constituent power can be exercised at any time, and whether to activate the latter is harder than to exercise the former (or vice versa) is not necessarily related to their nature but depends mostly on the rigidity or flexibility of the constitution at issue, as well as on the political context in which the constitution operates. It is not the case, for example, that original constituent power can only be exercised in cases of near unanimous support for constitutional change, and that the exercise of derived constituent power is merely a matter of complying

---

[7] It is telling that in a footnote to his *Constitutional Government and Democracy*, Carl Friedrich stated that: "It is very important to keep in mind that the 'constituent power' as used here is not identical with the *pouvoir constituant* of French constitutional law, which corresponds to the amending power of American constitutional law" (Friedrich 1950, 629n4).

with certain rules: ordinary amendment procedures can be designed in such a way that constitutional change is virtually impossible as long as it is opposed by a relatively small minority (a good example here is provided by Article V of the US Constitution, which involves supermajority requirements at the federal and state level that are notoriously difficult to meet).[8] When a constitution operates under the understanding that the derived constituent power is not subject to substantive limits (as in what I have called the second approach) it thus presents the same threat to the existing constitution than the original one: both the original and the derived constituent power can be used to replace the constitution with a new one, even though only the former would do it from outside of the legal order.[9]

Nevertheless, there is a fundamental difference between these two approaches. The first approach, while insisting in the extralegal character of constituent power and not subjecting it to any specific procedural rules, is permeated by the – natural law – notion that constituent power rests in the entire community. It is a power that groups of human beings have from the very moment they decide to enter civil society. Accordingly, it must be exercised in ways that somehow reflect the fact that during a constituent moment the nation, the community, or the people, acts. Otherwise, such an exercise of political power would lack legitimacy. During the French Revolution, it was concluded that only the representatives of the Third Estate could legitimately exercise constituent power; in the twenty-first century, a representative entity acting by itself is unlikely to be considered enough and some form of direct popular participation would probably be necessary. The second approach rejects that notion: whatever the process the law establishes for the alteration of the constitution will be sufficient to produce any constitutional content. There is no such thing as substantive limits not found in the positive law of the constitution, and there are no non-positive legal principles that require a participatory procedure of constitutional replacement.

These aspects of the second approach have nevertheless been superseded in practice. For example, some constitutions authorize the exercise of constituent power through mechanisms of "constitutional replacement" that, on the one hand, seem to escape the "legal" or "extralegal" categories and, on the other, lead to situations that are difficult to differentiate from popular constitution-making episodes. These types of mechanisms generally take the form of constituent assemblies attributed with a constitution-making power capable of producing any constitutional

---

[8] For a discussion, see Levinson (2008) and Jackson (2015).

[9] This helps to explain why, in one of its famous 1992 decisions on the Maastricht Treaty, the French Constitutional Council stated that "the constituent power is sovereign; it has the power to repeal, amend, and supplement constitutional provisions in such manner it considers appropriate," without any recourse to the well-rehearsed distinction between derived and original constituent power ("Le pouvoir constituant est souverain; qu'il lui est loisible d'abroger, de modifier ou de compléter des dispositions de valeur constitutionnelle dans la forme qu'il estime appropriée.") Decision n. 92-312 DC du 02 septembre 1992, para. 19.

content. From a strictly legal perspective, since they are convened according to preestablished rules, it could be argued that these assemblies are no different from ordinary amendment mechanisms. There are nevertheless strong reasons that point against that view. In particular, and unlike traditional amendment rules, these mechanisms allow for the convocation of an entity that operates separate from – and potentially against the will of – the ordinary institutions of government. In addition, once convened, constituent assemblies are usually not bound by constitutional rules and they sometimes even intrude in the exercise of the ordinary powers of government, claiming to represent the community in its full self-governing capacity and thus able to temporarily exercise the powers of the executive, legislative, and judicial branches.

From this perspective, they appear as entities that, although having originated in the legal order, exercise a truly sovereign power. They are manifestations of a new legal beginning, situations in which civil society exercises a primitive political force, coming closer than ever to a lawless state of nature. The highly participatory character of these assemblies (they can originate in a popular initiative – that is, through the collection of a number of signatures – and normally require authorizing and ratificatory referenda), to a great extent mimics what would be expected to happen in a democratic but revolutionary constitution-making episode. To the extent they do that, they become highly consistent with the Rousseauean view of constituent power as a popular power that can (and should) be exercised through law. The first national constitution exemplifying that approach, to the best of my knowledge, was the French Constitution of 1793 (which was ratified in a referendum but never came into effect after being suspended by a state of emergency) (Doyle 2002, 246). That constitution authorized the convocation of a National Convention at the request of a tenth of the primary assemblies in the majority of departments (Article 115). The National Convention could be given the authority to alter particular articles of the constitution or of "revising the constitutional text" (Article 115). In exercising that authority, it could adopt an entirely new constitution, even though its power could be limited beforehand (as Article 117 authorizes the National Convention to deliberate only on the topics for which it was convened).[10]

According to the Constitution of 1793, primary assemblies would comprise no less than 200 citizens (who resided in a particular canton) and no more than 600 (Articles 11–12). They would be held every year, but could also be convened in extraordinary circumstances at the request of one-fifth of the citizenry (Articles 31–34). The main purpose of primary assemblies, according to the constitution, was that of voting about particular proposals. For example, (and using Rousseau's language), the constitution established that while decrees could be issued by the

---

[10] See Article 28 of the Declaration of the Rights of Man and the Citizen of 1793, included in the constitution's preamble: "A people has always the right to revise, reform, and change its constitution. No generation can subject the future generations to its laws."

ordinary legislature alone, laws required the ratification of primary assemblies (if one-tenth of them, in the majority of departments, protested against a proposed bill) (Articles 54–61). Although the constitution does not explicitly state it, it seems that a newly proposed constitution would also be subject to popular ratification before coming into effect. This approach to constitutional reform was radically different from the one found in the French Constitutions of 1791 and 1795, where the exercise of the power to create a new constitution was left unregulated by law (and, where constitutional reform was, by and large, left in the hands of the ordinary institutions of government).[11] The French Constitution of 1793 not only attributed a National Convention with the ability to create a new constitutional order, but required that such a process took place through a participatory process (participatory, at least, according to the standards of the time) regardless of the many critiques to which it can be subjected.

This approach is to a large extent manifested in a number of Latin American constitutions. This is the case in the constitutions of Ecuador, Bolivia, Venezuela, and Panamá. These constitutions establish ordinary processes of constitutional reform normally led by a legislative supermajority that is unable to engage in the adoption of an entirely new constitutional text (being subject to a number of substantive limits specified in the constitution and potentially to implicit limits as well). That is to say, a process of constitutional reform that does not involve the exercise of constituent power (not even in its "derived" nature as conceived by Carré de Malberg and Vedel). At the same time, however, they provide for the possibility of the convocation, by popular initiative, of a constituent assembly capable of producing a new constitutional order.[12] These provisions, however, are highly

[11] The Girondin Constitutional Project, presented to the National Convention on February 1793 (which had, among its authors, the Marquis de Condorcet as well as Thomas Paine), also shared some of these features. *Plan de Constitution présenté à la Convention nationale les 15 et 16 février 1793, l'an II de la République.* Paine, it should be noted, had views similar to Jefferson about the periodic reconstitution of the state (Paine 1961, 251).

[12] See, for example, Article 444 of the constitution of Ecuador: "Installation of a Constituent Assembly can only be called by referendum. The President of the Republic can request this referendum, by two thirds of the National Assembly or by twelve percent (12%) of the persons registered on the voter registration list. The referendum must include how representatives must be elected and the rules for the electoral process. The new Constitution, for its entry into force, shall require adoption by referendum with half plus one of all valid ballots cast." Article 314 of the constitution of Panamá has an interesting approach, since it insists in the "parallel nature" of the Constituent Assembly (in order to ensure that it only engages in the exercise of constituent power and does not invade the jurisdiction of the constituted organs): "A new Constitution may be adopted by a Parallel Constituent Assembly (Asamblea Constituyente Paralela) which may be convened by decision of the Executive Branch, ratified by the Legislative Branch with absolute majority, or by the Legislative Branch with a favorable vote of two thirds of its members, or by popular initiative which must be signed by at least twenty percent (20%) of citizens enrolled in the Electoral Register on the thirty-first of December of the year preceding the initiative." See also Article 411 of the constitution of Bolivia and Article 348 of the constitution of Venezuela.

imperfect. In particular, they provide the executive with the power to trigger a referendum on whether a constituent assembly should be convened. Such a process is in tension with the participatory nature of an ideal exercise of constituent power and could lead to a number of different abuses.

Despite this problem (and perhaps others),[13] one can see in those provisions an attempt to regulate the exercise of constituent power. In regulating such an exercise, however, these constitutions do not attempt to limit its substantive force (i.e., the constituent assembly can produce any constitutional content, at least if it is explicitly authorized to do so).[14] At the same time, they establish processes of constitutional change of a highly participatory nature, at least when compared with other national constitutions. One might nevertheless ask: But are those provisions really facilitating the exercise of original constituent power, or are they just interesting reformulations of a power of constitutional reform that (despite Carré de Malberg's and Vedel's characterization of that power as an unlimited constitution-making force) can indeed be subject to a number of explicit or implicit substantive limits? If one looks at the ways in which these provisions are phrased, it seems that they are intended to channel a full power of constitutional change. For example, Article 411 of the constitution of Bolivia states that a number of fundamental principles that fall outside the jurisdiction of the ordinary power of constitutional reform can only be replaced by a constituent assembly described as "original" and "plenipotentiary." Article 347 of the constitution of Venezuela is even more explicit: "The original constituent power rests with the people of Venezuela. This power may be exercised by calling a National Constituent Assembly."

It is of course possible for an ordinary legislature (or for a legislature siting in a special capacity) to be authorized by law to replace an existing constitutional order. Whether such form of constitutional replacement can ever be reasonably understood as a legitimate exercise of constituent power would seem to largely depend on the political context and on the opportunities of popular participation provided. Consider, for example, the "constituent process" activated (but not concluded) in Chile between 2015 and 2017.[15]

---

[13] Article 411 of the constitution of Bolivia, for example, requires that the constituent assembly adopts a new constitutional text by a two-thirds majority. Congress added that requirement to the draft constitution before it was submitted for popular ratification. While it could be defended as an attempt to ensure that a proposed constitution is based on a wide consensus, such a requirement privileges the constitutional status quo in a way that is arguably in tension with the very idea of constituent power. As a result, it is possible that it will not be respected by a future constituent assembly. If that happened, a legal rupture would occur and, therefore, one would no longer be able to speak about an exercise of constituent power through law.

[14] If a constitution-making body is seen, as in Rousseau, as an entity that is authorized only to propose a constitution to the people, then there is no reason why its powers cannot be limited beforehand (for example, through conditions that could be part of the question put to the electorate when the assembly is convened).

[15] On this process, see Soto and Welp (2017).

According to the way it was originally designed by Bachelet's government, the constitution-making process in Chile would begin with multiple citizen fora at local and regional levels. These instances of consultation would result in the adoption of a list of principles (*bases ciudadanas*), which would then inform the constitutional drafters. Later in the process, a newly elected congress would have the authority to choose among four alternative constitution-making mechanisms, including that of convening a constituent assembly or that of having the constitution drafted by an assembly that would take the form of a joint sitting of both legislative houses (in both cases, the constitution would become law if ratified in a referendum). The latter option, at least in theory, could be seen as resulting in a legitimate exercise of constituent power if, for instance, the views expressed by citizens during the consultation process are actually reflected in the previously mentioned "list of principles," the new congress is elected amidst a national debate on constitutional replacement, and the candidates who eventually prevail in that election had made clear their intention of supporting the calling of a constituent legislature. Of course, if used as a means of suppressing the possibilities of more "radical" constitutional changes (that is, of preventing the adoption of certain type of content), constitution making by a "constituent legislature" would raise important questions of legitimacy.

IV THE LEGAL REPLACEMENT OF CONSTITUTIONAL REGIMES

In Section III, I attempted to show that Carré de Malberg's and Vedel's approach to constituent power as exercisable through a process regulated by law is reflected, for example, in the French Constitution of 1793 and in a number of Latin American constitutions. Unlike other constitutions that may also regulate the exercise of a substantively unlimited power of constitutional change, these constitutions require such a power to be exercised through participatory legal procedures. They seem to assume that constituent power may be exercised through law, but only if the process of constitutional change is a legitimate one. That is to say, a process that provides for the participation of the entire citizenry, or that approximates, to the extent possible, to that ideal. From this perspective, the question of whether constituent power can be exercised through law is not only a question about the nature of the power at issue (about whether it can produce any constitutional content), but about the mode of its exercise (about whether it can be reasonably understood as a constitution-making act of the people). In this sense, the tradition of constituent power that began with the Constitution of 1793 can be seen as having the potential of avoiding the need for legal ruptures, revolutions, and informal constituent episodes, while retaining the popular character of constitution making. In this last section, I will consider whether this conception can be firmly grounded on the idea of constituent power as the unlimited constitution-making power of the people, or whether it would require the rejection of that idea.

Constituent power is the power to create new constitutions. If a constitution maker is subject to legally enforceable limits of a substantive nature, it would not have constituent power: the content of the new constitution would have been determined in advance, perhaps by the true constituent subject (e.g., a foreign power, a political elite, an absolute monarch). The question is whether a substantively unlimited people could nevertheless be subject to procedural limits and that, when acting according to the established procedures, it could be seen as legally exercising original constituent power. That idea is controversial because, if accepted, the people would be subject to – potentially enforceable – limits of a legal nature. An attempt to exercise constituent power in violation of the legally established procedures (even if the chosen means are more participatory than the established ones), would be illegal and subject to constitutional control. In such a situation, the people would no longer exist in an extralegal terrain; it would no longer be "sovereign" in the traditional sense of the term (a supreme and unlimited power). This would entail, to use Carré de Malberg's phrase, a "pacification" of the constituent subject. To the extent that this approach would make extralegal ruptures unnecessary and therefore promote the stability of the constitutional regime, its attraction is obvious.

But can it be legitimate? Taking into account the previously discussed theoretical literature and comparative examples, it seems that a constitution that regulates constitutional replacement and therefore seeks to establish limits on the people's constituent power would need to, at the very least, satisfy the following criteria in order to have a claim to legitimacy. *First*, it must not set legal limits of a substantive nature. As noted earlier, a constitution maker subject to substantive limits would be unable to create new constitutions (as the content of any constitution it creates would have been previously determined); it would lack constituent power. This does not mean that a constitutional replacement clause could not identify a number of substantive limits that should guide a future constitution maker. For example, a replacement clause could state that any new constitution should respect human rights or comply with certain international treaties. But those substantive limits could only aspire to guide the constituent subject morally or politically, not legally. *Second*, the constitutional replacement rules should involve participatory procedures that come as close as possible (according to the understandings of the relevant society at any given moment) to something that can be reasonably described as an act of the people. If any of the previous two requirements were violated, an extralegal exercise of constituent power through a participatory process would be legitimate, even if illegal under the established constitutional regime. In such a situation, the relation of the people to the (non-participatory) constitutional replacement clause would be that of any sovereign: a sovereign can act according to law for political or prudential reasons but not because it is bound by it.[16]

---

[16] At the same time, if the ordinary institutions of government attempt to use the established process of constitutional change to adopt a new constitution, the judicial application of the

Even if one agrees with this approach, the question would remain as to whether, as a matter of constitutional practice, it is desirable for a democratic regime to attempt to regulate constitutional replacement in the ways described above. If the replacement of a constitutional regime is seen as a negative occurrence, then perhaps the law should not facilitate it. But this is not necessarily the case. It could be, for example, that the existing constitution arguably has illegitimate origins. If a social consensus emerges that such a constitution needs to be replaced in order for a legitimate constitutional order to emerge, there is no reason to conclude that such replacement should necessarily take place extralegally. The constitution, for example, could itself be amended in order to provide for a democratic process of constitution making leading to its own replacement. Or, if the amendment of the constitution is not possible (for example, it could involve a threshold that is virtually impossible to meet), such a procedure could be created extra-constitutionally. That is to say, through an ordinary law that makes the exercise of constituent power possible (e.g., a law that calls for a referendum on whether a constituent assembly should be convened). The fact that the procedure is brought into existence by law is not an impediment to seeing it as facilitating the exercise of constituent power, as long as it can be reasonably understood as channeling an "act of the people."

V CONCLUSION

This chapter argued that the exercise of the constituent power of the people could be subject to legal limits of a procedural nature. Those limits, I have attempted to show, do not necessarily take away the radical democratic potential of constituent power, at least not if they are consistent with a participatory conception of constitution making. In a certain way, the idea that constituent power can be subject to procedural limits should not even be controversial. If, for example, the arguably extralegal and participatory process used for the creation of the current Colombian constitution had been established by a previous constitutional amendment (as partially happened in Bolivia some years later), should it have been seen as involving the exercise of a lesser power of constitutional change that that which was in fact exercised in 1990–1991? It is difficult to see how that question could be answered in the affirmative without falling into the trap of defending extralegality for its own sake. Such a perspective could lead one to absurd conclusions. For example, it would involve preferring a less democratic but extralegal process over a highly democratic but legal one *just* because of the relationship of the process to the legal

---

doctrine of unconstitutional constitutional amendments would be justified. This is not the place to engage in a discussion about this doctrine, but suffice to say that it would also be applied in cases where a single change to an established constitution is so fundamental that it amounts to the creation of a new one. The reason is that those types of changes are under the exclusive jurisdiction of the constituent subject. See Roznai (2017).

system. None of this means that the extralegal exercise of constituent power can never be justified, or that in particular contexts it could in fact be the most desirable constitution-making practice. It just means that it is possible to establish a procedure of constitutional replacement that genuinely channels the constituent power of the people.

REFERENCES

Archives Parlementaires, vol., XXX (3 September 1791).

Böckenförde, E. W. 2000. *Estudios sobre el Estado de Derecho y la Democracia*. Madrid: Editorial Trotta.

Carré de Malberg, Raymond. 1948. *Teoría General del Estado*. México D.F.: Fondo de Cultura Económica.

Colón-Ríos, Joel. 2016. "Rousseau, Theorist of Constituent Power." *Oxford Journal of Legal Studies* 36(4): 885–908.

Doyle, William. 2002. *Oxford History of the French Revolution*. Oxford: Oxford University Press.

Friedrich, Carl. 1950. *Constitutional Government and Democracy: Theory and Practice in Europe and America*. Boston: Ginn.

Gözler, Kemal. 2004. *Pouvoir Constituant*. Bursa: Ekin Kitabevi.

Jackson, Vicki. 2015. "The (Myth of Un)Amendability of the U.S. Constitution and the Democratic Component of Constitutionalism." *International Journal of Constitutional Law* 13(3): 575–605.

Jefferson, Thomas. 1984. *Writings*. New York: Library of America.

Kalyvas, Andreas. 2008. *Democracy and the Politics of the Extraordinary: Max Weber, Carl Schmitt and Hannah Arendt*. Cambridge: Cambridge University Press.

Levinson, Sanford. 2008. *Our Undemocratic Constitution: Where the Constitution Goes Wrong (And How We the People Can Correct It*. Oxford: Oxford University Press.

Negri, Antonio. 1999. *Insurgencies: Constituent Power and the Modern State*. Minneapolis: University of Minnesota Press.

Paine, Thomas. 1961. "The Rights of Man" in *The Life and Major Writings of Thomas Paine*. Philip Foner (ed.) New York: Citadel.

Rosenblatt, Helena. 1997. *Rousseau and Geneva: From the First Discourse to the Social Contract, 1749–1762*. Cambridge: Cambridge University Press.

Rousseau, J. J. 1772. *Considerations on the Government of Poland and on Its Proposed Reformation*. ISN ETH Zurich. https://css.ethz.ch/en/services/digital-library/publications/publication.html/125482.

1973. *The Social Contract*. London: Everyman's Library.

Rossiter, Clinton (ed.) 1961. *The Federalist Papers*. New York: New American Library.

Roznai, Yaniv. 2017. *Unconstitutional Constitutional Amendments: The Limits of Amendment Powers*. Oxford: Oxford University Press.

Sánchez Viamonte, Carlos. 1957. *El Poder Constituyente*. Buenos Aires: Bibliográfica Argentina.

Sieyès, Emmanuel. July 20–21, 1789. *Préliminaires de la Constitution. Reconnoissance et Exposition Raisonnée des Droits de l'Homme et du Citoyen*.

2014. "The Opinion of Sieyès Concerning the Tasks and Organization of the Constitutional Jury" [Second Thermidorian Intervention] in *The Essential Political Writings*. Leiden: Brill, 170–185.

Soto, Francisco, and Yanina Welp. 2017. *Los Diálogos Ciudadanos: Chile ante el Giro Deliberativo.* Santiago de Chile: LOM.

Wall, Illan. 2012. *Human Rights and Constituent Power: Without Model or Warranty.* New York: Routledge.

Wenman, Mark. 2013. *Agonistic Democracy: Constituent Power in the Era of Globalisation.* Cambridge: Cambridge University Press.

Vedel, Georges. 1992. "Schengen et Maastricht (à propos de la décision n. 91-294 DC du Conseil constitutionnel du 25 julliet 1991." *Revue Française de Droit Administratiff* 8: 173–184

1993. "Souveraineté et Supraconstitutionalité." *Pouvoirs* 67: 79–97.

2002. *Manuel Élémentaire de Droit Constitutionnel.* Paris: Dalloz.

3

Expanding Revision Clauses in Democratic Constitutions

William Partlett

Major formal constitutional change can be an important moment of popular renewal in constitutional democracies (Levinson 2008, 173–175; Colón-Ríos 2010, 240). It allows the people themselves to reshape their governmental structure in order to improve governance and modernize institutions. For instance, Iceland's constitutional replacement process from 2009 to 2013 came as a response to large political outcry against an entrenched and corrupt status quo elite. To live up to this promise, however, the institutions in the constitution-making process must enhance popular representation, deliberation, and participation while avoiding a process captured by a factional majority.

The prevailing view – taken from democratic theory – is that the best process of large-scale, formal constitutional change is an "open" one involving extraordinary institutions. This democratic openness solves two problems stemming from the tyranny of the "status quo." First, openness avoids major constitution making in ordinary institutions. This will hinder status quo interests from exploiting their dominance of ordinary institutions to push through "abusive" constitutional changes that entrench themselves in power (Landau 2013b). Second, it allows the people to circumvent attempts by an entrenched "status quo" to *block* constitutional change by allowing them to act through extraordinary institutions (Levinson 2008).

Comparative experience of formal constitutional change in democracies shows that this openness and use of extraordinary institutions can carry dangers of another kind to democratic constitution making (Partlett 2016a). In particular, a self-interested factional majority can dominate the extraordinary institutions of constitution making and unilaterally reshape the constitutional order in a self-interested and abusive manner. This factional problem of a majority circumventing ordinary institutions and entrenching itself has become "peripheral ... to subsequent constitutional theorists" and has therefore largely been ignored by constitution-making theorists (Levinson 2011, 662). But it remains a practical problem in formal constitutional change in many democracies around the world (Partlett 2012).

The problem of faction was not a peripheral question in eighteenth-century American constitutional theory. James Madison warned of the dangers of majority factions that would become "adverse to the rights of others citizens or to the permanent and aggregate interests of the community" (*The Federalist Papers*, No. 10). His solution lay in clear rules of structure that would undermine factionalism by engendering "a multiplicity of interests" (*The Federalist Papers*, No. 51). This solution – which accords with Gabriel Negretto's argument and empirical findings in Chapter 5 on the importance of political pluralism in the drafting of new constitutions within democratic regimes – suggests that textual rules in *democratic* constitutions should have a role in regulating and therefore improving the process of constitution making.[1]

As a complement to Colón-Ríos' analysis in Chapter 2 of this book about the possibility of constitution making through law, this chapter seeks to reflect on the balance between the status quo and factional concerns in the design of a democratic process of formal constitutional change.[2] To do this, it will look at comparative constitution-making experience around the world. It will also draw on the subnational constitution-making experience of the American states. This subnational American constitutional experience is particularly instructive because state constitutions have more than two hundred years of experience balancing the competing demands of openness and regulation in democratic processes of constitution making.

Drawing on this comparative experience, this chapter will employ two concepts to guide this normative inquiry. First, it will describe constitution-making institutions as serving two different *roles*. At the drafting stage, constitution-making institutions play a predominantly representative role, as they are the site of drafting and deliberation by representatives of the people. At this stage, the people's representatives *propose* a constitutional draft; it is therefore a first step in a process of constitutional change. At the ratification stage, by contrast, constitution-making institutions reflect the direct preferences of the people and in the case of the most common and democratically legitimate ratifying institution – the referendum – is not representative at all. Thus, at this stage, the people directly exercise their unlimited constituent power to *consent* to a new constitution.

Second, this chapter will examine what I call the law of constitution making. This law can be organized into three different categories: selection rules (i.e., electoral rules), decision rules (i.e., internal voting rules), and relationship rules (i.e., rules determining the interaction of constitution-making institutions).[3] The details of

---

[1] See also Chapter 1 in this volume on legal regulation and continuity in intra-democratic constitution making.

[2] Although by formal constitutional change I understand both amendments and replacements, this chapter is more closely focused on the latter.

[3] See Brown (2008, 675) describing how scholarly analysis places emphasis on "deliberation, considerations of the general public interest, and long-term political reasoning" in constitution making.

these rules frequently determine whether constitution making is inclusive and representative of the people as a whole.

This chapter will then explore how these concepts can help to improve democratic constitutional design. In particular, it will suggest that democratic constitutions should include directive principles that guide the law of constitution making. At the *drafting* stage, directive principles should address the various problems of specific institutional choices. For instance, in constitution making through the institutions of ordinary politics (e.g., appointed commissions or ordinary legislatures), the status quo "abuse" of constitutional change to entrench their own power is of most concern (Landau 2013b). Constitutions should include directive principles requiring super-majority decision rules as well as relationship rules requiring popular ratification to ensure that entrenched status quo interests cannot use their dominance of ordinary institutions to push through self-interested constitutional norms. In extraordinary drafting institutions like constituent assemblies, by contrast, directive principles should call for laws that avoid the capture and manipulation of these institutions by factional majorities. One clear requirement would state that laws clearly specify extraordinary drafting bodies to be *proposing* bodies without the power to reshape the entire landscape unilaterally.

At the *ratification* stage, directive principles should call for laws that ensure ratification bodies are suitably inclusive while remaining difficult to capture. For referendums, these principles should require legislation that ensures that referendums best capture the informed consent of the people. One way to do this is to require an enabling act that agrees on the key rules of the referendum, including the wording and media rules.

This analysis thus provides lessons for constitutional drafters considering expanding revision clauses in democratic constitutions. As Joel Colón-Ríos argues in Chapter 2, the constitutional regulation of constitution making need not violate the people's right to exercise their constituent power. On the contrary, if devised carefully, laws made under these sort of directive principles can help structure a constitution-making process so that any new constitution can be "reasonably understood" as an "act of the people." Furthermore, expanded revision clauses can ensure more certainty with regard to the use of extraordinary institutions. This can allow the people to more confidently circumvent ordinary institutions without the fear of the process becoming captured by a powerful faction. In sum, this regulation can allow the people to express their original constituent power more effectively while curbing the dangers of factional majority.

To make this argument, this chapter will be divided into six parts. Section I will describe the neglected tension within democratic constitution making between an open process and one that is not susceptible to factional manipulation. Section II will introduce the importance of legal rules and roles for the institutions involved in constitution making. Section III will describe rules that can help improve constitutional *drafting*. Section IV will examine how rules can better structure constitutional *ratification*. Section V will explore how expanded revision clauses in democratic constitutions might respond to these lessons. Section VI will conclude.

I COMPETING DEMANDS OF DEMOCRATIC CONSTITUTION MAKING

A significant, but largely unexplored, tension lies at the center of democratic constitution-making theory. On one hand, theorists argue that democratic constitution making requires an open process that can allow the people to circumvent entrenched elites in ordinary institutions. On the other hand, democratic constitution making requires rules that will ensure the pluralism necessary to reduce the chances that partisan factions will run away with the process of constitution making and impose constitutional rules that entrench their own power. Both sides are responding to legitimate threats of elite self-dealing. Those advocating an open process are concerned that a "status quo" will either use its dominance of existing institutions and law to block constitution making or pass new constitutional changes that buttress its power. Those on the other side are concerned that too much openness will lead to a "factional problem" where elite factions representing popular majorities will use their control over the constitution-making process to ignore minorities and entrench their own power through constitutional law. It is important to strike a balance between these competing concerns in the design of a democratic constitution-making process.

I.A *The Status Quo Problem*

The status quo problem – the possibility that elites will use constitutional law to block democratic expression – is a key issue in democratic constitutional theory.[4] In fact, a central "dilemma" in democratic theory has long been the fear that constitutional law will allow a powerful and entrenched minority (often a court) to stifle the will of the majority of the people. The solution to this tyranny of the minority problem is found in allowing the people to remake constitutional law by circumventing the existing rules. This "democratic openness" seeks to solve two status quo problems. First, it ensures that elites cannot rely on *existing* constitutional law or institutions to block formal constitutional change. Second, it seeks to stop an entrenched elite from using its domination of ordinary institutions to pass *new* constitutional language that further entrenches their power.

We see this concern strongly reflected in the normative literature on constitutional change since the eighteenth century. During the revolutionary period in the United States, Thomas Jefferson famously argued that constitutions should be

---

[4] See Levinson (2011, 666) describing one of the problems in democratic theory to be "how to prevent venal and corrupt federal officials from tyrannizing and plundering the citizens they were supposed to serve." This problem has also been called the "dead hand problem."

returned to the people for revision every nineteen years in order to avoid "one generation of men binding another" (Kurland and Lerner 2000, ch. 2, doc. 23). This impulse is reflected in the current practice of some American state constitutions, which periodically submit a question to the people about formal constitutional revision.[5] This viewpoint has also been strongly expressed in work on the possibilities of formal amendment in the United States Constitution (Fritz 2008; Levinson 2008). Sanford Levinson argues that the formal rules for amendment in the United States Constitution are an "iron cage" that block the American people from changing their own constitutional order (Levinson 2008, 165).

To solve this problem, many American constitutional theorists have argued that the people have the inherent right to pursue a more open process involving extraordinary institutions like referendums and constituent assemblies to circumvent established constitutional revision procedures. For instance, Akhil Amar argues that "a majority of voters" retain an "unenumerated, constitutional right" to "call a convention to propose revisions . . . [and] that an amendment or new Constitution could be lawfully ratified by a simple majority of the American people" (Amar 1994, 459). Sanford Levinson endorses Amar's "visionary argument" that a national electorate could call a convention and then could ratify the new constitution that emerges from this convention in a referendum (Levinson 2008, 177).

The status quo problem remains an issue in formal constitutional change around the world today. For instance, Thorvaldur Gylfason's chapter on Iceland in this volume (Chapter 10) describes how an entrenched elite in the parliament have used their position to block popular constitutional change. In the wake of the 2008 global financial crisis, a near consensus emerged that Iceland needed a new constitution. This led to a highly participatory process, which yielded a constitutional draft that garnered a strong majority in a referendum (Landemore 2015). Yet, despite this clear message from the people for change, the status quo has (so far) used its control of the parliament to block this draft going into effect. Gylfason's analysis strongly condemns the "disrespect" of the legislature for the results of the referendum. The veto power of the legislature after a referendum is a key example of the status quo problem where the process is overregulated by pre-existing institutions.

I.B *The Factional Problem*

The factional problem is less well discussed in democratic constitutional theory. In this tyranny of the majority scenario, a faction undermines genuine participation and deliberation by advancing a self-interested agenda that seeks to use formal constitutional alterations to entrench their own power or policy preferences. This concern dates back at least to James Madison's famous warning about the threats to

---

[5] N.Y. Const. art. XIX, § 2 states that every twenty years, the people must vote on whether they want a constitutional convention to propose alterations to the Constitution.

both minority rights and the "aggregate interests of the community" when "a majority [is] united by a common interest" (*The Federalist Papers*, Nos. 10 and 51). The solution has generally been seen in rules that are more likely to engender "a multiplicity of interests" (*The Federalist Papers*, No. 51). The importance of rules to solving this problem, however, has not comprised a large part of constitution-making theory, largely because of the centrality of the status quo problem in this theory.

Although not part of constitution-making theory, the problem of faction is a significant problem in the practice of constitution making (Partlett 2016a). From Latin America to the former Soviet republics, self-interested factions have taken advantage of the openness of constitution making to run away with the process and entrench self-interested constitutional orders (Partlett 2012). They have done this by dominating institutions that have then claimed the legal power to "run away" from the limitations of the preexisting legal order. This kind of runaway constitution making can lead to two problems. First, runaway constitution-making institutions controlled by self-interested factions can degrade preexisting democratic institutions – particularly courts and legislatures – by issuing laws or ordinances removing individuals from power or disbanding institutions. Second, the products of these runaway processes themselves – written constitutional text – can themselves become the partisan tool of political entrenchment and rights reduction.

A classic example is Venezuela in 1999. In Venezuela, President Chavez issued a decree calling for a referendum to ask the people whether to call a constituent assembly to "transform the state and to create a new juridical order that would allow for the effective functioning of a social and participatory form of democracy" (Colón-Ríos 2011, 369). Chavez then took advantage of the openness to unilaterally draft rules for this constituent assembly. David Landau describes how these rules "brilliantly maximized his electoral representation and completely marginalized the opposition" (Landau 2013a). In particular, Chavez created a majoritarian system of voting, which over-represented forces with majority support nationally (Landau 2013). This allowed him to win 60 percent of the votes but take 95 percent of the seats (Landau 2013a).

With control of the drafting assembly, Chavez then unilaterally declared that all existing institutions would have "to subordinate themselves not only to the word but to the concrete fact, before the sovereign mandates that emanate from here, before this center of light" (Landau 2013a, 46). Chavez's assembly then went on to severely curtail the powers of the existing constituted powers (including the legislature). With control of this unlimited constituent assembly, Chavez reshaped the institutional landscape of the country in his own interests. As discussed by Bejarano and Segura in Chapter 6, the legacy of this process was one that both degraded institutions (particularly the court and the legislature) as well as one that allowed for the concentration of constitutional power.

The danger of factions has also become a reason to avoid formal constitution making through extraordinary institutions altogether. In the United States, for instance, the openness of constitution making through a federal constitutional convention has been seen as a fundamental threat to the democratic order. For instance, Chief Justice Earl Warren declared that a federal constitutional convention could "destroy the foundations of the Constitution" (Caplan 1988, 74). Justice William Brennan described the prospect of a convention to be "the most awful thing in the world" (quoted in Caplan 1988, viii). The governor of New Jersey said that a "convention would intimidate all branches of government, confuse the financial markets, and chill international relations" (quoted in Caplan 1988). In 1967, Senator Tydings of Maryland warned that a convention could "ignore the limitations placed on it by Congress and instead purport to speak for 'the people'" (113 Cong. Rec. 10,103, 10,104 [1967]).[6] Underlying all of these concerns is the danger that a united faction poses to genuine participation as well as to existing democratic institutions.

I.C *Solutions to These Problems?*

The institutional solutions to these competing elite self-dealing problems of constitution making seemingly present contradictory solutions. On one hand, the status quo problem requires institutions that allow the people to circumvent established government and law in creating a new constitution. These extraordinary institutions – including constitutional conventions, constituent assemblies, and referendums – frequently act outside legal regulation. Solving the factional problem, on the other hand, requires rules and structures that reduce the likelihood of the capture of institutions – and, particularly, extraordinary ones – by a majority faction. Section II of this chapter explores how to balance these competing demands.

II THE LEGAL RULES AND ROLES OF CONSTITUTION-MAKING INSTITUTIONS

To find an adequate balance between the status quo problem and the factional problem, I will examine two key concepts. These concepts will in turn help us to better understand how democratic constitution-making institutions work in practice.

II.A *The Law of Constitution Making*

Democratic theory has tended to ignore the importance of the legal rules governing constitution making. Experience shows, however, that even the most open and

---

[6] In legal academia, the debate has been strangely legalistic, centering on whether the states can limit a convention to certain topics. *Compare* Black (1972, 198) (arguing that neither Congress nor the states can limit a constitutional convention to a certain agenda) *and* Dellinger (1979, 1624) (same) *with* Van Alstyne (1978, 1305).

revolutionary process of constitution writing involves law; legal rules are necessary to ensuring coordination during the process. It is also critical in ensuring that institutions are sufficiently open to popular participation but also less likely to be manipulated by factions. In fact, these legal rules play a critical role in determining whether something functions as and is therefore rightly called a "constituent assembly" or "referendum."

There are three categories of the "law of constitution making." First, law sets the selection rules for constitution making. A good example is the electoral law for choosing representatives to a certain institution or legislation regulating how language is chosen for a referendum. Second, laws set decision rules that determine whether a decision has been made. In representative bodies, these might be minimum voting thresholds required to pass constitutional provisions; in referendums, they might be rules that determine that a constitutional text is adopted. Finally, laws include relationship rules that determine how constitution-making institutions interact with other institutions. These include both how these institutions are activated as well as their powers and capacities in relation to other institutions once they are activated.

These laws can be found in different sources. For constitutional amendment through ordinary institutions, these rules are frequently contained in the constitution itself. But, in most other cases (and particularly for constitution making through extraordinary institutions), they are usually left to ordinary legislation or executive decrees. I will examine what kind of legal rules are best for advancing both a more open process and a regulated one that is less likely to be captured by a faction.

II.B *Roles of Constitution Making: Drafting and Ratification*

Democratic theory generally views constitution making as a monolithic process where the people speak in the creation of new constitutional law. Experience, however, shows that constitution making is actually a two-stage process where the people act in two distinct roles.[7] The first is the drafting stage. Because the people themselves cannot gather together to engage in drafting, this is a representative process in which popular delegates deliberate over language. This drafting process raises both problems of status quo entrenchment and factional capture. To what extent are the status quo and factional problems linked to the type of institution in the drafting stage? Are there rules that can address both problems? And, if not, how to balance rules of constitution making to ensure that the people cannot be blocked in proposing new constitutional language but also avoid factional manipulation?

---

[7] See Saunders (2012) describing constitution making as a multi-stage process.

The second stage is one of ratification. In this stage, constitutional changes are approved. In most cases, the people themselves perform this task directly by accepting or rejecting the constitutional draft in a referendum or special election. Similar problems of balance between openness and regulation arise. What concerns are most problematic in ratification referendums? In particular, what rules might best allow a referendum to be an inclusive process but also one that is not so inclusive that it allows an entrenched elite to block it?

I will begin to explore these questions by looking at some of the key selection, decision, and relationship rules that exist at the center of the process of constitution making in its drafting and ratification stages. This exploration will not be exhaustive, but will seek to illuminate how best to regulate a constitution-making process from the point of view of seemingly opposed democratic principles.

III DRAFTING INSTITUTIONS

The drafting stage is a critical part of the process of constitution making. This is the period when key decisions are made that potentially affect both the structure of government as well as the rights of individuals. Although the people may participate directly through submissions, drafting is largely a representative process carried out politicians who act in the name of the people. The competing problems of factional capture and status quo entrenchment differ according to the institutional choices made. In ordinary constitutional drafting institutions, we should be most concerned about a status quo elite using its control over ordinary institutions to further entrench itself without popular input (either by blocking change or pushing through changes that reduce threats to their power). Conversely, constitutional drafting through extraordinary institutions triggers concerns about factional circumvention. It therefore requires legal rules that ensure that these extraordinary institutions are not captured by mobilized factions or that, if they are, these institutions are not able to dominate the constitution-making process.

III.A *Ordinary Institutions: Appointed Commissions*

The first institution frequently used in constitutional drafting is an appointed commission.[8] These bodies are frequently viewed as more efficient and cost-effective than elected drafting bodies as well as less of a threat to legislative power than elected constituent assemblies. These bodies – appointed by either the legislative or executive branch or a combination of both – can potentially undermine a deliberative and participatory constitution-making process. Because

---

[8] See Williams (1996) describing the increasing number of appointed commissions in constitution-making in the American states.

they are appointed, these commissions can become an opportunity for the defenders of the status quo to use formal constitutional law to their advantage. Thus, legal rules must be developed that help these bodies overcome the status quo problem.

Selection rules. Selection rules are critical for improving the functioning of appointed commissions. If the originator of the commission can appoint partisan political allies to sit on a committee, the commission will draft a constitution that reflects the current position and self-interest of the originator. A recent constitution-making process in Ukraine was criticized for this very problem (Partlett 2016b). On the other hand, if selection rules are chosen that generate a genuine bipartisan commission, this can allow the commission to play a productive role in constitution making. In the American states, independent constitution-making commissions are frequently convened to propose minor updates to the constitution. For instance, the Florida Constitution itself contains detailed rules about the composition of a Constitutional Revision Committee, which includes the attorney general, as well as representatives chosen by the governor, chief justice, Senate president, and House speaker (Fla. Const. art. XI, § 2. See also Adkins, 2016). In Utah, a law requires members of a permanent commission to be "bipartisan" (Williams 1996, 15). Finally, experts or academics can be placed on these commissions. In certain circumstances, this can be a way to ensure a better outcome or a device for salvaging the legitimacy of these commissions.

Decision rules. Decision rules are also important in determining how appointed commissions operate. Assuming a committee is relatively bipartisan, rules that are inclusive and require more consensus are more likely to ensure that the commission cannot be manipulated for partisan ends. Furthermore, rules that require these bodies consult with the public in their deliberations are another important way of ensuring that constitution making by commissions is more participatory. For instance, the Utah commission is required to consider recommendations from "responsible segments of the public." (Williams 1996, 15).

Relationship rules. Perhaps the most important rules about commissions are those concerning their relationship with other institutions. A rule requiring the people to approve a draft in a referendum before it goes into effect can help ensure that the proposers take into account the interests of the people. For instance, the Florida Constitutional Revision Committee only has the power to directly propose amendments to the people. In Utah, by contrast, a permanent appointed commission has the power to suggest amendments to the state legislature (Williams 1996). Whatever the choice, the American state examples suggest that appointed commissions should not have the power to circumvent existing institutions; instead, they should submit their drafts to the legislature and the people in a referendum before ratification. This kind of rule enhances popular participation in constitutional drafting while also checking the ability of legislative or executive elites to use these bodies to push through self-interested change.

III.B *Ordinary Institutions: Legislative Amendment and Dual-Purpose, Constituent Legislatures*

Ordinary elected legislatures also frequently play an important role in constitutional drafting. Legislative constitution making poses a threat of status quo entrenchment, in particular, the use by the status quo of their dominance in the legislature to entrench power. This risk is frequently mitigated by clear constitutional rules that regulate the process of legislative amendment. It is unclear, however, whether these rules apply when ordinary legislatures become "dual-purpose bodies" or "constituent legislatures" that formulate both ordinary law as well as major constitutional change. In these circumstances, legal rules are necessary to address the problem of status quo entrenchment.

Selection rules. Selection rules for legislatures engaging in formal constitutional amendment are well established. First, ordinary legislatures are elected according to the preexisting electoral law. Second, democratic constitutions themselves often include mechanisms such as unamendability clauses that limit the *topics* that constitutional amendment can cover. Many American states, for instance, create an amendment-revision distinction that seeks to limit the major constitutional changes that can be made by ordinary legislatures (Colantuono 1987). Enforced by courts, these types of rules are critical in ensuring that the legislature cannot change key constitutional provisions without a more open and representative process.

For dual-purpose constituent legislatures, however, different selection rules often need to be introduced. Most important, normal electoral law should be revised in order to ensure that these bodies function in a more representative manner. For instance, in Tunisia, the dual-purpose constituent legislature that drafted the constitution was elected according to a special proportional representation rule, which maximized representativeness and encouraged the election of particular groups such as women (The Carter Center 2011–2014, 24). These rules, in turn, help to ensure that the drafting process is more representative.

Decision rules. Decision rules are also important in improving legislative involvement in constitutional drafting. Legislatures are too numerous to actually carry out formal constitutional drafting themselves; instead, they generally choose representatives who in different committees will draft the language that is then considered. A key rule determines how these committees are chosen and how they will make decisions. In many cases, democratic legislatures have rules in place requiring committee membership to be selected only after agreement amongst different parties. These rules should be extended to dual-purpose constituent legislatures as well.

Another key decision rule is how textual changes are approved by the full legislature. Democratic constitutions normally specify super-majoritarian rules for making these kinds of decisions (Lijphart 2012, 47–48). Such rules frequently include a two-thirds majority to approve specific changes. These super-majoritarian rules should also be extended to dual-purpose bodies as well. In both contexts, by requiring broader support to agree to any change, super-majority rules can prevent a bare majority from changing the constitution in order to entrench their own power. Furthermore, they can ensure more deliberation by forcing participants to push for a consensus through attention to reasons that appeal to the common good.[9] Finally, super-majoritarian decision rules can also increase participation by incentivizing coalition-formation and the publicizing of private information to garner larger majorities (Lieb 2006, 116).

Relationship rules. Finally, key laws describe the legal relationship between drafting legislatures and other institutions. For ordinary legislatures drafting constitutional amendments, there are commonly clear –and often judicially enforceable– rules outlining how constitutional amendments in ordinary legislatures are brought into force. For instance, an increasing number of democratic constitutions require constitutional amendments drafted by ordinary legislatures to be ratified in a binding referendum (Elkins, Ginsburg, and Blount 2008, 377). In Australia, for example, any proposed alteration to a constitution must be ratified by a majority of the people as well as a majority of the states (Australian Constitution, s. 128).

The relationship of dual-purpose, constituent legislatures to preexisting institutions is less clear. This ambiguity could allow a partisan majority in a constituent legislature to claim the runaway power to ignore existing constitutional limitations, disband existing institutions, or ratify its own draft. To avoid this, a relationship rule should state that constituent legislatures have the power to propose a new draft but not to unilaterally reshape the existing constitutional order. A final relationship rule for a constituent legislature is how it becomes a constituent legislature. The best rule allows the people to determine when a legislature will adopt a dual role. For instance, in France in 1946, voters answered the question "Do you want the assembly elected today to be a constituent assembly" (Elster 2013, 207). After answering yes, this constituent legislature drafted France's new constitution. This also provides the people the ability to debate and question candidates over key questions of constitutional design during the election.

III.C *Extraordinary Institutions: Constituent Assemblies*

Extraordinary drafting institutions are generally seen as the most democratic institutions for large-scale constitutional changes (including replacement) because they respond directly to the status quo problems of constitution making through ordinary institutions. When elected, these bodies are thought to be "more consistent with people's sovereignty than a parliament (where sectional interests may dominate)" (Ghai 2005, 10). They are also viewed as allowing the people to break with a corrupt past or avoid the deficiencies of ordinary politics. They are also seen as better at

---

[9] McGinnis and Rappaport (2002) discuss how super-majoritarian rules improve consensual decision-making by encouraging negotiation and compromise.

deliberation. Because these bodies are temporary, they therefore avoid the "noise" of "regular politics" and will be more likely to operate behind a veil of ignorance (Ghai 2005, 10).

Despite their strong support in the normative literature, extraordinary institutions pose considerable dangers to a representative, deliberative, and participatory process of constitution making. Because of claims about inherent powers, these institutions raise serious concerns of capture by majority factions. This capture can endanger existing institutions as well as lead to constitutional norms that undermine political competition. As a result, proper constitutional revision rules must block elected factional majorities from running away with the process and dominating the process.

Selection rules. One of the most important rules for constitutional drafting bodies is how these bodies are selected. The choice of these rules in turn plays a critical role in determining the position of the drafting body within the constitutional landscape (thus, determining its relationship rules). The most common way of selecting these specialized bodies is through elections. Elected drafting bodies – called constituent assemblies or constitutional conventions – have the strongest democratic credentials of all the potential drafting institutions.[10] Selection rules that encourage representativeness and a plurality of interests are most likely to secure this normative vision. Selection rules for an extraordinary assembly should seek to generate as much as possible what Bejarano and Segura in this volume (Chapter 6) see as being so important in ensuring the success of Colombian constitution making: a broader distribution of power in the assembly.

The American states have experimented with a number of different ways of pursuing a more representative body. The first thing that many do is requiring the rules for forming an extraordinary drafting body to be the product of a bipartisan legislative act. The Kentucky Constitution requires the state legislature to create an ordinary statute calling a convention if a majority of citizens vote for a new one at the election.[11] The California Constitution also states a clear relationship rule for a constitutional convention: The people can call a convention through a vote and the legislature then calls the convention into effect.[12]

These statutes creating extraordinary drafting bodies should similarly focus on the most representative selection rules. The Panama Constitution, for instance, specifies that any law governing the makeup of the constituent assembly itself must be "proportional."[13] The Missouri Constitution includes a very elaborate provision that seeks to ensure that more than one political party will be represented in the

---

[10] But see Article V of the United States Constitution that allows the states to call a convention to amend the constitution: U.S. Const. art. V.

[11] Ky. Const. § 258. www.lrc.state.ky.us/legresou/constitu/258.htm (December 9, 2016).

[12] Calif. Const. art. XVIII. http://leginfo.legislature.ca.gov/faces/codes_displayText.xhtml?law Code=CONS&division=&title=&part=&chapter=&article=XVIII (December 9, 2016).

[13] Panama Constitution, art. 314. www.constituteproject.org/constitution/Panama_2004.pdf (December 9, 2016).

convention from each district.[14] A number of other approaches have also been tested. In other American states, elections to specialized constitutional conventions are non-partisan. For instance, Rhode Island had a non-partisan election for its 1985 constitutional convention (Morse 2014). It also provides that the election for at-large delegates be nonpartisan (Morse 2014). New York introduced a bill in 2015 entitled the People's Convention Reform Act, which sought to introduce nonpartisan elections for the New York constitutional convention.[15] In order to reduce the influence of the political elite, the bill therefore suggests that "proced-ures should be established in both the selection of delegates and in the running of the convention that will reduce partisanship."[16] These procedures include rules against party affiliation and involvement in the election.

In other cases, laws creating selection rules have instead sought to enhance participation by underrepresented groups by avoiding election altogether. One recent innovation involves constitution-making bodies that are selected by lot. These bodies are intended to serve a brainstorming purpose. The idea behind this is to avoid politics-as-normal and to give the people a stronger say in the drafting of constitutional language. Sanford Levinson has explored this idea in his work on constitutional reform in the United States. He argues that lottery selection in constitution making can help to avoid the corruption at the heart of ordinary representative politics (Levinson 2012, 124–125). Akhil Amar's work also describes how selection of assemblies by lottery helps lead to fewer insider representatives, more rotation in office, and weaker political partisanship (Amar 1984).

There has recently been a large amount of experimentation in this area. Iceland is a good example. In 2009, a National Forum was convened (Landemore 2015, 169). It included 1,500 representatives, most of whom were randomly selected from the Population Register. This National Forum engaged its participants in brainstorming that would seek to ensure the broad principles for the drafting process. After this, a twenty-five–member body drafted the constitution. This body was open to anyone who was not "President of the Republic of Iceland, members of parliament, their alternates, cabinet ministers and members of the Constitutional Commission and the Organising Committee."[17] In the United States, the state of Oregon created a

---

[14] Missouri Constitution, art. XII, § 3(a). www.moga.mo.gov/mostatutes/moconstn.html (Decem-ber 9, 2016).

[15] Bill No. A4674, N.Y. State Assembly, Last action, June 2, 2016. http://assembly.state.ny.us/leg/? default_fld=&bn=A4674&term=2015&Memo=Y (December 9, 2016).

[16] Assembly Bill A4674: Relates to the creation of the People's Convention Reform Act, 2015–2016 Leg. Sess., Last action, June 2, 2016. http://open.nysenate.gov/legislation/bill/A4674-2015 (December 9, 2016). The bill is a reaction to the fact that New York's last two constitutional conventions were "dominated by the politically connected (two-thirds of the delegates to the 1938 convention and about 83 percent of the 1967 delegates were present or former elected or party officials).

[17] Act on a Constitutional Assembly, art. 6. www.thjodfundur2010.is/other_files/2010/doc/Act-on-a-Constitutional-Assembly.pdf (December 9, 2016).

Citizen Initiative Review Commission.[18] Each review panel is randomly chosen and demographically balanced and is brought together to evaluate a ballot measure. Finally, in Australia, a citizens' parliament was convened in 2009 that included a large number of randomly selected citizens who matched the demographics of the area that they represented. This was intended to produce recommendations for "those in leadership that reflect the considered views of the broader community" (Australia's First Citizens' Parliament, 2009, 3).

Decision rules. Another set of important rules for extraordinary drafting bodies includes the way that these specialized bodies make decisions on draft constitutional language. These rules should operate much as the decision rules for appointed commissions or legislatures. In general, super-majority decision rules in extraordinary drafting bodies can help to block a majority faction from pushing through self-interested language.

Relationship rules. A crucially important rule relating to extraordinary drafting bodies is the relationship of extraordinary drafting institutions with ordinary institutions. This is particularly true with regard to *elected* constitution-making bodies. Normative theory – with its emphasis on openness – generally contends that these elected constituent assemblies must be sovereign and superior to the legal system. They are therefore seen as "a gathering of the nation" (Ghai 2005, 10) that allows the people to "reactivat[e] [their] constituent power and becom[e] the author[s] of a radically transformed constitutional regime" (Ghai 2005, 10). This specialized institution is about "recognizing a power superior to the constitution and giving citizens, acting outside the ordinary institutions of government, the institutional means to exercise it" (Colón-Ríos 2010, 240). Under this conception, these institutions should have full power to reshape the institutional landscape. Many Latin American constitutions follow this approach. For instance, the Venezuelan constitution states that existing authorities cannot obstruct the constituent assembly "in any way," suggesting it has unlimited powers.[19] In Bolivia, the constitution states that the "total reform" of the constitution requires "an original plenipotentiary Constituent Assembly."[20]

The danger of majority factions capturing these bodies, however, strongly counsels against allowing extraordinary elected drafting bodies to possess unlimited legal power. Law should therefore create clear boundaries on the powers of these drafting bodies. For instance, Panama's constitution is one of the few Latin American constitutions to contain a relationship rule that limits the power of the constituent assembly to make "retroactive" laws or to alter the terms of office of officials "exercising their functions at the moment when the new constitution

---

[18] Citizens' Initiative Review Commission. www.oregon.gov/circ/pages/index.aspx (December 9, 2016).
[19] Venezuelan Constitution, ch. III, art. 349. www.constituteproject.org/constitution/Venezuela_2009.pdf?lang=en (December 9, 2016).
[20] Bolivian Constitution, pt. V, art. 411. www.constituteproject.org/constitution/Bolivia_2009.pdf (December 9, 2016).

enters into effect."[21] An even better rule would state that these bodies – much as with constituent legislatures – are unlimited in their ability to propose constitutional language but not in other capacities. There is support for this concept in the practice of American constitution making. During the American founding period, elected constitutional conventions were viewed not as all-powerful but instead as proposing bodies (Partlett 2017). One of the key participants in the Philadelphia Convention, James Wilson, explained that the Philadelphia Convention was "authorized to conclude nothing" but was "at liberty to *propose* any thing" (Farrand 1966, 253). Later on, one of the most important American treatises on constitutional conventions was written to dispel the idea that conventions had sovereign powers.[22] Underlying this approach was the idea that the people themselves could not be sovereign if they delegated their full power to a representative body.

Another key relationship rule for constituent assemblies is how they are activated. As long as constituent assemblies are simply proposing bodies, a rule that allows the people themselves to call a constituent assembly into place is a desirable way of ensuring that an entrenched elite cannot block popular constitutional change. We see examples of this type of relationship rule across Latin America. For instance, in Bolivia, 20 percent of the citizens can petition for a referendum on calling a constituent assembly. If the referendum is successful, a constituent assembly must be called.[23] In Ecuador, the constitution states that a referendum is the only way to call a constituent assembly and that this referendum must allow the voters to also vote on the selection rules for how the constituent assembly is elected.[24] Finally, the American states also require the state legislature to convene a constitutional convention in the event of a majority vote calling for one.

IV RATIFICATION INSTITUTIONS

The ratification stage represents a moment when the people themselves consent to or reject a proposed constitutional document. For this reason, the rules for the bodies that are involved in this process must seek to ensure that the people speak in the clearest way possible.

IV.A *Ordinary Politics: Legislative Ratification*

From a normative point of view, ordinary institutions are disfavored as ratifying institutions. In contrast with the representative requirements of drafting, ratification

---

[21] Panama Constitution, art. 314. www.constituteproject.org/constitution/Panama_2004.pdf (December 9, 2016).

[22] See Jameson (2013).

[23] Bolivian Constitution, pt. V, art. 411. www.constituteproject.org/constitution/Bolivia_2009.pdf (December 9, 2016).

[24] Ecuador's Constitution, art. 444. www.constituteproject.org/constitution/Ecuador_2008.pdf (December 9, 2016).

generally requires the direct participation of the people through voting or other form of participation. There are two exceptions to this rule. First, a new constitutional norm can be ratified if two successive legislatures approve the language with an intervening election. This form of ratification allows an intervening election to serve as a referendum on draft constitutional changes and can provide time for a partisan majority to fade after a period to "cool down and reconsider" following from the "passion of the moment" (Venice Commission 2010, 19, para. 95). Second, ordinary subnational legislatures sometimes ratify new constitutional text. For instance, in the United States, state legislatures ratify constitutional amendments proposed by the federal legislature (U.S. Const. art. V).[25] The rules concerning legislative ratification are generally well-settled laws of ordinary politics; they are therefore less likely to be manipulated by a status quo elite or a majority faction.

IV.B *Extraordinary Politics: Constitutional Referendums*

The institution favored by democratic theory for ratifying a constitutional amendment or replacement is a referendum. Referendums are seen as giving the people an opportunity to directly ratify or reject constitutional law. In general, they are widely considered to be a critical institution in unleashing popular participation and deliberation (see generally, Morgan 2015). This is underpinned by an idea that they allow "the people" to circumvent the old regime institutions of the preexisting regime and "return the direct power to the people" (Tierney 2009, 367).[26] Referendums therefore play a highly important role in "the most fundamental acts of constitutional self-definition" (Tierney 2009, 366). Furthermore, because of their capacity to engage the public, referendums can also help to ensure a better form of elite deliberation at the drafting stage. In particular, they place a "downstream constraint" on drafting that can help to improve the deliberation process at the earlier drafting stage.[27]

As with drafting institutions, the rules regarding referendums are critical to ensuring that referendums live up to these normative ideals. Despite the importance of these rules – including the timing of the referendum, the setting of the question, defining the franchise, regulating the campaign and ballot procedure – these rules are generally unregulated by constitutions. Recent work has sought to find some of the best ways to improve the nature of referendums. For instance, Stephen Tierney's research has sought to better understand what legal rules can be introduced to render referendums more deliberative (Tierney 2014). Looking to recent examples in Northern Ireland and Australia, Tierney argues that legal regulation can transform

[25] Brown (1935) describing how there was some disagreement about the way in which specialized constitutional conventions should be constituted in ratifying the twenty-first amendment.
[26] For more on dualism and referendums, see Tierney (2009, 366).
[27] Setala (2006, 718) exploring the benefits of ex post referendums in encouraging better deliberation.

referendums into mechanisms that enhance "deliberative decision-making" (Tierney 2009, 44).

Selection rules. Selection rules for referendums involve important questions about the selection of the electorate as well as the rules about the way that constitutional language is proposed and understood. Rules should seek to avoid the manipulation of language for partisan outcome. With constitutional amendments, for instance, some American state constitutions contain referendum rules such as the single subject rule (Cooter and Gilbert 2010). The Florida Constitution states that any revision or amendment of the Constitution "shall embrace but one subject and matter directly connected therewith" (Fla. Const. art. XI, § 3). These rules seek to ensure that referendum voting is clearer and transparent.

Another key selection rule should state that voters have access to impartial information. Some constitutions include these requirements. The Colorado Constitution, for instance, includes provisions requiring that a "nonpartisan research staff" should present a "fair and impartial analysis of each measure" that is then distributed to registered voters state-wide (Colo. Const. art. V, § 1(7.5)(a)). In other cases, these rules exist at the level of ordinary legislation. For instance, Australia has a clear law on referendums that regulates the way in which information is given to voters in the election process. In particular, it provides a short case "for and against" a proposal for constitutional change to be prepared by members of parliament who voted for and against the bill as it went through parliament.[28] Australian law also has extremely strict regulations governing political advertising during referendum campaigns (AEC 2015).

Decision rules. Another important rule is the threshold required for the proposed constitutional language to be ratified in a referendum. There are generally two options: the requirement of a simple majority or one of an absolute majority. For major constitutional changes, an absolute majority requirement is to be preferred as it ensures that constitutional text is only ratified in a vote that engages a large percentage of the population. For instance, in Estonia, an electoral commission decreed that the referendum would only be valid if more than 50 percent of the voters participated. This wide participation helped to enhance popular engagement with the new constitution (Partlett 2015).

Relationship rules. A final set of rules involves the relationship between referendums and preexisting institutions. These rules determine both when and how referendums are activated and their effect (Australian Constitution, s. 128). One important principle for these rules should recognize that referendums are a second ratification step after the drafting step. Thus, referendums should automatically be called to allow the people to directly consent to language formulated at the drafting stage. Many constitutions require this, including following extraordinary bodies such as constitutional conventions. The Arizona Constitution states that a

---

[28] Referendum (Machinery Provisions) Act 1984 s. 11.

convention is for "propos[ing] alterations, revisions, or amendments" and that any changes require them to be "submitted" to the people before they become "effective."[29] Another important relationship rule should state that referendums present the binding final word on specific issues. For instance, the Colorado Constitution states that all aspects of the referendum process of amendment are "self executing."[30]

A final set of relationship rules governs the extent to which referendums can be used to activate a formal constitution-making process in the first place. In these cases, rules should be adopted that ultimately ensure that there is broad popular support for a referendum. For instance, many states include rules that require a certain percentage of the electorate to call a petition. In Oregon, for instance, a popular petition for a referendum requires it to be signed by 8 percent of the total number of votes cast for the previous gubernatorial election (Ore. Const. art. IV, §§ 1, 2(c)). Rules should be careful not to allow the unilateral calling of a referendum by one group; for this reason, the executive branch should not be given unilateral power to call a referendum.

V EXPANDED REVISION CLAUSES

This analysis has clear implications for expanding revision clauses in democratic constitutions. These expanded provisions in turn provide legal rules that facilitate more frequent and more inclusive formal constitutional change.

V.A *Nature of Regulation*

Before we consider the expansion of the constitutional regulation of constitutional change, we must confront some objections. First, one might object that the people's original constituent power requires the possibility of a constitutional replacement process that takes place outside of the legal track. Under this view, any expansion of constitutional rules governing constitutional change seemingly violate the original right of the people to draft a new constitution outside of preexisting law (Kay 2011, 745).

This objection, however, is answerable. As described in Joel Colón-Ríos' chapter in this book (Chapter 2), the constituent power is not necessarily extinguished through regulation. Rules about certain institutions themselves need not hinder the openness of a process; they can actually help to ensure the expression of the people's constituent power. Furthermore, even the most revolutionary period of constitution making must have rules to ensure coordination. This position accords

---

[29] Ariz. Const. art. XXI, § 2. www.azleg.gov/FormatDocument.asp?inDoc=/const/21/2.htm (December 9, 2016).
[30] Colo. Const. Section 10. art. XIX, § 2(1) law.justia.com/constitution/colorado/ (December 9, 2016).

with the view of constituent power held at the American founding. The Massachusetts General Court proclaimed in 1776 that the people have "Supreme, Sovereign,
absolute, and uncontroulable Power" but this power *"never was, or can be delegated,
to one Man, or few"* (Wood 1969, 362).[31] In this view, delegating the full power of the
people to a constitution-making body violates the concept of original constituent
power because it would mean giving up popular power to a group of representatives.
In Delaware, radicals called a runaway convention a body of "usurpers and tyrants"
(Wood 1969, 333). Thus, they were careful to stress that the convention must simply
propose a constitution or leave the people "with no rights at all" (Wood 1969, 337).
They argued that this body was to be "invested with powers to form a plan of
government only, and not to execute it after it is framed. For nothing can be a
greater violation of reason and natural rights, than for men to give authority to
themselves" (Wood 1969, 338).

Another related concern is that judicial enforcement of these rules itself raises
concerns about status quo entrenchment (Tribe 1983, 436 and n. 13). In particular, if
given too much power over constitution making, an elite could use the court to
block any change. One way to respond to this objection is to give courts a less active
role in regulating the process. A way to do this is to place directive principles in
expanded revision clauses rather than regular constitutional rules. If inserted as
directive principles, these provisions could themselves be suited to local context
while also helpfully structuring the politics of constitution making. Courts can
review this legislation – rather than any constitutional language itself – for its general
adherence to these principles (Weis, N.d.). Thus, courts would be acting in a far less
intrusive way than they would be in reviewing the substance of constitutional
language (Weis, N.d.). In fact, a set of directive principles could help courts – as
David Landau describes in Chapter 4 – "shape" the process of constitution making.
These constitutional provisions would then be performing what Mark Tushnet
describes as a "political" role by structuring political "dialogue" about the best
expression of popular will in constitution making (Tushnet 2006).

Comparative experience suggests that constitutional provisions can play an
important political role in structuring the lawmaking of constitutional replacement.
Bolivia's constitution included a newly drafted constitutional provision that covered
the convoking of a constituent assembly. This replacement clause stated that the
"total reform" of the constitution must be carried out by a constituent assembly,
convoked by a "special law" approved by two-thirds of the members of the congress,

---

[31] Underlying this concern was a deep fear of concentrating all power in one body. James Madison
argued that "the accumulation of all powers, legislative, executive, and judiciary, in the same
hands, whether of one, a few, or many, and whether hereditary, self-appointed, or elective, may
justly be pronounced the very definition of tyranny": *The Federalist Papers*, No. 47 (James
Madison). Thomas Jefferson also worried about the dangers of concentrating all power in the
hands of one body, commenting that "one hundred and seventy-three despots would surely be as
oppressive as one": *The Federalist Papers*, No. 48 (James Madison quoting Jefferson).

and which could not be vetoed by the president (Landau 2013a, 952). During a highly contested constitution-making process, this clause forced both sides to compromise on the rules governing the constituent assembly. In particular, it placed significant constraints on President Evo Morales, because "it ruled out a strategy of making an end-run around Congress, as Chávez had done, and forced him to negotiate with the opposition in Congress" (Landau 2013a, 952). It also helped to generate an electoral rule that led to a highly representative electorate. Second, the law provided a key decision rule stating that the Assembly "will approve the text of the new constitution with two-thirds of the members present," and that once so approved the text would be put to the people in a referendum convoked by the executive, which would require approval by an absolute majority of votes. This in turn played a critical role in leading to what Landau has described as "a novel synthesis of ideas, particularly in the incorporation of indigenous groups and in constructing a multicultural state" (Landau 2013a, 958).

V.B *Expanded Revision Clauses*

What might such an expanded revision clause look like? One possible approach would divide it into two sections, one covering drafting institutions and the other ratification institutions. Each would contain a set of directive principles that would guide the law of constitution making. These directive principles would ultimately seek to improve constitution making by creating laws that avoided both status quo entrenchment and the threat of factions.

Drawing on the insights from this chapter, a section on "drafting institutions" should include a baseline directive principle that any legal regulation governing the selection, decision, and relationship rules of drafting institutions involved in formal constitutional change must be highly representative and participatory. This drafting institution section could then specify more detailed directive principles. First, a selection principle could state that the selection of drafting bodies should be formulated in the most representative way possible. This would allow some different legislative solutions for elected bodies, including a proportional representation system or one that set aside a number of seats for minorities. It would also reduce the possibility that status quo interests could manipulate appointed commissions. Second, a decision principle could require drafting bodies to employ a version of a super-majority rule in making decisions – whether on text or those individuals actually drafting text. This would encourage compromise and negotiation. Finally, a relationship principle would call for laws limiting any drafting institution – whether elected or not – from itself having the legal power to do anything other than propose constitutional text. Another relationship principle would state that the people cannot be blocked from calling an extraordinary drafting body. This would require legislation affording the people themselves the ability to circumvent ordinary institutions in calling a drafting body.

The section on "ratification institutions" should take a similar approach. A key baseline directive should state that all laws detailing selection, decisions, and relationship rules for ratifying institutions should be aimed at allowing the people to broadly consent to draft constitutional language. More specific rules should be built from this. First, a selection principle should ensure laws that provide the people with a clear choice on constitutional language. This could trigger a number of different legislative responses, which seek to ensure that the people are making an informed choice. Second, a decision principle could state that laws should be passed requiring more than a simple majority to ratify constitutional language. This would allow legislative flexibility in seeking to ensure that more people are engaged in the process of consenting to major constitutional changes. Finally, a relationship principle might call for laws stating clearly that the specified majority in the referendum is the *final* word on a constitutional draft and is not subject to review or refusal by any existing institutions.

VI CONCLUSION

This chapter has considered how the text of democratic constitutions might improve the high-stakes process of formal constitutional change. This responds to a real problem. Despite its romantic portrayal in much of the literature, formal constitutional change is a dangerous moment for democracies. In fact, recent experience suggests that this process can be a powerful tool for those seeking to undermine democratic governance. Democratic constitutions must engage with these dangers, and seek to minimize the possibility of status quo or factional entrenchment.

This chapter suggests two main insights for improving formal constitutional change. First, it draws our attention to the critical role that normal legal rules play in ensuring that democratic constitution-making institutions allow the people to remake their constitutional order or enable an entrenched status quo or factional majority to consolidate power. Rather than ignoring the importance of these rules, democratic constitutions should include a set of directive principles that help ensure that the law of constitution making is better designed and more productive.

Second, it demonstrates how the different *roles* played by constitution-making institutions can help devise directive principles for expanded revision clauses. During the drafting stage, the people's representatives are involved in *proposing* constitutional language. These drafting bodies should therefore have no special power to alter the constitutional landscape without the direct consent of the people. During the ratification stage, the people consent to language. If popular consent is given according to certain rules, this is an unreviewable statement of validity.

This more regulated approach to constitution making is not just able to overcome the danger of faction. It is also more likely to encourage the people to engage in formal constitutional change in the first place. In fact, by reducing the significant uncertainty underlying this high-stakes process, it will allow the people to more fully take part in their constitutional order. In this way, increased regulation will actually encourage the people to more frequently express their constituent power and improve the nature of their constitutional democracy.

REFERENCES

Adkins, Mary. 2016. "Organizing Florida's Next Constitution Revision Commission: A Historical Perspective." UF Law Faculty Blogs. https://facultyblogs.law.ufl.edu/210-2/.

Amar, Akhil Reed. 1984. "Choosing Representatives by Lottery Voting." *Yale Law Journal* 93(7): 1283–1308.

1994. "The Consent of the Governed: Constitutional *Amendment* outside Article V." *Columbia Law Review* 94(2): 457–508.

Australian Electoral Commission (AEC). "Electoral Backgrounder: Referendum *Advertising*." Last updated, February 17, 2015. www.aec.gov.au/about_aec/Publications/Back grounders/ref-advert.htm.

Australia's First Citizens' Parliament. 2009. newDemocracy Foundation. www .newdemocracy.com.au/docs/newDemocracy_Citizens_Parliament_Handbook.pdf.

Black, Charles L. Jr. 1972. "Amending the Constitution: A Letter to a Congressman." *Yale Law Journal* 82(2): 189–215.

Brown, Everett S. 1935. "The Ratification of the Twenty-First Amendment." *The American Political Science Review* 29(6): 1005–1017.

Brown, Nathan J. 2008. "Reason, Interest, Rationality, and Passion in Constitution *Drafting*." *Perspectives on Politics* 6(4): 675–689.

Caplan, Russell L. 1988. *Constitutional Brinksmanship: Amending the Constitution by National Convention.* Oxford: Oxford University Press.

The Carter Center. 2011–2014. *The Constitution-Making Process in Tunisia.* Final Report. Atlanta, GA. www.cartercenter.org/resources/pdfs/news/peace_publications/democracy/ tunisia-constitution-making-process.pdf.

Colantuono, Michael G. 1987. "The Revision of American State Constitutions: *Legislative* Power, Popular Sovereignty, and Constitutional Change." *California Law Review* 75(4): 1473–1512.

Colón-Ríos, Joel. 2010. "The Legitimacy of the Juridical: Constituent Power, Democracy, and the Limits of Constitutional Reform." *Osgoode Hall Law Journal* 48(2): 199–245.

2011. "Carl Schmitt and Constituent Power in Latin American *Courts*: The Cases of Venezuela and Colombia." *Constellations* 18(3): 365–388.

Cooter, Robert D., and Michael D. Gilbert. 2010. "A Theory of Direct Democracy and the *Single* Subject Rule." *Columbia Law Review* 110(3): 687–730.

Dellinger, Walter E. 1979. "The Recurring Question of the "Limited" Constitutional Convention." *Yale Law Journal* 88(8): 1623–1640.

Elkins, Zachary, Tom Ginsburg, and Justine Blount. 2008. "The Citizen As Founder: Public Participation in Constitutional Approval." *Temple Law Review* 81(2): 361–382.

Elster, Jon. 2013. *Securities against Misrule: Juries, Assemblies, Elections.* Cambridge: Cambridge University Press.

Farrand, Max (ed.) 1966. *The Records of the Federal Convention of 1787.* Vol. 1. New Haven: Yale University Press.

Fritz, Christian. 2008. *American Sovereigns: The People and America's Constitutional Tradition before the Civil War.* Cambridge: Cambridge University Press.

Ghai, Yash. 2005. "The Role of Constituent Assemblies in Constitution Making." *International* Institute for Democracy and Electoral Assistance. www.agora-parl.org/sites/default/files/the_role_of_constituent_assemblies_in_constitution_making.pdf.

Jameson, John Alexander. 2013. *A Treatise on Constitutional Conventions: Their History, Powers, and Modes of Proceeding.* Clark: Lawbook Exchange.

Kay, Richard S. 2011. "Constituent Authority." *American Journal of Comparative Law* 59(3): 715–762.

Landau, David. 2013a. "Constitution-Making Gone Wrong." *Alabama Law Review* 64(5): 923–980.

2013b. "Abusive Constitutionalism." *UC Davis Law Review* 47(1): 189–260.

Landemore, Hélène. 2015. "Inclusive Constitution-Making: The Icelandic *Experiment.*" *The Journal of Political Philosophy* 23(2): 166–191.

Levinson, Daryl J. 2011. "Parchment and Politics: The Positive Puzzle of *Constitutional* Commitment." *Harvard Law Review* 124(3): 657–746.

Levinson, Sanford. 2008. *Our Undemocratic Constitution: Where the Constitution Goes Wrong (And How We the People Can Correct It).* Oxford: Oxford University Press.

2012. *Framed: America's Fifty-One Constitutions and the Crisis of Governance.* Oxford: Oxford University Press.

Lieb, Ethan J. 2006. "Supermajoritarianism and the American Criminal Jury." *Hastings Constitutional Law Quarterly* 33(2): 141–196.

Lijphart, Arend. 2012. *Patterns of Democracy: Government Forms and Performance in Thirty-Six Countries.* 2nd ed. New Haven: Yale University Press.

McGinnis, John O., and Michael B. Rappaport. 2002. "Our Supermajoritarian *Constitution.*" *Texas Law Review* 80(4): 703–806.

Madison, James, Alexander Hamilton, and John Jay. [1788] 1987. *The Federalist Papers.* London: Penguin Books.

Morgan, David Gwynn. 2015. "Referenda: Like the Egg That Was Excellent in Parts." *Constitutional* Making & Constitutional Change. February 16, 2015. http://constitutional-change.com/referenda-like-the-egg-that-was-excellent-in-parts/.

Morse, Carroll Andrew. 2014. "A Constitutional Convention for Rhode Island? The History and Legal Framework." The Ocean State Current. http://oceanstatecurrent.com/interview/a-constitutional-convention-for-rhode-island-the-history-and-legal-framework/.

Ntwari, Daniel S. 2015. "Rwandan Controversial Constitutional Reform Commission *Members* Sworn in Amidst Lawsuit." Afrika Reporter, September 16. www.afrikareporter.com/rwandan-controversial-constitutional-reform-commission-members-sworn-in-amidst-lawsuit/.

Partlett, William. 2012. "The Dangers of Popular Constitution-Making." *Brooklyn Journal of International Law* 38(1): 193–238.

2015. "Restoration Constitution-Making." *Vienna Journal of International Constitutional Law* 9(4): 514–547.

2016a. "The Elite Threat to Constitutional Transitions." *Virginia Journal of International Law* 56(2): 407–458.

2016b. "Reforming Centralism and Supervision in Armenia and *Ukraine*" in *Annual Review of Constitution-Building Processes: 2015.* Sumit Bisarya et al. (eds.) Stockholm: International Institute for Democracy and Electoral Assistance, 85–98. www.idea.int/publications/catalogue/annual-review-constitution-building-processes-2015?lang=en.

2017. "The American Tradition of Constituent Power." *International Journal of Constitutional Law,* 15(4): 955–987.

Saunders, Cheryl. 2012. "Constitution-Making in the 21st Century." *International* Review of *Law* 2012(1): 1–10.

Setala, Maija. 2006. "On the Problems of Responsibility and Accountability in *Referendums*." *European Journal of Political Research* 45(4): 699–721.

"Thomas Jefferson to James Madison, September 6, 1789." 2000. *The Founders' Constitution*. Philip B. Kurland and Ralph Lerner (eds.) http://press-pubs.uchicago.edu/founders/documents/v1ch2s23.html.

Tierney, Stephen. 2009. "Constitutional Referendums: A Theoretical Enquiry." *Modern Law Review* 72(3): 360–383.

　　2014. "The Independence Referendum in Scotland: *Constructing* a Deliberative Process?" Presented at "Constitutional Challenges: Global and Local," IXth World Congress of the International Association of Constitutional Law (IACL), Oslo, Norway (June 16–20, 2014). www.jus.uio.no/english/research/news-and-events/events/conferences/2014/wccl-cmdc/wccl/papers/ws16/w16-tierney.pdf.

Tribe, Laurence H. 1983. "A Constitution We Are Amending: In Defense of a *Restrained* Judicial Role." *Harvard Law Review* 97(2): 433–445.

Tushnet, Mark. 2006. "Popular Constitutionalism As Political Law." *Chicago-Kent Law Review* 81(3): 991–1006.

Tydings, Joseph. 1967. Statement of Senator Tydings, Maryland, 113 Congressional Record 10103.

Van Alstyne, William W. 1978. "Does Article V Restrict the States to Calling *Unlimited* Conventions Only?: A Letter to a Colleague." *Duke Law Journal* 1979(6): 1295–1306.

Venice Commission. 2010. *Report on Constitutional Amendment.* No. CDL-AD(2010)001. 81st Plen. Sess. www.venice.coe.int/webforms/documents/?pdf=CDL-AD(2010)001-e.

Weis, Lael. N.d. "Environmental Constitutionalism: Aspiration or Transformation?" (On file with author).

Williams, Robert F. 1996. "Are State Constitutional Conventions Things of the Past? The Increasing Role of the Constitutional Commission in State Constitutional Change." *Hofstra Law & Policy Symposium* 1(1): 1–26.

Wood, Gordon S. 1969. *The Creation of the American Republic, 1776–1787.* Chapel Hill: University of North Carolina Press.

4

Courts and Constitution Making in Democratic Regimes

A Contextual Approach

David Landau

Recent experience has highlighted the important role that courts can play during constitutional replacement processes. In transitional cases such as South Africa and Egypt, judicial interventions in key moments helped legitimate or undermine constitution making. And in a number of recent episodes of constitutional replacement from a democratic starting point, ranging from Bolivia to Iceland, courts have been key players in enabling, blocking, or shaping the constitutional moment.

This chapter aims chiefly to develop a typology of the functions and modes of judicial intervention in constitutional replacement processes in democratic regimes. It distinguishes between three different functions played by courts during these constitution-making moments: catalytic, blocking, and shaping functions. In a first set of cases, courts have played out a catalytic role by empowering constitution making to go forward when it had an ambiguous legal justification. In a second set of cases, courts have performed a blocking role by issuing decisions that have attempted to stop constitution making from occurring. Finally, in a third set of examples, courts have played a shaping role: here they have neither blocked nor enabled constitution making, but have sought to exercise an influence on particular aspects of the process.

The chapter also explains that courts have used several different theories or justifications for intervention, and argues that each of these modes makes more sense in carrying out certain functions and in certain contexts, and less sense in others. A constituent power approach, which emphasizes the ability of the "people" to remake their political institutions even absent specific legal authority in the existing constitutional text, is most useful at playing a catalytic function but less beneficial at providing restraint where it is needed. A "legalist" approach, where courts insist that political actors play strictly by the existing constitutional rules, may block some problematic attempts at constitutional replacement and force those actors to stick to an existing roadmap, but it may also prevent exit from an untenable situation. Finally, an approach that focuses on enforcement of sub-constitutional rules, like those governing elections and referendums, may show the most promise in shaping constitutional replacement processes, but it may also threaten to saddle those processes with rules that are a poor fit to govern constitution making.

Both the functions that courts can and should play during constitutional replacement processes, and the theories they use to justify those actions, are likely to be highly contextual. The political context influences which functions courts can reasonably carry out and which tasks are most important. Furthermore, because different modes and theories of intervention have different strengths and weaknesses, different approaches will be appropriate in different contexts. Rather than seeking a unified jurisprudential theory of constitutional replacement, in other words, scholars should focus on the contexts in which different approaches are most useful and most likely to be successful.

The rest of this chapter proceeds as follows. Section I explores the importance of political context for understanding judicial function during constitution making in democratic regimes, both at a descriptive and normative level. Section II outlines the three major functions that courts can play during constitutional replacement – catalyzing, blocking, and shaping. Sections III, IV, and V explore the uses of three different modes or justifications for judicial intervention – constituent power theory, legalist approaches, and sub-constitutional interventions – in recent episodes of democratic constitution making. The aim in each section is to show that each mode is more effective at playing some of the functions than others. Finally, Section VI concludes by suggesting some ways in which the contextual approach developed in this chapter could drive future research.

I THE CONTEXT OF CONSTITUTIONAL REPLACEMENT IN DEMOCRACIES AND THE ACTIVATION OF COURTS

The political context within which constitution making occurs exercises a significant impact on both the ability of courts to carry out interventions and the kinds of interventions that are needed. This context has varied widely across different democratic constitution-making processes. At times constitutional replacement in democracies has occurred in contexts where the institutional order is in crisis or has become delegitimized (Negretto 2012). Some recent examples from Latin America fit this model of "institutional crisis" well – Colombia (1991), Venezuela (1999), Ecuador (1998 and 2008), and Bolivia (2009), for example. Yet not all crises are created equal – in some cases political institutions may be undermined to a degree where they are effectively nonfunctioning, while in other cases institutions are under stress but still functional. Moreover, and as Negretto notes in Chapter 1 of this volume, constitutional replacement in democratic regimes has often occurred in contexts without a crippling institutional crisis. Other factors – such as the need to update or democratize major institutional structures – also explain a large number of democratic constitution-making episodes.[1]

The extent of an institutional crisis faced by a country may bear on the likelihood that courts will be successful in carrying out different kinds of tasks. The judiciary, for example, is usually part of the existing institutional order. If that order faces a severe crisis, it may be more difficult for courts to carry out at least those tasks that place obstacles in the way of constitution makers, and in fact attempts at intervention may be met with backlash. A context of deep institutional crisis with delegitimized institutions is of course analogous to that often faced when constitution making occurs during regime transitions, rather than being triggered within a democratic order. Judicial intervention within such a process is far from impossible, but it can be both difficult and risky.

As an illustration of this challenge, in Ecuador, both the Supreme Electoral Tribunal and the Constitutional Tribunal attempted to shape aspects of the 2008 constitution-making process (Conaghan 2008). The former initially intervened by allowing the opposition-controlled congress to weigh in on President Correa's unilateral plan to hold a plebiscite on whether a constituent assembly should be called. But after the congress did so, agreeing to hold the plebiscite but also insisting that any resulting constituent assembly would be subject to legal limits, the Electoral Tribunal allowed Correa to substitute his own proposal removing those limits. When the congress tried to fire the head of the Electoral Tribunal, the Tribunal responded by removing fifty-seven members of Congress. Those members of congress in turn filed a case protesting their dismissal with the Constitutional Tribunal, which ruled in their favor. However, the new congress (now controlled by Correa's allies) removed nine of the Tribunal's justices and refused to comply. In the particular context of Ecuador, judicial intervention on either side of the debate may have worsened rather than ameliorated an institutional crisis, in addition to feeding a backlash against the judiciary.

This kind of deep institutional crisis is not one faced in all democratic constitution-making moments. For instance, in Chile between 2015 and 2017, president Bachelet attempted to replace the existing constitution during a period of relative institutional normality (Coddou McManus 2016). The promoters of this change were also proceeding inside rather than outside of the existing legal framework. Part of the reason for this is a perception that if they attempted to step outside

---

[1] A related issue, also discussed in Chapter 1, is whether constitutional designers make a break in legal continuity, which in turn tends to have a relationship with a series of design choices such as a constituent assembly versus a legislature as the constitutional drafter. As the remainder of this chapter shows, courts in some contexts have been able to influence whether designers are able to work outside the existing institutional order. Nonetheless, by making choices before courts intervene, constitutional designers affect the context in which courts work. It may be more difficult for courts to exercise effective restraint – through blocking or shaping – when the constitutional process is being carried out outside of the existing institutional framework and by an extraordinary body such as a constituent assembly.

of that framework, opposition actors would turn to the courts, which in turn would likely be successful in shutting down the process. In short, where institutions making up the existing order have a higher degree of legitimacy, courts will probably have more capacity to issue rulings that restrain or influence that process (see Couso 2018).

Relatedly, the political configurations underlying constitutional replacement will exercise a significant influence on any potential judicial intervention. A key variable appears to be whether there is substantial support from political actors for a court's ruling. Iceland offers an example: as Gylfason notes in Chapter 10, the country's deep economic and institutional crisis created surging pressure for constitutional change, but the design of the process largely sidelined traditional political elites, many of whom opposed the process. The Supreme Court issued a controversial ruling nullifying the elections for the constituent assembly on the basis that the election had ignored certain provisions of electoral law; the parliament then reappointed those same members to a Constitutional Council (Landemore 2015). The Court's decision arguably aided the position of members of the political class, who feared an independent constituent assembly.

In comparison, in Venezuela, President Hugo Chavez won the presidency as an extreme outsider (he had previously led a coup against the incumbent regime) in a context where existing political parties and institutions had largely imploded. In 1999, the Supreme Court allowed Chavez to call elections for a specialized constituent assembly outside of the existing institutional order, but it subsequently attempted to place some restraints on his actions and those of the assembly (Brewer-Carias 2010). These responses not only failed to stop Chavez from electing an assembly almost completely dominated by his supporters, but also eventually led to a chain of events in which the Court itself was shut down and replaced. The timid nature of the Court's response may in part be explained by the fact that the Court would have had little organized support had it attempted to impose stronger limits.

Another variable that may affect the nature and success of any judicial intervention are the rules governing access to the judiciary. These rules may be important to determining whether courts are triggered at all. In Colombia's 1991 constitution-making process, for example, the president's decisions to hold a referendum on the calling of a constituent assembly, and then to call for elections, were carried out using state of siege decrees (Cepeda-Espinosa 2005). Under the Colombian Constitution of 1886 (as reformed in 1968), these decrees were automatically sent to the Supreme Court to review, and thus the Court had to weigh in before the process could go forward. In most other cases, however, judicial intervention may need to be triggered by particular actors with standing to make the charge, or in extreme cases challenge may be impossible.

It is also worth noting which court (or chamber) the issue is sent to. Constitutional challenges to laws or other measures contemplating a constitution-making process are often sent to constitutional courts (or supreme courts exercising judicial review). But other courts, such as electoral courts and administrative courts, have also played a role in recent democratic constitution-making episodes. In some countries, electoral tribunals have jurisdiction over matters relating to the preparation of referendums or elections, and may review questions like the content or wording of referendum questions or the electoral rules used to elect a constituent assembly. Administrative courts may have power over certain kinds of decrees that may also be used by the executive branch to initiate or shape constitution-making processes. The nature of the court that is empowered to review acts related to the constitution making may matter on a case-by-case basis. As the Ecuadorian example suggests, different courts may sharply disagree on key legal issues, either because of legal-cultural reasons or political factors.

Finally, the timing in which judicial review occurs may be important. Where courts intervene closer to the beginning of a constitution-making process (say, to review a proposed referendum on whether to initiate a process or the electoral rules under which a constituent assembly will be elected), they may enjoy a greater opportunity to block or shape that process. Where courts intervene later in the process (say, to review a referendum approving the final constitutional text), it may be more difficult for them to shape the process in significant ways or to block it entirely. Nonetheless, as the Bolivian example explored below shows, under certain conditions courts can exercise a constraining role even quite late in the game: there, an Electoral Tribunal decision squashing a referendum to approve the constitutional draft forced bargaining between government and opposition, leading to a finalized constitutional text that was more a product of negotiation and less one of imposition.

II A TYPOLOGY OF JUDICIAL FUNCTIONS DURING CONSTITUTION MAKING

Experience suggests three broad classes of functions that courts tend to play during constitution making: a catalytic function, a blocking function, and a shaping function. Table 4.1 clarifies these three functions and maps them onto different justifications for intervention, which are explored in the next several sections along with a number of examples. At the outset, it is worth noting two points. The first is that the functions here are not necessarily mutually exclusive and courts can play multiple roles. For example, it is possible to imagine a court playing a catalytic role at one point in a process, and a shaping function at another point. The second is that, as illustrated in more detail below, the fit between "functions" and "justifications" are tendencies drawn from recent experience, not inevitabilities or logical relationships. All of the theories examined below could be deployed for any of the three functions.

First, courts play a *catalytic* role when they give political actors the legal authority to proceed with constitution making in contexts where this authority is contested or

TABLE 4.1 *Functions and justifications of judicial intervention during constitution making*

Judicial functions	Most characteristic mode or justification of intervention
catalytic – permit constitutional replacement to go forward when it would otherwise be definitely or potentially illegal	*constituent power theory* – "people" retain power to remake their institutional order
blocking – prohibit constitutional replacement from going forward	*"legalist" interventions* – require that constitution making be in accord w/ existing constitutional text
shaping – influence procedural rules through which constitutional replacement occurs	*enforcement of sub-constitutional rules* – use legal means like regulation of referenda or elections to channel replacement

ambiguous. In this way, courts can unblock processes of change that would otherwise be blocked or of dubious legality. Of course, in some cases judicial imprimatur of a process may be unnecessary – political actors may be able to move forward through political power or sheer force. But particularly when constitution making has a democratic starting point, opponents are likely to challenge any process and it may be difficult to move forward without legal approval (even when that approval occurs under immense pressure).

As the examples in Section III suggest, this function may be normatively desirable in cases where the existing constitution either contains no clause on its own replacement or the mechanisms for replacement are likely to be blocked because of political stalemate. It may also be important in cases where the existing constitutional order faces a political or economic crisis or has lost legitimacy from a broad swath of the public. In these cases, judicial intervention may provide an exit from a crisis that would otherwise continue to escalate, by allowing an act of constitution making that would not otherwise occur.

Second, judicial decisions can play a *blocking* function, effectively prohibiting political attempts to undertake constitution making. That is, if a court determines that an attempt at constitution making does not comply with rules found in the existing constitution or some other source of law, it can stop it from going forward. Such a decision obviously can raise risks for a court, which may be issuing a decision that frustrates the will of powerful political actors in a situation of high political tension and institutional instability. A court issuing such a decision thus may be risking significant backlash. Nonetheless, judicial decisions which block constitution-making processes from going forward are possible.

A court playing a blocking role faces two broad sets of questions. The first is about legal authority – what is the source of constraint through which the court is stopping the constitutional process? Theoretically, constraint might be found in a number of different sources – the nature of "popular will," the existing constitutional rules, sub-constitutional rules, or even norms drawn from international law. But each of these sources of constraint is contestable.

The second question is more normative: when might it make sense for a court to stop constitution making from going forward? Without developing a full answer here, one might emphasize the risk that constitution making can be used to erode the democratic order by entrenching incumbents and weakening institutions designed to check them (Landau 2012; Partlett 2012). This suggests that particularly where constitution making is undertaken in a manner that is exclusionary rather than inclusive, it may make sense for courts to step in. The Honduran case, examined in more detail below, is one where the risks of an abusive outcome were arguably significant enough to justify the courts in shutting down the constitution-making process altogether.

Finally, courts may be able to play a *shaping* function – rather than seeking to block the constitution-making process entirely, they may instead try to move the process in certain directions. For example, they might seek to influence the rules for the election of a constituent assembly, strike down referendums based on the wording of questions, timing of the vote, or rules for approval, or either remove or insist on adherence to certain stages or constraints in the process. Normatively, such a conception may be attractive because it allows a court to guide constitution-making processes in ways that limit the potential for abuse, while also allowing constitution making to go forward.

However, this conception too raises difficult questions about both the source of a court's authority to intervene in constitution making and the normative theory that it should use to guide its interventions. Again, without developing full answers to these questions, courts may be able to shape processes in ways that limit the risks of democratic erosion. The Bolivian case examined below offers an example – the judiciary's interventions may have played at least a modest role in preventing majoritarian forces from ignoring the interests of the opposition by forcing negoti-ations. Limiting the potential for abuse, of course, is not the only reason why courts may want to shape constitution making. They may also, for example, take steps to broaden the degree of public participation or remove obstacles that that give narrow interests too substantial a say in these processes, or which are likely to make them fail.

The remainder of this chapter uses a number of examples to explore the ways in which these different judicial functions during constitution making can be served by different justifications for intervention. My goal here is not to be exhaustive, but rather to cover the most common justifications of intervention during recent constitution-making episodes. One could also imagine, for example, that courts could rely on international law or transnational principles as a basis for their decision-making during constitution-making processes. Such an approach may be conceptually feasible and even normatively appealing, but it does not yet appear to play a significant role in judicial decision-making during acts of democratic constitution making.[2]

III CONSTITUENT POWER THEORY AND THE CATALYTIC FUNCTION

The constituent power model of constitution making has its origins in Sieyes and Schmitt (Colón-Ríos 2012). The basic conceptual argument is that "the people" are ultimately sovereign over their political institutions. As a result, they retain the power to remake those institutions by writing a new constitution, at any time. This theory has several major implications, laid out below.

It relies on a division between forms of constitutional change, and especially constitutional amendment versus constitutional replacement. Constitutional amendment, an exercise of "derivative constituent power," is constrained by the existing constitutional order. This means that amendment must ordinarily be done within the existing procedural rules laid out in the constitutional text. Courts will regulate compliance with those rules, determining which procedural route must be used for which type of change and striking down forms of change that do not comply with procedural requirements. Indeed, many courts now also strike down amendments that seek to alter core constitutional principles, holding that changes of that scope are really replacements of the constitution that can only be carried out via constituent assembly (Roznai 2013).[3] In contrast, constitutional replacement, an exercise of "original constituent power," can be carried out by the people outside of the constraints of the existing constitutional order. That is, even if the text of the constitution says nothing about constitutional replacement (or, more extremely, prohibits it), it can be undertaken by deploying the sovereign power of the people.

The constituent power theory of constitution making has echoes in other aspects of the constitution-making process. It suggests a preference for procedures of constitution making that work around the existing institutional order. Thus, specialized bodies like Constituent Assemblies seem more logical, if not inevitable, under these theories than constitution making by using ordinary institutions like parliaments. Constituent power theories also may imply that the bodies charged with constitution making are not constrained by the ordinary constitutional rules, but rather stand apart from and above those rules. This means that they need not follow ordinary

---

[2] In contrast, there may be more evidence that it has played a significant role in judicial decision-making during some transitional constitution-making processes. For example, the South African Constitutional Court relied in part on transnational consensus in its interpretations of the relevant principles in its certification decisions, even though the principles on which it relied were instantiated in a temporary constitutional text (Landau and Dixon 2015).

[3] It is possible that judicial decisions that have the effect of making constitutional amendment more difficult may increase the probability of constitutional replacement. Negretto, for example, in a study of Latin American constitutional change finds some evidence that the probability of replacement increases as amendment becomes more difficult. See Negretto (2012).

legal procedures and can instead set their own rules, for example, on how they vote or function. Indeed, since these special constitutional bodies have "original constituent power," they can shut down or limit the functioning of any other state institution during the constitution-making process. Recent experiences in Colombia (1991), Venezuela (1999), and Ecuador (2008) all give examples of this dynamic, with constituent assemblies in each case taking action to either limit the power of, or shut down, ordinary institutions of state.[4]

A constituent-power theory of constitution making gives courts the analytic tools needed to play a catalytic function. Where existing constitutional or legal rules appear to block constitution making entirely or to create obstacles to its proceeding, constituent-power theories may be helpful in sweeping away those barriers. Colombia in 1991 is the clearest example. The Constitution of 1886 contained no provision providing for its own replacement. During the National Front period of the 1950s through the 1970s, the two major political parties agreed on a pacted arrangement to share power in order to end a protracted period of inter-party violence followed by a brief dictatorship. The drafters thus designed institutions so that major decisions would require the agreement of both major parties in Congress, and required that Congress approve any constitutional amendment. This arrangement succeeded in stabilizing political institutions; however, it tended to exclude other political forces and over time it became resistant to change.

When constitutional changes did occur, the Supreme Court often blocked them. A proposal in 1977 to create a "small constituent assembly" to work on certain topics was blocked by the Court because it read the amendment powers of Congress to be exclusive and non-delegable; another major constitutional reform in 1979 was struck down because of supposed procedural errors in the process of passage through Congress (Cajas Sarria 2007). This led analysts to refer to Colombia in the 1970s and 1980s as a "blocked society." From a constitutional perspective, it was not just that the existing constitution contained no replacement clause, but in addition that there was a significant risk the Supreme Court would strike down any new attempt to insert such a clause because the sole constitutional procedure of amendment passage by Congress was held to be exclusive.

Meanwhile, and as described by Bejarano and Segura in Chapter 6, in the late 1980s there was a growing sense of both social and institutional crisis in Colombia, particularly fed by rising levels of violence. After the assassination of the Liberal-party presidential candidate in 1989, a student movement mobilized to demand

---

[4] The Colombian Assembly revoked the mandate of the Congress by calling new elections for that body, and in the meantime transferred its functions to a commission selected by the Assembly (Bejarano 2001). The Venezuelan Assembly reduced the Congress to a smaller commission exercising limited powers, shut down the Supreme Court, and replaced local government officials (Brewer-Carías 2010). The Ecuadorian Assembly declared the Congress in recess and assumed legislative powers, as well as shutting down several control institutions (the attorney general, national ombudsman, and comptroller, for example). See Conaghan (2008).

constitutional change and pushed for an informal vote to be held alongside local elections in March 1990. A more formal referendum was held alongside the presidential election of 1990 and then the new president issued a decree setting elections and rules for a constituent assembly. This decree was based on a multiparty pact.

The key Supreme Court decision in October 1990 (Decision 138 of 1990) held by a one vote majority that the decree establishing a constituent assembly was constitutional. In the face of a crisis, the Court retreated from its earlier doctrine that the constitutional reform powers of Congress were exclusive. The decision was a fairly orthodox statement of the constituent power theory – it emphasized the power of the people to remake their political institutions. Moreover, while the decree envisioned the assembly only having powers of constitutional reform over certain areas, the Court struck down those limitations and gave the assembly the power to undertake reforms of any part of the existing constitution (Colón-Ríos 2012). The assembly could not be limited by existing political institutions but, once constituted, could seek any type of reform over any aspect of the state that it wished to touch. The doctrine arguably provided an exit from a crisis that would otherwise have been difficult to overcome.

In Venezuela as well, the theory may have facilitated constitutional replacement in a situation where the two-party regime set up by a bipartisan pact had lost much of its legitimacy. In this case, however, the existing constitution included a replacement clause allowing for total reform, but the procedure required congressional approval. An initial Supreme Court decision allowed President Chavez to pursue constitutional replacement unilaterally. This decision relied heavily on constituent power theory and the original constituent power of the people, and had the practical effect of allowing constitutional replacement without requiring Chavez to negotiate with the opposition, which still controlled the Congress (Cameron and Sharpe 2010). In other words, in the Venezuelan case the use of constituent power theory was pivotal not so much for allowing constitution making to occur at all, but rather for allowing it to occur without need for compromise with the opposition.

Finally, it is worth mentioning the case of France in 1962, although in the context of a transformative amendment rather than a replacement. President De Gaulle proposed a referendum to establish direct popular election of the president in order to substantially strengthen the presidency within France's semi-presidential system. The Constitutional Council was asked to invalidate the referendum on the ground that the Parliament had exclusive powers of amendment, but in Decision 62-20 of November 1962, it refused, holding that it would not exercise constitutional control over a referendum, since it was a "direct expression of national sovereignty," or, in other words, an act of the people rather than their institutions (Morel 2012). The use of constituent power reasoning possibly allowed a significant change to the separation of powers to go forward when it would not otherwise have occurred.

These examples suggest two different ways in which the constituent power theory can play a catalytic role. First, if the mechanisms of change themselves are blocked by existing legal rules or political institutions, the theory suggests that the "people" can always find an exit that works above those political institutions. Second, if existing political actors allow change but place "upstream" or "downstream" constraints on constitution making (Elster 1995), for example, by limiting the topics on which an Assembly can deliberate or requiring that its actions be ratified by some institution associated with the old institutional order, the theory may give courts or other actors a basis to disregard those constraints.

On the other hand, the constituent power doctrine seems to have a more difficult time enabling courts to shape or block actions during the constitution-making process. In theory, constituent power doctrine could play a restraining as well as an enabling role. The doctrine gives "the people" the power to remake their institutions. Obviously, not all acts by political leaders or other groups outside of the existing institutional framework are plausible manifestations of the people. Some scholars have suggested that the concept of the "people" could be utilized by domestic or international bodies to nullify procedures or outcomes that do not plausibly represent the "popular will" (Braver 2016).

Judicial experience – although rather limited – suggests that the doctrine may have difficulty playing this role. The Venezuelan Supreme Court's decisions during the 1999 constitution-making process represent a relatively sustained effort at defining the meaning of "constituent power." The Court relied on the original constituent power theory in allowing Chavez to hold a referendum on whether a constitution-making process should go forward in the first place. But, in the *Gerardo Blyde* case, the Court then struck down an attempt by him to hold that referendum based on electoral rules that the president would write after the referendum; it instead forced him to define the electoral rules for the assembly before holding the referendum. In issuing its decision, the Court held that the constitution-making process was not fully above the constitution, instead it was bound by the basic principles or spirit of the existing text, including the principle of participatory democracy. In later decisions, the Court struck down an attempt by a Chavez resolution to declare the assembly sovereign over other institutions as well as declaring unconstitutional statements by him to that effect. However, in a case brought by the vice-president of Congress against the assembly the Court refused to intervene when the assembly sharply reduced the powers of the Congress, again citing the original constituent power doctrine.

Overall, the Court did not exercise a significant impact on the shape of the constitution-making process beyond catalyzing it at the outset. The only practical limitation the Court put on the process was the requirement that the electoral rules by which the assembly would be elected be publicized before the referendum was held, instead of afterwards. But the Court said nothing about the content of those rules or the process by which they should have been drafted. Thus, the rules were unilaterally drafted by the administration and heavily favored Chavez – he won over 90 percent of the seats with only about 60 percent of the votes, and thus was able to dominate the assembly (see Bejarano and Segura, Chapter 6). The later decisions had purely symbolic effect and did not stop the assembly from limiting or closing down rival institutions, effectively consolidating the president's power and setting the stage for a competitive authoritarian regime.

Some scholarship has noted that the failure of the Venezuelan Supreme Court to restrain the assembly was a product of the difficult political context in which the Court acted and of errors it made in the timing and content of its decisions (Landau and Dixon 2015; Braver 2016). The Court was obviously under tremendous pressure from Chavez and his allies. And there may well have been ways that the Court could have more effectively restrained the assembly, for example, by defining the content of the electoral rules to ensure pluralism rather than simply requiring that they be written in advance.

At the same time, the constituent power theory may be geared more toward playing a catalytic function than a restraint function. "The people" as used in the theory is primarily a legal fiction intended to explain and legitimize revolutionary constitution making (Tushnet 2015). Particularly when deployed against popular and insurgent politicians, it may be too ambiguous to play a role in shaping the constitution-making process. The doctrine, for example, could be consistent with either a majoritarian or more consensus-driven constituent assembly. It could allow for thick participation of civil society groups or a mere ratification of an imposed product through a referendum. Giving the theory more shape so that it has bite (for example, as a brake on majoritarian exercises of constitution-making) seems challenging.

The experience of constitution making in certain US states may suggest another way in which constituent power theory could be retooled to restrain constitution making as well as to enable it. In some US states, courts have issued decisions allowing processes of constitutional replacement where this is not contemplated in the existing constitutional text (generally through referendum ratification of a legislative proposal to call a constituent assembly), but they have also enforced limits on the power or jurisdiction of the assembly that were propounded in the enabling act (Partlett 2017). Thus, some US state courts have propounded a tradition of enforcing "limited constitutional conventions." The advantage of these conventions is that they combine the exit function of constituent power theory with at least some kind of restraint. However, the success of this model may have something to do with the peculiar nature of constitution making at the subnational level in the United States, where replacement has occurred against the backdrop of a constant federal constitutional order. And as the Colombian decision in 1990 shows, enforcing limited assemblies may also be counter to at least certain understandings of the constituent power theory, since it may limit the sovereign power of the people to remake their institutions at will.

IV "LEGALIST" INTERVENTIONS AND THE
BLOCKING FUNCTION

In contrast to a "constituent power" theory of constitution making, courts sometimes deploy a "legalist" view that envisions constitutional replacement as occurring wholly within the existing constitutional order and as regulated by rules arising out of that order. In this view, constitutional replacement has been carried out properly if it corresponds to the procedural or other rules found in the existing constitutional text; it will be struck down if it deviates from those rules.

Just as the constituent-power theory of constitution making is associated with a certain kind of institutional choice – a constituent assembly that prevails over the rest of the institutional order – the legalist conception also tends toward certain kinds of institutional dynamics. Constitution making under this theory of change seems somewhat more likely to be carried out by ordinary political institutions like parliaments, even though that choice is not inevitable (Arato 2016). If a constituent assembly is used, that assembly by definition will be limited by external constraints from the legal order. It may be limited to which subjects it can treat or how it must make decisions, for example.

This "legalistic" conception of constitution making insists that constitution-making bodies play by the rules, rather than working outside of them. The ability of courts to impose these demands may however depend on the political context, and particularly whether there is an explicit clause governing replacement and when and how it was put in place (see Partlett, Chapter 3). One can usefully distinguish three situations: where constitutional replacement clauses are put in place as a roadmap right before replacement occurs, where there is a significant lapse of time between the drafting of a replacement clause and its use during constitution making (especially where there has been a major change in the political context in the interim), and where the constitution says nothing about its own replacement at all (or explicitly bars it).

Courts will often be in a relatively strong position where contending forces have developed a pact immediately in advance of the constitution-making process about how that process ought to work. This is what Arato calls the "roundtable" model for democratic transition, although it may also be used for democratic constitution making (Arato 2016). In the South African transitional process, for example, the Constitutional Court acted as the guarantee to contending political forces that the final constitution (which was written by a democratically-elected parliament dominated by the ANC) would not depart from certain core principles found in the interim constitution (Klug 2011). The Court reviewed the final constitution and in fact rejected parts of it the first time around; those problems were fixed by the parliament and the Court then certified the final constitution in a second case. Should the Chilean constitution-making process move forward in the future on the basis of a clear and bargained-for roadmap, a court would likely have similar legitimacy in enforcing those constraints.[5]

In other cases, however, there is a significant time lapse between the drafting of clauses governing replacement and the actual process of replacement. The enforcement of replacement clauses in these contexts may be more difficult because the political context may have changed substantially between the drafting of the clause and its deployment. Bolivia (discussed in more detail below) is an example of this dynamic. A replacement clause was added to the constitution in 2004 during a deep political crisis and civil unrest. Two years later, an insurgent coalition led by President Evo Morales took power in the country and sought wholesale constitutional replacement. The Bolivian replacement clause was thus in an odd position at the start of the replacement process in 2006: It was recently enacted, but it was the product of a now-discredited regime that had been replaced by an insurgent who had led the civil unrest against the old order. With the help of a critical but ambiguous judicial intervention, the rules based on the replacement clause were contested by Morales' forces throughout the replacement process, but they did exercise a crucial influence on that process (Landau 2012).

Finally, there is a third class of cases of constitutional replacement in democratic regimes where the constitution says nothing about its own replacement or explicitly rules out constitutional replacement. In some cases, courts thus refuse to allow any change other than that through the exclusive channels of amendment. The risk of course is that courts acting this way may petrify the constitutional order or prevent a necessary exit from a political crisis. As noted above, the Colombian Supreme Court suggested this view of constitutional change for many years before, in the midst of a severe political crisis, finally using the constituent power doctrine in order to allow the 1991 constituent assembly to be held. The Colombian Constitution after 1957 plausibly went beyond silence and seemed to rule out the use of assemblies – in order to protect the bipartisan pact, it stated that reforms could "only" be carried out by the congress using designated procedures. In the early years after the National

---

[5] Of course, the legitimacy of judicial enforcement of even a recently enacted roadmap may depend in part on which actors imposed it, as well as the legitimacy of the court itself. During Egypt's constitution-making process in 2012, for example, the Supreme Administrative Court issued a ruling dissolving the constituent assembly appointed by the Egyptian Parliament, on the ground that it fell afoul of a provision added into the Egyptian constitution during the transition and which required the assembly to be representative of broader forces in Egyptian society (Brown 2013). Instead, the assembly was dominated by the Islamist forces that held a majority in the Parliament and the presidency. Forces close to those movements derided the Court's intervention, and several months later President Morsi issued an order effectively insulating the constitution-making process from judicial review. The backlash caused by the Court's intervention might be attributed both to the fact that the judiciary itself was perceived by many actors as allied with the military rather than as an independent arbitrator, and to the fact that the transitional amendments themselves were largely done by military imposition rather than consensus.

Front was put into effect, a court enforcing this limit could plausibly be viewed as defending a recent political settlement. But as time went on, this position became more problematic and was widely viewed as an attempt to block institutional change. The problem with the Supreme Court's jurisprudence in Colombia over time was not really the insistence that political actors follow rules found in the current constitution, but the suggestions that even consensual attempts to reform the constitution to add a replacement clause would be struck down. This effectively forced the major political parties to seek an extra-constitutional route through constituent power doctrine.

Thus, the context may in part determine whether a court can effectively block attempts at constitutional change that depart from the rules found in the existing constitutional text. The legalist conception can be deployed by courts to stop the constituent-power conception of constitution making "outside the rules," but that conception deployed indiscriminately may block opportunities where exit is needed. Just as there seems to be a risk that adherence to the existing rules may block too much (preventing necessary changes that a constituent power conception would have catalyzed), there is also a risk that they may block too little (essentially allowing unregulated or only weakly regulated constitutional change). They may stunt a court's ability to carry out the shaping function of judicial review on constitution-making processes. The reason why is the same one noted above – replacement clauses or other restrictions found in existing constitutional texts are written for one political context and may function differently once that context changes.

Hungary is relevant on this point. Like Bolivia, it is an example of a constitution where replacement provisions were contemplated in one political context and then utilized in another. The existing constitution was heavily amended during the transition to democracy after 1989, but the new text was thought to be a "temporary" constitution that was the first phase in a multistage constitution-making process (Arato 2010). Initially, drafters thus allowed it to be amended or replaced by a two-thirds vote. The initial two-thirds rule may have seemed like it would be enough to force effective consensus in the weak and fragmented political environment immediately after transition. In 1994, Parliament added a clause requiring the rules for the drafting of any new constitution to be approved by a four-fifths vote. This clause was intended to be temporary (one provision of the law inserting the amendment of the constitution stated that it would be in effect during the 1994–1998 legislative term), although it is somewhat more controversial whether it actually had a sunset date as finally codified in the constitution.[6]

---

[6] Arato (2010) argues that because the sunset clause was never actually codified in the constitutional text itself, it never actually became part of the constitution and the amendment may be viewed as permanent, while Sonnevand, Jakob, and Csink (2015) argue that its provisional intention should prevail and at any rate that it was properly removed from the constitution by a two-thirds vote.

In 2010, the Fidesz party, because of the nature of the electoral rules, gained over two-thirds of seats in Parliament with just over half of the votes (Bankuti, Halmai, and Scheppele 2012; See also Negretto and Wandan [Chapter 7]). This gave the party the ability to amend the existing constitutional text at will or indeed, to replace it altogether. In practice, it did both, passing a series of amendments affecting key institutions like the Constitutional Court, before writing a new constitution in 2011. Before undertaking replacement, the legislature also passed an amendment, by a two-thirds vote, removing the four-fifths clause from the constitution. Many scholars have criticized the new Hungarian constitution for helping perpetuate Fidesz in power while weakening horizontal checks on its authority (Bankuti, Halmai, and Scheppele 2012; Sonnevand, Jakob, and Csink 2015).

The Hungarian Constitutional Court took a relatively deferential role during the replacement process. It declined to review amendments to the old constitution (before it was replaced) that restricted the Court's jurisdiction on the ground that they were unconstitutional constitutional amendments because they conflicted with basic principles of the constitutional order. The Court held that fundamental unamendable principles might exist, but that it was beyond its competence to identify and apply them (Halmai 2012). On this point, the Court's jurisprudence was at variance with that of an increasing number of high courts around the world, which have embraced some notion of an unconstitutional constitutional amendment. Arato (2011) argues that this decision (as well as justiciability concerns) deterred the opposition or anyone else from bringing a complaint to the Court challenging the removal of the four-fifths clause as unconstitutional. At any rate, since the Court may well have concluded that the four-fifths clause had expired (or more dubiously that it was properly removed using a two-thirds vote), it is not clear that a review demanding that an intervention requiring Fidesz to play by the replacement rules would have been successful. If a two-thirds vote was all that was required, then Fidesz did play by the express constitutional rules. The problem here would be that the constitutional rules themselves were insufficient to ensure a consensual constitutional process.

V SUB-CONSTITUTIONAL MODES OF INTERVENTION AND THE SHAPING FUNCTION

Relatively frequently, courts acting during intra-democratic constitution-making processes seem to justify their actions on sub-constitutional grounds. They might, for example, hold that elections do not comply with the dictates of ordinary electoral rules, or that referenda do not comply with the rules applicable to those instruments in normal situations. In other words, rather than asking whether the replacement process follows rules found in the constitution itself, courts might ask instead whether it complies with other legal norms that bear on its procedures.

This mode of intervention may allow courts to play a shaping function that is more difficult to achieve with either the constituent power or legalist conceptions.

The constituent power conception tends to allow courts to catalyze processes by legitimizing them; the legalist conception allows courts to block attempts at constitutional change that are extralegal. By activating sub-constitutional norms governing elections, courts may be in a better position to shape processes so that they become more inclusive and participatory. They may also be able to inhibit elite manipulation of the rules to the advantage of those elites, which has been a problem in a number of recent constitution-making episodes.

It is also possible that courts feel more confident intervening at the sub-constitutional rather than constitutional level, and are less likely to face backlash if they act at this level. When courts answer questions as to whether or not political forces must follow procedures laid out in the existing constitution (which often may prohibit constitutional replacement altogether), they are wading into theoretically-contested questions and taking on those forces in a particularly high-stakes way. Courts may be more comfortable, and more likely to succeed, if they instead rely on ordinary law.

At the same time, reliance on ordinary law to block constitution making raises several difficult problems. The first is theoretical. A court may act at the sub-constitutional rather than constitutional level in order to elide the debate between "constituent power" and "legalist" schools of thought. But the application of sub-constitutional rules governing things like elections and referenda to constitutional processes may effectively be a choice to follow the legalist approach. It subordinates constitution making to existing legal processes rather than allowing it to play by its own rules outside of those processes. This in turn creates a potential political problem: forces seeking to carry forward with constitutional replacement can cast the restraints imposed by a court as illegitimate impositions on the power of the people.

A more practical concern is that application of ordinary law may limit constitution-making processes in ways that do not sufficiently acknowledge the special questions raised in that context. Laws that may be well suited to regulate ordinary politics may not work well when applied to constitutional replacement. To be sure, these ordinary rules are likely to include some valuable norms and provisions that would work to limit the manipulation of processes like referenda. But they may also place unnecessary or unsuitable constraints on replacement, for example, by requiring electoral rules that do not make sense in that context.

A few examples may help clarify these points. In Honduras in 2009, the populist President Zelaya sought to advance a "popular consultation," a name he later changed to an "opinion poll," on whether or not a constituent assembly should be elected in the country to replace the existing 1982 Constitution (Feldman et al. 2011). The opposition party and much of Zelaya's own political party opposed this effort. Zelaya's stated intent was to hold a nonbinding vote on the question of whether a formal vote to call an assembly should be held in conjunction with the next set of elections. An administrative court issued a preliminary injunction against a decree issued by Zelaya ordering the opinion poll, and Zelaya's attempt to appeal that denial to the Supreme Court failed. An Electoral Tribunal later declared the poll illegal.

The judicial rulings against Zelaya's position focused on sub-constitutional legal provisions governing the regulation of referendums and similar devices.[7] In particular, opponents argued that there was no provision in Honduran law allowing such a "non-binding poll" and that particular choices made by Zelaya, such as having the National Statistics Institute rather than the National Electoral Court monitor and count the vote, were illegal. The judicial decisions contained very sparse reasoning and focused heavily on technical issues (standing and the threshold needed to justify a preliminary injunction, for example), but they seem to be based in large part on these sub-constitutional arguments.

The risk of democratic erosion in the Honduran context was very high (Human Rights Foundation 2010). Zelaya set up a process that seemed designed to evade normal oversight carried out by institutions like the Electoral Court or even judicial review (he reissued similar decrees multiple times and delayed publishing them). He ominously ordered the military to assist in the process several weeks before the vote. And on the eve of the vote, with several courts having blocked the poll and the military refusing to help him carry it out, he and his followers broke into a military base to take the ballots and other materials needed to hold it. This is not a context in which one would be confident of the integrity of the vote.

At the same time, the use of ordinary law to constrain Zelaya proved difficult. The nonbinding poll requested by Zelaya was not expressly contemplated in existing law, but one could argue that that power could be implied based on existing legal instruments and particularly the nonbinding nature of the vote. The process that Zelaya stated he intended to follow – nonbinding "poll," followed by binding referendum, followed by election of an assembly – was superficially similar to the one used in Colombia, although the political context was completely distinct. Zelaya's allies argued that it was a reasonable way to proceed in the face of an existing constitutional text that seemed not to allow a constituent assembly and a hostile Congress that was unwilling to move forward with reforms. The opposition of the courts through ordinary instruments of legality allowed Zelaya and his supporters to respond with invocations of the constituent power theory.

---

[7] In contrast to these judicial rulings, the political discourse after Zelaya's removal focused on a distinct set of arguments grounded in the legalist approach outlined in Section IV. Opponents argued that the replacement of the existing constitution was illegal because the existing 1982 Constitution did not allow for constitutional change via constituent assembly, and moreover that a petrified or unamendable clause preventing the reelection of the president under any circumstances disallowed any form of constitutional change, including replacement, that would affect that article. The argument that the petrified no-reelection clause could not be touched by any method of constitutional change threatened to have a similar effect as the Supreme Court's National Front–era doctrine in Colombia, cutting off any possibility of wholesale constitutional replacement (Albert 2010).

The dispute escalated until Zelaya was removed in a military coup just before the poll was to have been held.

The recent constitution-making experience in Iceland offers an example of courts intervening through the use of ordinary law in a more clearly problematic way. After a parliamentary law was passed, the country held elections to a twenty-five–member Constitutional Assembly. However, the Supreme Court of Iceland nullified the election in 2011, holding that it violated certain technical requirements found in existing law and needed to ensure confidence in electoral outcomes, such as the design of ballot boxes and ballots themselves and the manner in which ballots were counted (Landemore 2015). Surely, basic norms of electoral fairness should be adhered to in any election, but the question is whether the use of highly technical arguments, without a credible argument of underlying fraud or malfeasance, should have been enough to nullify the election of a constituent assembly, or instead whether the Court should have been particularly deferential in that context. Moreover, the Court's decision did little to advance any underlying value of constitutional process (increased inclusiveness or participation, for example). The negative impact of the Court's decision may seem relatively insignificant – Parliament subsequently appointed the same twenty-five members to a special commission with the same functions. But one wonders whether the loss of electoral legitimacy may have impacted the final outcome, which ended when the Parliament refused to take action on the Commission's draft despite a nonbinding referendum requesting that it do so.

Bolivia, finally, offers a perhaps more successful experience with the use of ordinary law to constrain constitution making. As noted above, the Bolivian constitution-making process from 2006 until 2009 proceeded under the shadow of a constitutional replacement clause that had been added by a prior administration in 2004. The new president, Evo Morales, bargained with the opposition to obtain a law based on that clause, which allowed the convening of a constituent assembly but required a two-thirds vote in that assembly for the approval of the final text, which effectively gave the opposition a veto. Throughout the contentious three-year process, Morales's allies contested these restraints on the constituent assembly, both arguing about their proper interpretation and more broadly claiming that the assembly, now that it had been constituted, had original constituent power and was not bound by any external constraint (Landau 2012).

After a series of disputes and social disruptions, Morales's allies approved a final draft of the constitution in the assembly at a session in which social movements prevented the opposition from entering. But the opposition had sufficient numerical strength to block Congress from scheduling a required referendum on the approved draft. Morales's forces finally pushed through a vote calling a referendum approving the draft after his civil society allies blocked the opposition politicians from entering Congress. Concurrently, the law would have allowed for another referendum allowing the public to adjudicate between competing versions of certain articles on which the assembly had not reached two-thirds approval. Thus, the Congress passed two separate laws: first a law scheduling the two referendums simultaneously, and second an amendment to the law regulating the assembly to ensure that the two referendums could be held simultaneously (the previous version of that law had envisioned them being held sequentially).

In this context, in March 2008, the Bolivian National Electoral Court issued a key ruling (Resolution 013 of 2008): it nullified the referendum and required the Congress to pass a new law authorizing one. The Court's reasoning was highly technical: the amendment to the enabling law allowing parallel referendums had been passed just after the law calling those referendums (or at least was published afterwards), and thus went into effect one day later. Therefore, at the time the Congress tried to call the two referendums simultaneously, it acted in violation of the legal framework governing the assembly. In other words, Congress had passed the two laws out of sequence, and would need to pass the call for referendums all over again in order to have legal effect.

The Court's decision was silent regarding the bigger questions surrounding the case. The Court said nothing about the theoretical dispute between allies and opponents of Morales about constituent power. It did not mention the fact that the draft was muscled through the assembly and then Congress because actors on the streets stopped opposition politicians from entering. The Court in fact said very little about the overall shape of the referendum or constitutional process.[8] Its reasoning was not an attempt to examine and advance any reasonable constitutional values, but simply a technical conception of the rule of law. The effect of the decision, however, advanced those broader values by encouraging negotiations with Morales's political opponents. After the Court issued its decision, the two sides jointly agreed on a draft, which was presented and approved in a referendum the following January. The final draft gave Morales much of what he wanted but did represent a compromise on some key points.

In the Bolivian context, this may have been as much as the Court could have done. Judicial institutions have historically been quite weak; indeed, during a part of the constitution-making period the Constitutional Court was not operating because opposition-affiliated judges had quit after the allies of Morales started impeachment proceedings against them, and new judges could not be appointed (Lehoucq 2008). A broader and more theoretical decision would have been very risky in that context. And the Court's decision again was at least plausibly aimed at shaping the constitution-making process by advancing core values, even if those values are not apparent in the text of the decision.

---

[8] The Court did hold that any future referendum should be held at least ninety days following the announcement of the referendum and publication of the draft, in order to give both voters and officials time to prepare for the vote and ensure the integrity of the election.

VI CONCLUSION

This chapter has explored the myriad ways in which courts have influenced constitution making in democratic regimes, and has argued for a contextual approach to understanding judicial interventions during constitution-making moments. Just as democratic constitution making is carried out under a number of different conditions, courts might pursue a number of different functions during those processes. Moreover, any single theory or mode of intervention will carry out some functions well and others poorly, and will work better in some contexts than in others.

From a descriptive perspective, this chapter suggests the need to explore the conditions under which courts can successfully intervene in processes of constitutional replacement in democratic regimes. Many of these factors are beyond a court's control: the political conditions under which replacement is carried out, and, in particular, whether a court has institutional and political support for its decisions, are likely to be particularly important (Landau and Dixon 2015). But courts also have some control over the framing of their interventions. Appeals to the text of the existing constitution or to ordinary laws governing elections and referendums as a source of restraint may be more persuasive in some contexts than in others, for example.

From a normative perspective, more work must be done in identifying the tasks for which courts are most needed in different kinds of constitutional replacement processes. In some cases, as this chapter has argued, the core function is to restrain "abusive" forms of constitution making, either by blocking it altogether or by shaping it to ensure that the rules adequately protect minority groups. In other cases, the most important task may be allowing a peaceful exit from a crisis and preventing certain groups from vetoing necessary change. The context in which each of these tasks is paramount, and how each can be carried out in different conditions, remain underexplored.

The analysis here may give scholars at least rough tools for evaluating the interventions of courts in constitution making. In some cases, courts seem to be pursuing a counterproductive goal, as in Iceland where the Supreme Court was focused on restraint in a situation where exit may have been the major concern, or no clear goal, as in Ecuador where the Supreme Electoral Tribunal first ruled that the president must bargain with the Congress over the process but then allowed him to replace a bargained-for proposal with his own unilateral plan. In other cases, such as Venezuela, it may be that courts are pursuing an important goal (shaping) but doing so in a sub-optimal way (constituent power theory).

A systemic consideration of the fit between the needs of a given context and the likely nature of any judicial intervention suggests a disconcerting possibility. Judicial interventions to restrain or reshape constitutional replacement processes may be most normatively desirable in contexts where democratic institutions are in crisis and opposition forces are disorganized, because these contexts may raise the most significant risk of democratic erosion. But numerous examples suggest that restraint in these contexts is difficult to achieve, precisely because of the weakness of institutions and lack of organized political support for courts. Restraining constitution making through legal means may be far easier where existing institutions are stronger and opposition forces more entrenched, and courts may also be more likely to have incentives to provide such restraint. Yet in these contexts, as the examples from Chile and Iceland suggest, the chief concern may not be the need for restraint, but rather that political actors and institutions associated with the existing order will ossify a political order in need of change. This observation, if correct, may serve less as a cause for despair and more as a challenge to consider how courts can best be conceptualized during the wide range of institutional and political pressures that accompany moments of constitutional replacement in democratic orders.

REFERENCES

Albert, Richard. 2010. "Constitutional Handcuffs." *Arizona State Law Journal* 42(3): 664–715.
Arato, Andrew. 2010. "Post-Sovereign Constitution-Making in Hungary: After Success, Partial Failure, and Now What?" *South African Journal on Human Rights* 26: 19–44.
   2011. "Arato on Constitution Making in Hungary and the 4/5 Rule." International Journal of Constitutional Law Blog, April 6, 2011. www.iconnectblog.com/2011/04/arato-on-constitution-making-in-hungary-and-the-45-rule.
   2016. *Post-Sovereign Constitution-Making: Learning and Legitimacy*. Oxford: Oxford University Press.
Bánkuti, Miklós, Gabor Halmai, and Kim Lane Scheppele. 2012. "Hungary's Illiberal Turn: Disabling the Constitution." *Journal of Democracy* 23(3): 138–146.
Bejarano, Ana Maria. 2001. "La constitucion de 1991: un Proyecto de construccion institucional" in *Colombia ante los retos del siglo XXI: Desarrollo, democracia y paz*. Manuel Alcantara Saez and Juan Ibeas Miguel (eds.) Salamanca: University of Salamanca Press, 77–97.
Braver, Joshua. 2016. "Hannah Arendt in Venezuela: The Supreme Court Battles Hugo Chavez over the Creation of the 1999 Constitution." *International Journal of Constitutional Law* 14(3): 555–583.
Brewer-Carias, Allan. 2010. *Dismantling Democracy in Venezuela: The Chavez Authoritarian Experiment*. Cambridge: Cambridge University Press.
Brown, Nathan J. 2013. "Egypt's Failed Transition." *Journal of Democracy* 24(4): 45–58.
Cajas Sarria, Mario. 2007. *El control judicial a la reforma constitucional Colombia 1910–2007*. Cali: ICESI University Press.
Cameron, Maxwell A., and Kenneth E. Sharpe. 2010. "Andean Left Turns: Constituent Power and Constitution Making" in *Latin America's Left Turns: Politics, Policies, and Trajectories of Change*. Maxwell A. Cameron and Eric Hershberg (eds.) Boulder: Lynne Rienner, 61–80.
Cepeda-Espinosa, Manuel Jose. 2005. "The Judicialization of Politics in Colombia: The Old and the New" in *The Judicialization of Politics in Latin America*. Rachel Sieder, Line Schjolden, and Alan Angell (eds.) New York: Palgrave McMillan, 67–103.
Coddou Mc Manus, Alberto. 2016. "The Chilean Constituent Process: A Long and Winding Road." International Journal of Constitutional Law Blog, May 4, 2016. www.iconnectblog.com/2016/05/the-chilean-constituent-process-a-long-and-winding-road.

Colón-Ríos, Joel. 2012. *Weak Constitutionalism: Democratic Legitimacy and the Question of Constituent Power*. London: Routledge.

Conaghan, Catherine M. 2008. "Ecuador: Correa's Plebiscitary Presidency." *Journal of Democracy* 19(2): 46–60.

Couso, Javier. 2018. "Reflections on Latin American Constitution-Building from a Chilean Perspective" in *Constitution Building Processes in Latin America*. Gabriel L. Negretto (ed.) The Hague: IDEA International.

Elster, Jon. 1995. "Forces and Mechanisms in the Constitution-Making Process." *Duke Law Journal* 45(2): 364–396.

Feldman, Noah, David Landau, Brian Sheppard, and Leonidas Rosa Suazo. 2011. Report to the TRC of Honduras: Constitutional Issues, March 2011. http://papers.ssrn.com/sol3/papers.cfm?abstract_id=1915214.

Halmai, Gabor. 2012. "Unconstitutional Constitutional Amendments: Constitutional Courts As Guardians of the Constitution?" *Constellations* 19(2): 182–203.

Human Rights Foundation. 2010. The Facts and the Law Behind the Democratic Crisis of Honduras, 2009. http://humanrightsfoundation.org/uploads/The_Facts_And_The_Law_Honduras_2009.pdf.

Klug, Heinz. 2011. "South Africa's Experience in Constitution-Building" in *Reconstituting the Constitution*. Caroline Morris, Jonathan Boston, and Petra Butler (eds.) Heidelberg: Springer, 51–82.

Landau, David. 2012. "Constitution-Making Gone Wrong." *Alabama Law Review* 64(5): 923–980.

Landau, David, and Rosalind Dixon. 2015. "Constraining Constitutional Change." *Wake Forest Law Review* 50(4): 859–890.

Landemore, Helene. 2015. "Inclusive Constitution-Making: The Icelandic Experiment." *Journal of Political Philosophy* 23(2): 166–191.

Lehoucq, Fabrice. 2008. "Bolivia's Constitutional Breakdown." *Journal of Democracy* 19(4): 110–124.

Morel, Lawrence. 2012. "Referendum" in *The Oxford Handbook of Comparative Constitutional Law*. Michel Rosenfeld and Andras Sajo (eds.) Oxford: Oxford University Press, 501–528.

Negretto, Gabriel L. 2012. "Replacing and Amending Constitutions: The Logic of Constitutional Change in Latin America." *Law and Society Review* 46(4): 749–779.

Partlett, William. 2012. "The Dangers of Popular Constitution-Making." *Brooklyn Journal of International Law* 38(1): 193–238.

    2017. "The American Tradition of Constituent Power." *International Journal of Constitutional Law* 15(4): 955–987.

Roznai, Yaniv. 2013. "Unconstitutional Constitutional Amendments: The Migration and Success of a Constitutional Idea." *American Journal of Comparative Law* 61(3): 657–720.

Sonnevand, Paul, Andras Jakab, and Lorant Csink. 2015. "The Constitution As an Instrument of Everyday Party Politics: The Basic Law of Hungary" in *Constitutional Crisis in the European Constitutional Area: Theory, Law, and Politics in Hungary and Romania*. Armin von Bogdandy and Pal Sonnevend (eds.) Oxford: Hart, 33–109.

Tushnet, Mark. 2015. "Peasants with Pitchforks, and Toilers with Twitter: Constitutional Revolutions and the Constituent Power." *International Journal of Constitutional Law* 13(3): 639–654.

5

Replacing Constitutions in Democratic Regimes

Elite Cooperation and Citizen Participation

Gabriel L. Negretto[*]

Normative theories of constitution making have made competing claims about which features of this process have the potential to establish or improve a democratic regime. In one widely shared view, the active involvement of citizens before, during, and after constitution writing is supposed to enhance the sense of collective ownership over the new text, promote a democratic institutional design, and facilitate its enforcement. A different perspective emphasizes the importance of elite accommodation and cooperation to promote legality and consensus building among the major political forces. Neither theory, however, has examined the relative weight of these arguments by conceptually and empirically analyzing the exact mechanisms by which the actions of citizens and elites may affect democratization.

In this chapter, I discuss the impact of direct citizen participation and elite cooperation in constitution making on the deepening of an already existing electoral democracy. I argue that cooperation among a plurality of elected political representatives at the constitution-making stage is likely to improve the liberal dimension of democracy after the enactment of the new constitution. Inclusive constitutional agreements at the elite level and the dispersion of power that makes them possible not only facilitate the creation of legal limits on state action but also provide opposition parties and citizens alike with the means to make institutional constraints on executive power and civil liberties effective. This effect is usually observed during the early years of life of the new constitution, when the balance of power among the political forces that created the constitution tends to remain stable. I find preliminary support for this argument analyzing aggregate data and selected case studies from all episodes of democratic constitution making in the world between 1900 and 2015.

[*] I would like to thank Zach Elkins, Lourdes Jiménez Brito, Saúl López Noriega, Mariano Sánchez-Talanquer, Georg Vanberg, and all the participants at the conference "Constitution Making in Democratic Constitutional Orders: Theoretical and Comparative Perspectives" (Mexico City, August 11–12, 2016) for their comments on a previous version of this work.

Section I offers a critical review of existing theories on constitution making and democratization and derives from it some hypotheses about the potential impact of elite cooperation and direct citizen participation in constitution making on a democratic regime. Sections II and III offer quantitative and qualitative evidence that is consistent with the proposal that it is elite cooperation and not citizen participation in constitution writing that contributes to improving democracy in its liberal dimension. Section IV concludes.

I CITIZENS, ELITES, AND DEMOCRACY
IN CONSTITUTION-MAKING THEORY

Most theories of constitution making are predominantly normative, as they attempt to respond to the question of what rules political actors should choose if they intend to create a legitimate constitution. These theories, however, often imply that following their normative prescriptions at the constitution-making stage would result in a stable democracy, or a stronger one if it already existed.

One view emphasizes the role of public participation in constitution making in enabling citizens to monitor the actions of elected officials through their increased awareness of existing rules and rights. An alternative position stresses the importance of elite cooperation during constitution writing for the creation of a consensus among the main political forces about the constitutional rules that would regulate democratic competition. As we will see, both theories share several limitations. However, the proposition highlighting the importance of elite accommodation during constitution making provides the most appropriate starting point for examining the impact of constitutional change on democratization in comparative perspective.

The most traditional and still very influential theory of constitution making emphasizes the role of the people as the founder of democratic constitutions through indirect channels of citizen involvement. This theory was born out of the great revolutions of the late eighteenth century and presupposes a radical rupture with the preexisting political and legal order. As a reflection of its historical struggle against oppressive monarchical government, a distinctive claim of the revolutionary theory of constitution making was that only the people are the legitimate holders of constituent power.[1] As Thomas Paine summarized it, "a constitution is not the act of a government but of a people constituting a government" (Paine 1995, 467–468).

The idea of the people as a collective author of the constitution was subject to different conceptualizations in the American and French revolutionary traditions. Whereas in America "the people" was understood as a plural association of pre-constituted territorial entities, in France, "the nation" was conceived as a single

---

[1] On the historical and conceptual evolution of the constituent power theory, see Loughlin (2003); Kalyvas (2005); and Colón-Ríos (2012).

collective subject that was legally unbound in relation to existing institutions.[2] However, in respect to how the people should express its will, revolutionary theories were inspired in a republican view that usually rejected direct forms of citizen participation (see Manin 1997). For this reason, the popular origins of constitutions often referred to a founding principle that could be satisfied by representative channels, such as the election of a constituent assembly or the ratification of the constitution through elected conventions.[3]

Recent formulations of participatory constitution making have in mind either the adoption of a new constitution in societies affected by the complete breakdown of representative institutions or the involvement of ordinary citizens in important democratic reforms. As regards how citizens should be involved, contemporary advocates of participatory constitution making take the idea of popular authorship to its natural conclusion and claim the need for actual and direct citizen participation in constitutional change (Banks 2008; Hart 2011). Although this perspective does not presuppose discontinuity with the preexisting political and legal order, it does assume either the inability to resort to normal representative procedures, as in the adoption of a new constitution in some post-conflict societies, or the need to complement representative institutions with direct citizen involvement in significant democratic transformations (see Banks 2008; Fishkin 2011). Cooperation among the elite is not excluded from this analysis but plays a normatively less important role than direct engagement by citizens in processes of deliberation and voting on constitutional change (Fishkin 2011; Tierney 2012).

In relation to the potential consequences of constitutional change for the inauguration or deepening of democracy, some advocates of participatory constitution making take a more or less strict principled position. In this perspective, citizens have a right to participate in the making of the constitution because they must consent to the higher norm that will bind them in the future (Hart 2011). In a similar vein, it has been argued that regardless of its effects on democracy or other outcomes, citizen participation in constitution making enhances a collective sense of ownership over the constitution and thus its legitimacy (Miller 2011). More often, however, arguments supporting citizen participation in constitution making tend to emphasize, either implicitly or explicitly, its potentially positive consequences for democratization.

Some works have hypothesized that participatory processes, in particular, the popular ratification of new constitutions, are likely to lead to the formal expansion

---

[2] See Madison, Hamilton, and Jay ([1788] 1987, 302–322); Sièyes ([1789] 2003, 94–98).

[3] There were variations, however, within each revolutionary tradition. The proposal of the 1787 Federal Convention needed the consent of a qualified majority of representatives of the people of the states to become the new constitution. Yet in the states, some local constitutions, such the 1778 Massachusetts constitution and the 1792 New Hampshire constitution, were submitted to direct popular vote. The constitution adopted by the 1789–1791 Assemblée Constituante did not require any form of popular ratification to be enacted. Later on, however, a popular referendum was required to ratify the 1793 constitution.

of rights and reforms strengthening citizen influence and control over representatives (Elkins, Ginsburg, and Blount 2008; Ginsburg, Elkins, and Blount 2009). Others have proposed that participatory constitution making may lead to more constraints on government authority (see Carey 2009). However, the most general argument about the democratizing effects of participatory constitution making is that citizen involvement in this process increases public awareness of accepted behavior under the new constitution, which, in turn, enables citizens to monitor elected officials and prevent transgressions (see Widner 2008, 1516). Similarly, a recent study proposes that public participation during the drafting of a new constitution is likely to improve subsequent levels of democracy because such participation makes it possible for citizens to monitor the process and prevents elites from easily modifying the rules of the game as they play it (Eisenstadt, LeVan, and Maboudi 2015; 2017).

A perspective that differs from both the traditional constituent power doctrine and contemporary theories of participatory constitution making highlights the importance of legal continuity, gradualism, and above all, the central role that negotiation and deliberation among political elites should have for the foundation of democratic constitutions (Holmes and Sustein 1995; Preuss 1995; Arato 2009; 2010; 2016). This theory has been mostly inspired by some of the gradual and negotiated transitions to democracy that took place in countries such as Hungary and Poland in the late 1980s.[4] The most prominent example is Arato's "post-sovereign" constitution-making model.

According to Arato, the central features of a democratic constitution-making process should include: (1) a two-stage process with initial adoption of an interim constitution whose rules constrain the adoption of the final constitution, (2) drafting of the interim constitution by a non-elected round table, and drafting of a final constitution by a freely elected constituent legislature, (3) the use of existing amendment rules to provide legal continuity to the process, and (4) enforcement of the interim constitution by a constitutional court. Direct forms of citizen involvement, particularly popular referenda, are not required and may even be counterproductive for the realization of this model (Arato 2016, 64).

The post-sovereign theory has a clear normative goal, which is the rejection of the idea of a unified popular sovereign, characteristic of some versions of the constituent power doctrine. However, it also proposes that following the main components of the model would help not only to construct democratic legitimacy for the new constitution but also to facilitate the consolidation of a democratic regime by promoting consensus among the major political forces, a plurality of channels to

---

[4] To be sure, several authors have also highlighted the potentially democratizing effects of inclusiveness at the level of representative elites (even in the absence of direct popular participation) in constitutional change based on the analysis of particular cases in different countries and areas of the world. See, for instance, Horowitz's study (2013) of constitutional change in Indonesia.

express popular consent, publicity, and the rule of law (see Arato 2016, 161; 1995). Moreover, this theory also has a practical, political dimension. Just as legal discontinuity, special conventions, and popular authorship suppose a revolutionary setting in which the old regime lost legitimacy and its elite must be displaced from the new order, the ideas of legal continuity, parliamentary constitution making, and indirect citizen involvement reflect the need for elite cooperation in some transitions to democracy. In particular, gradualism and multi-party round table agreements are key elements when it is important to protect the interests of the outgoing authoritarian elite who might obstruct the initiation of the transition or the consolidation of the new democratic regime. Non-reliance on referendums, in turn, is intended to secure outcomes negotiated beforehand among elites, either in non-elected forums or in a newly elected parliament.

These theories have similar shortcomings as frameworks for comparative analysis of the relationship between constitutional change and democratization. They tend to portray constitution making as merely a formal, legalistic process and fail to analyze, both conceptually and empirically, the exact mechanisms by which the actions of citizens and elites during the creation of a constitution may affect democracy after its promulgation. Theories on constitution making also lack generality; they were inspired and are meant to apply to specific political environments, such as constitutions drafted after a revolution, a civil war, or as a result of a negotiation between outgoing authoritarian rulers and democratic forces. Nevertheless, a perspective emphasizing the key role of elite cooperation provides a critical vantage point for understanding how the dynamics of constitution making might have an effect on democratization.

Although the interdisciplinary dialogue between comparative constitutional theory and comparative political science on this matter has been sparse, there is a long tradition of research in the social sciences that focuses on the central importance of decisions made by political elites for the inauguration of a stable democracy and, potentially, its future improvement.[5] Seminal works in this research agenda have argued and provided a significant amount of evidence in support of the idea that the existence of a formal or informal procedural compromise among the leaders of contending political forces is crucial for a democratic opening (O'Donnell and Schmitter 1986). One key role of this compromise is to create a set of rules of mutual security that make it unlikely that the subsequent competitive political process would result in outcomes highly adverse to the interests of any of the main political and social groups (Przeworski 1988). Inspired by this line of reasoning, it has also been proposed that elite settlements and pacts in which the main political actors commit to follow rules of mutual security are the very foundation of a self-enforcing or consolidated liberal democracy (see Weingast 1997; Higley and Burton 2006;

---

[5] On this point, see also Saati (2015).

Alberts, Warshaw, and Weingast 2010). The relevance of these propositions to constitution making is clear.

There is no doubt that in several cases mass mobilization can be crucial for promoting a democratic opening or for making possible reforms to a deficient democracy.[6] It is also likely, particularly in the face of preceding events of mass action, that channels of citizen participation may make constitutional changes more legitimate in the eyes of the general public. Yet the drafting of constitutions has historically been a predominantly elite affair. Representatives of political parties and leaders from the most important social groups have usually been the ones who decide how constitutions should be drafted and what content they would have. This content, in turn, depends on the distribution of political power among the main political forces.

When none of the political groups and leaders that participate in constitutional negotiations has the popular support or the institutional resources to make decisions alone or form a coalition with a like-minded partner, they are likely to cooperate in creating institutions that protect the interests of all the parties involved. While these institutions do not need to take a full consociational form, they are likely to create legislative and judicial constraints on incumbent governments, reduce the power of electoral and legislative majorities, and establish rights that protect the interests of all the relevant groups in society (see Przeworski 1988; Jung and Shapiro 1995; Alberts, Warshaw, and Weingast 2010). More specifically, a constitution created by contending forces will tend to include formal rules that provide a standard for the detection of constitutional transgressions and legal mechanisms to react against them.[7] In other words, accommodation and compromise among different fractions of the political elite at the time of writing the constitution are likely to produce a constitutional design that enhances the principles of liberal democracy and provides legal means for their realization.[8]

To be sure, there is no reason to expect that liberal institutions would matter for the future democratic regime if the constitution is not implemented and observed in practice. What matters is an actual change in behavior, not just in formal rules. The role of political elites is again crucial in this respect (see Burton, Gunther, and Higley 1992). When a plurality of representatives of organized political and social interests has participated in the constitutional agreement, more actors are likely to

---

[6] On the role of mass mobilizations in transitions to democracy, see Collier (1999) and Haggard and Kaufman (2017).

[7] Institutions such as executive term limits, for instance, may work as devices that signal compliance or transgression of agreements. Several types of judicial and administrative actions may provide citizens and opposition parties with the capacity to challenge irregular government decisions. See Haggard and Kaufman (2017) on how specific institutional rules may help contending groups to monitor each other and act against transgressions.

[8] The liberal model of democracy is identified with limits on both the power of the executive and the power of electoral and institutional majorities. See Held (1987); Coppedge, Gerring et al. (2011).

have both the incentives and the resources to enforce that agreement later on.[9] After the constitution is enacted, it is generally the opposition political leaders who are more inclined to react when those in power renege on the initial constitutional compromise. And they would not act alone. Representatives of opposition political groups would, among other actions, mobilize public opinion or organize mass actions in defense of the constitution.

Changing preexisting forms of collective interaction, such as shifting from a pattern of polarized conflicts in multiple dimensions to stable cooperative relations, may depend on economic and social processes that precede constitution making and transform the preferences of individual agents.[10] For this reason, unless this transformation had already taken place at the time when the constitution is being adopted, political actors would attempt to renegotiate the terms of a constitutional agreement or renege on it ex post if they have the capacity to do so. Most political agreements are opportunistic or induced by the temporary influence of exogenous factors. This suggests, in turn, that for most constitutional agreements to be enforced over time it is crucial that the dispersion of political forces that made them possible in the first place remains relatively stable during electoral competition. If one of the participants in the initial constitutional compromise gains control over the government and becomes a dominant actor in the electoral arena, it would be more difficult to prevent, monitor, and sanction transgressions to the constitution.[11]

Because the power of political elites depends on their social support, the actions of citizens matter for the effective implementation of a democratic constitution; in particular, it matters whether citizens are willing and able to vote against incumbents, or engage in massive acts of social protest when the government infringes constitutional provisions. Yet these actions are not determined by the direct participation of citizens during constitution writing. This participation may indeed be an empowering experience. It is also reasonable to suppose that among those motivated to participate and obtain information about the process, involvement in constitution making will increase their knowledge about the content of the constitution and its importance in political life. It is doubtful, however, that participatory constitution making alone would deepen democracy after the new constitution is in force. Although some arguments about the democratic benefits of participatory constitution making have been tested, with positive results, the underlying logic that links

---

[9] Some authors have made a very similar argument regarding the enforcement of constitutions in general, yet without distinguishing between inclusion at the elite and citizen level. This is the case of Voigt (2004) and Elkins, Ginsburg, and Melton (2009).

[10] According to Boix (2003, 9–10), for instance, democracy cannot emerge as a self-enforcing equilibrium out of elite pacts unless previous transformations in the economic structure (such as declining inequality or a shift from fixed to mobile assets as a source of wealth) reduce the costs of tolerance for democracy among economic elites and their political agents.

[11] On this point, see also Alberts, Warshaw, and Weingast (2010).

citizen involvement during the writing of the constitution with actual levels of democratization after the event is generally weak.

The hypothesis that makes the most sense is that citizen involvement in constitution making may provide reformers with an incentive to expand citizen rights.[12] Ratification referendums, for instance, create what Elster calls a "downstream" constraint on the decisions that reformers can make (Elster 1995). If reformers know or anticipate the preferences of those who have the power to accept or reject their proposals, they have every incentive to satisfy those preferences beforehand. Regardless of whatever else they include in the proposal; the expansion of citizen rights can be presented and is likely to be regarded by significant segments of the population as an improvement in collective welfare. If citizens express demands for the inclusion of various rights during processes of consultation, reformers may also decide to expand the list of rights to address some of these demands. However, there is no reason to think that citizen voting or consultation during constitution making would lead to the creation of a set of rights that protects all major social groups. More importantly, even if reforms were designed in an impartial manner, majority voting or other forms of citizen involvement during their adoption does not guarantee that they will be effectively implemented after the new constitution is enacted.

Unlike the case of reforms related to the expansion of rights, the rationale behind the proposal that citizen involvement in constitution drafting may lead to a strengthening of constraints on the executive power is not apparent. In the first place, ordinary citizens are not likely to have well-defined and fixed general preferences on this matter. Moreover, one can think of many cases of constitution making against the background of a deep economic or political crisis, where people may be willing to support the strengthening of executive authority and the curtailment of rights.[13] And of course, even if there were circumstances under which citizens would demand increased formal constraints on the executive, there is no reason to suppose that these constraints would in fact be implemented after the constitution is approved.

Finally, and crucially, the argument that citizen involvement during the drafting or approval of new constitutions will increase public awareness about existing rules and rights, facilitate the detection and sanction of transgressions, and thus prevent self-serving behavior by elected authorities, rests on dubious assumptions about the preferences of citizens regarding the content of constitutions and their collective capacity to act in defense of legality. Citizen participation in the

---

[12] This logic may also apply to the inclusion of mechanisms of public participation in future governance.

[13] In his analysis of recent participatory processes of constitutional change in Latin America, Roberto Gargarella argues that while citizen rights have been expanded, the powers of the executive have increased, in particular, the power to stand for consecutive reelection. See Gargarella (2013).

formulation, discussion, or promulgation of a new constitution does not generate consensus about the rules and rights that should be included in it. As Weingast (1997) has argued, the most natural equilibrium in a society is a nondemocratic one in which citizens are unable to coordinate on punishing constitutional transgressions by the state because they are divided along ethnic, religious, ideological, or socioeconomic lines. Clearly, these divisions are not likely to disappear just because the citizens participate, even through deliberation channels, during the writing of a new constitution.

If it emerges at all, a general agreement among citizens about the rules and rights that should be respected by the state initially depends on successful negotiation of the content of the constitution among a plurality of political leaders representing the diversity of interests in society. In other words, elite bargains usually come before liberal democratic precepts and practices are adopted by any large number of citizens (Higley and Burton 2006, 3).[14] In addition, even if they were to agree on what rights should be universally protected, citizens do not normally have the ability to mobilize spontaneously against an incumbent government that transgresses the constitution. Aside from some episodic outbursts of protest, the capacity of the masses for sustained and effective mobilization is usually dependent on the leadership or organizational resources provided by political and social elites that oppose incumbents (see Albertus and Menaldo 2018).[15]

This discussion suggests that while citizen involvement in democratic constitutional replacements may be normatively desirable or politically convenient, only elite cooperation at the constitution-making stage is likely to improve the liberal dimension of democracy after the enactment of the new constitution. Inclusive constitutional agreements at the elite level, which occur when political power is dispersed at the constitution-making stage, are not only likely to promote the establishment of legal limits on state action but also provide the organized political opposition and ordinary citizens with the means to make institutional constraints on executive power and civil liberties effective. This effect should be observed during the early years of life of the new constitution, when the balance of power among the political forces that created the constitution tends to remain stable. Except in the rare circumstances where a constitutional agreement formalizes a deeper consensus on democratic norms, the only factor that prevents incumbents from reneging on the constraints accepted at the constitution-making stage is the existence of an opposition with enough resources to defend it.

These propositions are sufficiently general to apply to a wide variety of political environments. There are several reasons, however, why it is worth examining them in relation to constitutional replacements that take place in a regime that is already

---

[14] See also Weingast (2004).
[15] On a similar point about the importance of mass mobilization for forging and sustaining elite settlements, see Burton, Gunther, and Higley (1992, 19–20).

democratic in at least a minimal, electoral sense. The first is that, unlike some cases of revolutionary ruptures and democratic transitions, both citizen participation and elite cooperation may be required when a constitution is adopted after the establishment of free and fair elections. Whereas in revolutionary overthrow situations established elites tend to be displaced, in some transitions to democracy citizen mobilization may be disruptive to sustaining necessary inter-elite agreements. Democratic constitutional replacements, in turn, are often necessary to address public criticism of the working of inherited representative institutions. To achieve legitimacy and placate disaffected citizens, these reforms are likely to demand direct public involvement during drafting and approval of the constitution. At the same time, even if suddenly discredited by a crisis, preexisting parties and political leaders in an electoral democracy usually express the preferences of a significant number of citizens because they have achieved power positions through free and fair elections. For this reason, they have a legitimate claim to inclusion in the negotiations and deliberations leading to the adoption of a new constitution.

Second, whereas cooperation among political elites can take place under authoritarian or democratic conditions, direct citizen participation is less likely to be genuine when civil liberties and competitive elections have not been fully re-established. Determining when processes of public consultation are consequential for the design or implementation of a new constitution is always a difficult matter. Yet it is clear that these processes are more likely to be meaningful when the basic rights of assembly and freedom of expression are enforced. Voting in referendums can be informative as to popular preferences and may constrain the decisions of reformers only if we assume that citizens are free to participate and their votes are counted fairly. In other words, although elite manipulation of citizen participation is always possible, true citizen involvement in constitution making is more likely when a regime is already at least minimally democratic.

Finally, studying constitutional change once an electoral democracy is in place is also appropriate because it allows a better appreciation of the difference that adoption of a new constitution makes in terms of improving or not improving dimensions of democracy that go beyond the mere existence of free and fair elections. One of these dimensions, the most basic after equitable conditions of electoral competition are met, is the deepening of liberal principles, such as the implementation of legislative and judicial constraints over the executive and the effective protection of citizen rights. This dimension is crucial not only because it improves a merely competitive regime but also because it relates to the success of the ideal of limited government of classic constitutionalism (Sartori 1962). By contrast, when the reference point prior to the creation of a new democratic constitution is an authoritarian regime, democratic conditions in a country are likely to improve in almost every dimension, not necessarily because a new constitution is in place.

II AGGREGATE STATISTICAL ANALYSIS

As noted in Chapter 1 of this volume, the number of constitutions adopted in the world within an established electoral democracy is not negligible and may increase in the future. Yet there are relatively few cases, a mere twenty-five if we use the criterion of observing a new constitution at least five years after the first competitive election. We can expand the sample to forty-three observations if we shorten the time span and include all constitutions in the world enacted at or after the third year of free and fair elections in a country. The observations in this larger set incorporate some constitution-making events that took place in close connection with a recent transition to democracy, such as the adoption of South Africa's 1996 constitution and Brazil's 1988 constitution. Nonetheless, all the constitutions in this analysis will still have been enacted after the holding of democratic elections and after a few years of experience with representative institutions.[16]

A universe of forty-three observations is still admittedly small for testing causal claims. It is suitable, however, for a basic statistical analysis to observe whether empirical patterns exist and whether these patterns are consistent with existing hypotheses relating citizen participation and elite cooperation during the drafting stage of new constitutions to levels of democracy after their implementation. More-over, in order to persuade the reader that the observed effects are not an artifact of a restricted sample, I will report the results of the same analysis using data on all the episodes (ninety-four observations) of constitutions adopted in an electoral democracy, regardless of the year of their enactment, between 1900 and 2015.[17]

II.A *The Liberal Dimension of Democracy*

I have argued that only cooperation among representative elites at the constitution-making stage is likely to improve the liberal dimension of democracy by making institutional constraints on executive power and citizen rights effective during the early years of life of the new constitution. The empirical analysis of this proposition should focus, then, on the actual implementation of liberal principles after a new constitution is enacted in the context of an existing electoral democracy.

In order to measure the implementation of liberal principles and the level of liberal democracy after the enactment of the new constitution, I have used variables that capture the extent to which legislative and judicial constraints over the

---

[16] The constitutions added to those discussed in Chapter 1 of this book are Finland (1919), Italy (1948), Bosnia and Herzegovina (1995), Czech Republic (1920), Czech Republic (1993), Estonia (1933), Latvia (1922), Lithuania (1922), Moldova (1994), Poland (1921), Serbia (2006), Slovakia (1992), Nigeria (1963), South Africa (1996), Mongolia (1992), Brazil (1988), Venezuela (1961), and Nicaragua (1987).

[17] The observations have been obtained from the *Comparative Constitution Making Database*. See Chapter 1, n. 8.

executive are observed and citizen rights protected in practice after the new constitution is enacted. For this purpose, I have relied on four indexes taken from the *Varieties of Democracy* (V-DEM) project: judicial constraints, legal constraints, liberal component, and liberal democracy.[18] The first two indicate the extent to which the national executive in a political regime abides by the constitution and respects court rulings and how effective the legislature is in exercising oversight over the executive. The third averages these measures along with an index that captures respect for the rule of law and individual liberties.

The fourth index is the most relevant for the argument presented in this chapter because it measures the quality of a democratic regime by the effective limits placed on the exercise of executive power through the protection of civil liberties, checks and balances, rule of law, and an independent judiciary. Like the other three, it takes values from 0 to 1, where 0 is the minimum and 1 the maximum score. Unlike the others, this index takes into account the existing level of electoral democracy. As a robustness check, I will also report the results if I use as dependent variable the polity score of democratization from the Polity IV database.[19] It measures democratization in a scale that goes from −10 (pure dictatorship) to 10 (complete democracy). Although not specifically designed to estimate the effective implementation of liberal institutions, the polity score not only captures the degree of competition in the election of representatives, which is a key feature of electoral democracy, but also the extent of institutional constraints over executive power, which is one of the components of liberal democracy.

I have proposed that the impact of elite cooperation during constitution making on liberal democracy should be observed during the early years of life of the new constitution, when the level of popular support and institutional resources that organized political forces had at the drafting stage are likely to persist. For this reason, the dependent variables under analysis consist of the average value of each index during the first five years of life of the new constitution (i.e., t+1 to t+5). This is a reasonable time span because electoral cycles across parliamentary and presidential systems vary, on average, from four to five years.[20]

II.B *Elite Cooperation and Citizen Participation in Constitution Making*

The degree of elite cooperation is associated with certain characteristics that provide various political actors with mutual guarantees of inclusion and control over constitution making, such as legal continuity, institutional checks, and a politically plural

---

[18] See Coppedge et al. (2016).
[19] See Marshall, Gurr, and Jaggers (2019).
[20] However, using a shorter term, such as three years, does not alter the results that I present below. For effects in periods longer than five years, see n. 26.

representative body responsible for drafting the constitutional text. Legal continuity between the old and the new order makes the process more predictable and enables the courts to supervise compliance with the rules. Institutional checks refer to the involvement of various independent collective institutions in the activation and regulation of the process. However, the key feature that signals the presence of elite cooperation is a politically plural democratic constitution-making body. Such a body exists when (1) two or more political parties or groups achieved representation in it through free and fair elections and (2) cooperation between at least two of these parties or groups is necessary according to the decision rule established for the approval of the constitution.

Following this logic, I measure the impact of elite cooperation during democratic constitutional change using a dummy variable that takes a value of 1 when cooperation between two or more freely and fairly elected parties was necessary to pass the constitution according to the decision rule, and 0 otherwise.[21] A value of 0 in this variable indicates that a dominant party was able to pass the constitution unilaterally or that the executive or a single political force appointed the constitution-making body. This measure is correlated with legal continuity between the old and the new constitution and, particularly, with the existence of institutional checks over the process, suggesting that these variables are internally consistent and tapping into the same phenomenon.[22] Nevertheless, since only some of these features may be present in a single episode of constitutional replacement, it is the existence of a politically plural democratic constitution-making body that should be preferred as a measure of elite cooperation because it is a factual, not formal indicator.[23]

As indicated in Chapter 1, citizens might be actively involved in constitutional change through electoral and nonelectoral mechanisms. Accordingly, I provide here two different measures of direct citizen participation. Nonelectoral participation is captured using a dummy variable that takes the value of 1 if ordinary citizens were involved in the formulation, discussion, or submission of reform proposals at any stage in the process. The voting alternative is measured through a dummy variable coded as 1 if citizens participated in popular referendums either at the beginning, in authorizing the process or deciding on a particular issue, or at the end, to ratify the new constitutional text.

[21] My concept and operationalization of elite cooperation thus differs from what Eisenstadt and Maboudi (2019) call "group inclusion," which refers to the sheer number of groups included in a constitution-making process (both social and political) without taking into consideration their relative influence in the final adoption of the constitution according to the decision rule.

[22] Pluralism in political representation and decision making has a correlation of 0.58 with institutional checks in constitution making, and is statistically significant at $p < 0.001$. Institutional checks, in turn, have a correlation of 0.36 with legal continuity, significant at $p < 0.05$.

[23] The results reported for elite cooperation in the following analysis are stronger if we use an aggregate scale including legal continuity, institutional checks, and plural representation. Yet the latter is the strongest variable driving the effects.

Regardless of what sample of constitutions adopted in a democratic regime we use, there is no significant correlation between a politically plural constitution-making body and direct citizen involvement, either in electoral or nonelectoral forms. In addition, there is no statistical association between these two channels of direct popular participation, suggesting that they are not only different at a conceptual level but also that, in practice, constitution makers tend to see them as alternative and not necessarily complementary ways of engaging citizens in the process.

The most important variables added to control for alternative explanations are the lagged value of the dependent variables and the age of democracy before the enactment of the new constitution. The success of democracy in the present is likely to be explained by its success in the past. For this reason, I will use the average of the indices of legal constraints, judicial constraints, liberal component, and liberal democracy during five years before the new constitution was adopted as a standard of comparison to determine whether actual practices changed as a result of constitutional change. The age of democracy is also a key control variable because it is very likely that the deepening of democracy in any dimension is associated with the time passed since its inauguration. Additional variables included are the GDP per capita the year before the new constitution was adopted, the level of ethnic fractionalization in the country, the year the new constitution was enacted, and the region of the world to which the country experiencing the change belongs.[24] Just as democratic success in a given country may very well be linked to its level of economic development, internal social divisions may determine democratic failure. Temporal and regional trends may also be responsible for the level of democracy observed in a given country.[25]

II.C *Results*

Given the structure of the data and the nature of the dependent variables, I used an OLS regression with robust standard errors clustered by country to provide a basic test to the proposed hypotheses. Table 5.1 shows the results of this analysis.

The first models include the main explanatory variables along with the lagged score of the dependent variable and the accumulated years of electoral democracy before the adoption of the new constitution. The second models in each case incorporate the rest of the control variables. The results of all the tests are consistent

[24] Data on GDP per capita comes from the Maddison Project Database (2018), available at www .rug.nl/ggdc/historicaldevelopment/maddison/releases/maddison-project-database-2018. Data on ethnic fractionalization comes from Alesina et al. (2003), available at www.nsd.uib.no/ macrodataguide/set.html?id=16&sub=1. Regions of the world have been divided into Latin America and the Caribbean, Africa, Asia, and Europe. The Latin American and Caribbean region is omitted and used as a baseline.

[25] The results reported below do not change significantly if we add additional control variables, such as population size and a measure of civil unrest based on the addition of general strikes, riots, and antigovernment demonstrations at the time of change.

Dependent variables

Explanatory variables	Legislative constraints[a]		Judicial constraints[b]		Liberal principles[c]		Liberal democracy[d]	
	Model 1	Model 2	Model 1	Model 2	Model 1	Model 2	Model 1	Model 2
Elite cooperation	0.127**	0.121**	0.066	0.098*	0.082*	0.081*	0.120**	0.108**
	(0.062)	(0.057)	(0.042)	(0.055)	(0.041)	(0.044)	(0.052)	(0.047)
Citizen consultation	−0.035	−0.019	0.016	0.077	−0.002	0.050	0.015	0.061
	(0.058)	(0.068)	(0.049)	(0.067)	(0.045)	(0.047)	(0.052)	(0.068)
Citizen voting	−0.084	−0.029	−0.060	−0.041	−0.063	−0.016	−0.103**	−0.060
	(0.053)	(0.054)	(0.045)	(0.054)	(0.040)	(0.041)	(0.044)	(0.051)
Lagged DV t−5	0.368*	0.257	0.862***	0.657***	0.563***	0.180	0.707***	0.499**
	(0.206)	(0.279)	(0.112)	(0.133)	(0.156)	(0.196)	(0.128)	(0.193)
Democratic age (ln)	−0.016	−0.037	−0.035*	−0.039	−0.020	−0.024	−0.030	−0.044
	(0.030)	(0.037)	(0.018)	(0.024)	(0.017)	(0.022)	(0.023)	(0.028)
GDPPC t−1(ln)	—	0.079	—	0.063	—	0.105**	—	0.084
		(0.052)		(0.046)		(0.039)		(0.050)
Enactment year	—	0.002	—	−0.002	—	−0.002*	—	−0.002
		(0.001)		(0.001)		(0.001)		(0.001)
Ethnic fractionalization	—	−0.156	—	−0.166	—	−0.190	—	−0.152
		(0.197)		(0.163)		(0.144)		(0.191)
Africa	—	0.161	—	0.120	—	0.131*	—	0.029
		(0.113)		(0.093)		(0.073)		(0.077)
Asia	—	0.136	—	0.108	—	0.122	—	0.090
		(0.144)		(0.141)		(0.132)		(0.149)
Europe	—	−0.002	—	0.022	—	0.051	—	0.025
		(0.071)		(0.055)		(0.043)		(0.075)
Constant	0.491***	3.926	0.209*	3.940	0.387***	3.405*	0.250**	3.481
	(0.130)	(2.673)	(0.108)	(2.484)	(0.131)	(1.767)	(0.093)	(2.322)
Adjusted R2	0.18	0.25	0.64	0.63	0.33	0.49	0.44	0.55
N	40	35	40	35	40	35	40	35

(A) Sample of constitutions adopted at or after the third year of free and fair elections from 1900 to 2015;

[a] Average V-DEM legislative constraints index from t+1 to t+5;

[b] Average V-DEM judicial constraints index from t+1 to t+5;

[c] Average V-DEM liberal component index from t+1 to t+5;

[d] Average V-DEM liberal democracy index from t+1 to t+5.

*** p < 0.01; ** p < 0.05; * p < 0.10.

with the proposition that elite cooperation at the constitution-making stage facilitates the implementation of liberal principles and the improvement of liberal democracy during the early years of life of the new constitution.[26]

In particular, when the agreement between two or more freely and fairly elected parties is required to pass the constitution, there is a statistically and substantially significant improvement in the implementation of institutional constraints on executive power and citizen rights during the first five years after enactment of the constitution. By contrast, direct citizen participation, either through electoral or nonelectoral mechanisms, does not generally have a significant impact on liberal principles or liberal democracy after the new constitution is in force. The direction of the effect of voting in constitutional referendums is consistently negative. Yet only in one basic model (model 1 of liberal democracy) is this effect statistically significant and it disappears once we add the rest of the controls.[27]

Among the control variables, the lagged scores of institutional constraints, liberal principles, and liberal democracy all have an expected positive impact. The level of GDP per capita the year before a constitutional replacement takes place also appears to be associated with an improvement in the implementation of liberal principles, suggesting that richer countries are more likely to make institutional constraints over the executive and citizen rights effective.

The positive impact of elite cooperation on liberal democracy is confirmed if we employ a larger database including all ninety-four new constitutions created in the world between 1900 and 2015 in an electoral democracy. This result also holds if we use the Polity IV score, which captures only some aspects of the liberal dimension of democracy, as the dependent variable.[28] The test confirms the positive effect of income per capita and provides evidence that as a democracy becomes older it is less likely to experience further improvements in its liberal dimension. It also indicates that a high level of ethnic fractionalization may be an obstacle to deepen democratization. Table 5.2 shows these results.

These findings do not suggest that citizens play no role in the effective implementation of liberal institutions. Nor do they imply, more specifically, that public participation in democratic constitution making is worthless. Comparing political conditions before and after the adoption of a new constitutional text, cases such as the adoption of Colombia's 1991 constitution show that cooperation among fractions of the political elite and citizen involvement in both consultation and voting during the process can

---

[26] Similar short-term effects are observed in a different test using longitudinal data comparing levels of liberal democracy ten years before and ten years after a plural constitution-making process took place. Depending on the specification used, the positive impact of elite cooperation on liberal democracy ceases to be statistically significant after the fifth or seventh year. On this analysis, see Gabriel Negretto and Mariano Sánchez-Talanquer (2019).

[27] For this reason, this analysis does not indicate, as Eisenstadt, LeVan, and Maboudi (2015; 2017) suggest, that there is a significant difference in the impact of voting and non-voting forms of participation on democracy.

[28] See n. 19.

TABLE 5.2 *Democratic constitution making, liberal principles, and liberal democracy* (B)

	Dependent variables					
	Liberal principles[a]		Liberal democracy[b]		Democracy polity IV[c]	
Explanatory variables	Model 1	Model 2	Model 1	Model 2	Model 1	Model 2
Elite cooperation	0.098***	0.075**	0.120***	0.089**	2.795***	1.739**
	(0.030)	(0.031)	(0.040)	(0.038)	(0.855)	(0.788)
Citizen consultation	−0.002	0.024	−0.017	0.010	0.548	0.899
	(0.029)	(0.036)	(0.035)	(0.041)	(0.749)	(0.922)
Citizen voting	0.012	0.013	0.002	0.012	0.032	0.032
	(0.032)	(0.026)	(0.039)	(0.031)	(0.818)	(0.729)
Lagged DV t−5	0.423***	0.283***	0.574***	0.380***	0.004	0.054
	(0.089)	(0.101)	(0.081)	(0.099)	(0.103)	(0.111)
Democratic age (ln)	−0.015*	−0.024**	−0.021*	−0.027**	0.303	0.041
	(0.009)	(0.001)	(0.011)	(0.012)	(0.334)	(0.370)
GDPPC t−1(ln)	–	0.102***	–	0.117***	–	0.979
		(0.031)		(0.039)		(0.650)
Enactment year	–	−0.000	–	−0.000	–	0.003
		(0.001)		(0.001)		(0.018)
Ethnic fractionalization	–	−0.185**	–	−0.232**	–	−4.551*
		(0.091)		(0.110)		(2.415)
Africa	–	0.137**	–	0.118*	–	1.043
		(0.056)		(0.066)		(1.851)
Asia	–	0.129	–	0.142	–	2.714**
		(0.087)		(0.091)		(1.208)
Europe	–	0.040	–	0.027	–	1.118
		(0.041)		(0.049)		(1.274)
Constant	0.428	0.781	0.252	−0.216	4.146	−7.762
	(0.061)	(1.578)	(0.038)	(1.901)	(0.998)	(32.080)
Adjusted R2	0.35	0.54	0.41	0.59	0.14	0.29
N	83	73	83	73	79	72

(B) Sample of all constitutions adopted in years of free and fair elections from 1900 to 2015.
[a] Average V-DEM liberal component index from t+1 to t+5.
[b] Average V-DEM liberal democracy index from t+1 to t+5.
[c] Average Polity IV polity score from t+1 to t+5.
*** $p < 0.01$; ** $p < 0.05$; * $p < 0.10$.

be a fruitful combination for the strengthening of liberal democracy. Other cases, such as Brazil's 1988 constitution and South Africa's 1996 constitution illustrate the benefits of mixing elite cooperation with popular consultation channels. Even simply voting in referendums may enhance liberal democracy if it follows an inclusive elite agreement, like the adoption of Italy's 1948 constitution with the support of the Christian Democrats, Communists, and Socialists. What the preceding analysis clearly indicates, however, is that no form of direct citizen participation is likely by itself to improve levels of liberal democracy after the new constitution is in force.

Gabriel L. Negretto

III QUALITATIVE EVIDENCE: KENYA 2010 AND BOLIVIA 2009

The results of the above analysis may not be sufficient to provide conclusive evidence of a systematic positive effect of cooperation among political elites during constitution making on democratization.[29] Its negative findings, however, strongly suggest that direct citizen involvement in constitution making does *not* contribute to improving the liberal dimension of democracy after the adoption of a new constitution. A way to complement and make this analysis more persuasive is by examining particular cases to show how the dynamics of elite cooperation at the constitution-making stage are linked to democratic developments once a new constitution is in force.

I have selected the making of Kenya's 2010 constitution and Bolivia's 2009 constitution for comparative analysis. These constitutions were both made in the context of an electoral democracy that persisted after they were enacted. The countries where these episodes took place shared a number of key economic, social, and institutional background conditions. Yet the outcomes were different in terms of the levels of liberal democracy observed before and after constitutional replacement.[30]

Both Kenya and Bolivia are lower middle-income countries with a high level of ethnic fractionalization, a presidential form of government, and a relatively recent authoritarian past. In both cases, the new constitution was adopted in the context of preexisting free and fair elections (since 2002 in Kenya and since 1982 in Bolivia) and after a political crisis (in 2007 in Kenya and in 2003 in Bolivia) that called the working of representative institutions into question. In both cases, also, the crisis made a high degree of direct popular participation necessary, which was achieved through channels of consultation and voting during constitution making. Furthermore, in both Kenya and Bolivia, approval of the constitution required cooperation between the incumbent and main opposition party so that according to the operationalization provided in this chapter, they also qualify as cases of elite cooperation. In spite of these shared characteristics, the liberal components of democracy temporarily improved in Kenya but relatively declined in Bolivia in the years that immediately followed enactment of the new constitution.

Given the similarities between these cases, it seems difficult to account for the divergent outcomes by looking at constitutional origins alone. I will argue, however, that a careful analysis of the political context in each case reveals that the reason for the contrasting results resides in the fact that the balance of political forces that sustained a cooperative constitutional agreement was more short-lived in Bolivia than in Kenya. In both episodes, the agreement was to a large extent

---

[29] For a more exhaustive analysis of this matter, see Negretto and Sánchez-Talanquer (2019).

[30] In terms of case selection methods, one of the cases (Kenya) represents a typical case in terms of the argument presented in this chapter, while the other (Bolivia) plays the role of a seemingly negative case that, upon inspection, is similar to the first except on the way in which the independent variable of interest (elite cooperation) worked in reality. See Gerring (2006).

induced and constrained by exogenous factors. The incumbent party in Bolivia was deterred from imposing the constitution unilaterally in order to get the constitution approved and avoid greater political costs. Similarly, as Murray notes in Chapter 9, political elites in Kenya behaved in a consensual fashion due both to international pressures and to the perceived high costs of continuing the violence unleashed after the 2007 election. In neither case did the agreement reflect a genuine consensus on norms of democratic behavior. The difference was that whereas in Bolivia the largest party during the process soon became a hegemonic incumbent able to implement and interpret the constitution at will, in Kenya the electoral and institutional power that the incumbent and main opposition party had at the time of passing the constitution remained relatively stable after the first round of elections. This condition made it possible for the leaders of the political opposition in Kenya, at least in the short term, to prevent the incumbent party from reneging on the constitutional agreement.

Kenya transitioned from a one-party state to a multiparty democracy in 2002, when the Kenya African National Union party, which had governed the country since independence, lost both the presidency and a parliamentary majority. Although the demand for a new constitution emerged strongly in the 1990s, it was only with the beginning of the transition to democracy in 2001 that Parliament enacted a Review Act outlining the steps for the adoption of a new constitution. These included initial drafting by a small review commission, deliberation on and revisions to the draft by a national convention, and ratification by Parliament (see Bannon 2007). Immediately after the 2002 election, however, a conflict between government and opposition over the structure of executive-legislative relations and the question of devolution derailed the process. The government decided to propose a presidential constitution without support from the opposition and submitted it for popular approval in 2005. The proposal was defeated.

The outcome of the 2007 presidential and parliamentary elections formed the immediate background for the 2010 constitution. The incumbent president, Mwai Kibaki, was re-elected with a very narrow margin over his opponent, Raila Odinga, leader of the Orange Democratic Movement (ODM). At the same time, the president's party, the Party of National Unity, won only 43 seats in the legislative election while the ODM became the largest party in Parliament, with 99 of 210 seats. Odinga claimed that the presidential elections had been rigged and demanded that a new election be held. Opposition supporters led street protests, and violence rapidly spread across the country, leading to the death of more than 1,000 people (see Final Report of the Committee of Experts on Constitutional Review 2010). Preexisting interethnic conflict in part fueled the violence. Whereas the incumbent president belonged to the Kikuyu tribe, the largest (but not majoritarian) ethnic group, Odinga belonged to the Luo people, the fourth largest ethnic group in the country. On the brink of a civil war that no party had the capacity to win, and with the help of international mediation and under strong international pressure, government and opposition signed a pact that led to a power-sharing coalition government that committed to enact a new constitution on a consensual basis.

As Christina Murray notes (Chapter 9 of this volume), like the 2001 Review Act, the 2008 Constitution of Kenya Review Act established a replacement procedure that contained several features aimed at preventing any single institution or actor from manipulating the process. Legal continuity was secured by following the reform procedure established in the existing constitution, as amended between 1997 and 2008. According to this procedure, a Committee of Experts was responsible for collecting public views and submitting a draft to a parliamentary committee, which in turn would revise the draft before submitting it to approval by the National Assembly (parliament). The latter could only pass the proposal if it received support by a qualified majority of 65 percent of the total membership. This design, along with party fragmentation in the approval body, contributed to a high degree of cooperation among the representatives of the main political groups.

The making of the new constitution in Kenya also involved a relatively high degree of direct citizen participation. Before the draft was written, the Committee of Experts held public consultations to identify contentious issues. Later, before submitting the proposal to the parliamentary committee, and following the requirements of the Review Act, it released the draft for a month of public consultations that led to the writing of an amended version in response to public views (see Final Report 2010; Kirby and Murray 2016). In a last stage, after involvement by the parliamentary committee and the final vote in parliament, the text was submitted to a popular referendum, where the constitution was approved by 67 percent of the valid votes cast.

Although the new Kenyan constitution maintained a presidential structure of government, it constrained the powers of the executive in several ways. In the first place, the president would be elected by majority runoff instead of plurality rule, thus potentially increasing the probability of party fragmentation and reducing the president's ability to count on the support of a legislative majority.[31] Provisions that sought to strengthen the Independent Electoral and Boundaries Commission limited interference in the electoral process by the president. The government powers of the executive were also curtailed by a process of political decentralization that allowed for popular election of county (subnational) governors. At the same time, both legislative and judicial controls over the government were strengthened and the number of citizen rights expanded.[32] Finally, additional checks and

---

[31] On the party system effects of plurality and majority runoff presidential elections, see Shugart and Carey (1992).

[32] According to the indexes created by Elkins, Ginsburg, and Melton (2017) based on data from the *Comparative Constitutions Project* (CCP), the powers of the legislature in Kenya's 2010 constitution went from 0.10 to 0.29, the independence of the judiciary increased from 4 to 5, and the number of rights from 38 to 72. Complete database provided by Zachary Elkins and Tom Ginsburg. See http://comparativeconstitutionsproject.org/ccp-rankings/ (June 2017) for the coding of the variables.

balances were introduced by means of a Supreme Court and a bicameral legislature that replaced the preexisting unicameral assembly.

In terms of the actual implementation of the new constitution, although Kenya continued to be affected by strong ethnic rivalries and violence, public corruption, and a weak party system, the country experienced a relative democratic improvement. According to the Polity IV index, Kenya increased its score from 7 in 2009 to 8 in 2011 and 2012 and to 9 between 2013 and 2015. As a result of the new constitution, the Independent Electoral and Boundaries Commission was founded in 2011 and became responsible for organizing the coming 2013 elections. Although the presidential race was relatively close and the loser challenged the outcome in the courts, the opposition abided by the results. Institutional constraints on the executive improved after 2010, particularly due to the increased judicial controls over the administration. Due to ethnic and religious tensions, as well as terrorist threats, civil rights have remained fragile but their protection is stronger than in the previous period. For these reasons, and according to V-DEM indexes, the liberal democracy score improved from 0.31 in 2009 to 0.35 in 2015.

This outcome was made possible by the relative stability of the balance of power among the political forces that participated in the approval of the 2010 constitution. The two main contenders in the 2013 presidential election, Uhuru Kenyatta and Raila Odinga, were members of Kibaki's coalition government and participants in the making of the 2010 constitution. Although Kenyatta won the presidential election, his supporting coalition, the Jubilee Alliance, did not win a majority in either the assembly or the senate.[33] At the same time, the main opposition party, the ODM, remained a significant opposition force with institutional influence and capacity to mobilize its constituents in defense of the constitution.[34] However, it seems dubious whether this balance will hold in the future. Violence reemerged during the 2017 election and the incumbent president was reelected with an almost absolute majority in the legislature. The opposition protested against electoral irregularities and although it won a successful legal challenge in the Supreme Court, it refused to participate in the election rerun.

The constitution-making process in Bolivia between 2006 and 2009 had several features in common with the Kenyan case in terms of fostering the democratic legitimacy of the new constitution by means of citizen participation. The adoption of a new constitution in Bolivia stemmed from the extensive popular mobilizations that took place between 2000 and 2003, demanding changes in public policies and deep reforms to the exclusionary nature of existing representative institutions. In 2003, the incumbent president was forced to resign in the midst of widespread social protests

---

[33] In the assembly the Jubilee Alliance won 167 of 349 seats (47.8 percent) and in the senate 30 of 67 seats (44.7 percent).

[34] Between 2013 and 2017, the ODM controlled 27 percent of the Assembly, 25 percent of senate seats, and 15 of 47 governorships.

against his government, which included a demand to call a constituent convention to replace the 1967 constitution. As a response to these events, the provisional government and the parties represented in Congress organized a constitution-making process that was meant to involve citizens in a wide variety of ways.

The constitution was amended in February 2004 to allow Congress to convene an independently elected constituent convention and regulate its internal procedures. Based on this reform, in 2006 Congress passed a law establishing the system to elect constituent assembly delegates; the decision-making process of the assembly, the relationship between the constituent assembly and the Congress; and a final ratification of the constitution by referendum. Along with the election of delegates to the convention, Bolivians were also called to decide on the autonomy of regions in a referendum that would be binding on the convention. After the convention was installed, it organized deliberative forums in the different regions of the country and both ordinary citizens and civic organizations were allowed to submit reform proposals to the different committees on various aspects of the new constitution.[35]

What sets the Bolivian case apart from the Kenyan case lies not in the level of direct citizen involvement but in the short-lived nature of the balance of power that made an inclusive constitutional agreement among political elites possible. At the time of amending the Bolivian constitution to regulate its replacement (2004) the main party advocating reform, the Movimiento al Socialismo (MAS), was a minority political group with a radical left-wing platform. The situation started to change in 2005, when Evo Morales, the MAS candidate and a member of the Aymara ethnic indigenous group, won the presidential election with more than 50 percent of the vote.

Morales' party reached an absolute majority in the Chamber of Deputies but fell short of a majority in the Senate. In this context, the 2006 congressional law regulating the constituent convention was passed with the support of center-right Poder Democrático Social (PODEMOS), the main opposition party at the time, and included important safeguards to preserve a consensual process, such as the requirement for a two-thirds majority to pass the constitution. Yet after winning a majority of seats in the convention, the president and his party attempted to violate the convening law and adopt the constitution by majority rule. After a series of violent civil confrontations, the government backtracked from its attempt to impose the constitution and its final text was negotiated with opposition forces in Congress. It is clear, however, that in a context of high polarization between the incumbent and the main opposition party, agreement was forced by time constraints and the need to obtain congressional approval for the ratification referendum (Böhrt Irahola 2013).

The tug-of-war between government and opposition to control the process was reflected in the design of the new constitution. While citizen rights were

---

[35] On direct popular participation in recent constitution-making processes in the Andean countries, see Escudero (2017).

significantly expanded, the powers of the executive were strengthened in various ways.[36] The threshold of votes to elect the president was reduced from 50 to 40 percent and the consensual Bolivian system that required Congress to intervene if no candidate reached that threshold was eliminated.[37] The president was allowed to compete for one consecutive reelection and his legislative powers were increased by the power to submit urgency bills to Congress for approval. At the same time, both the formal independence and powers of the judiciary were enhanced. After the promulgation of the new constitution, however, the legal institutional constraints over the executive failed to be implemented.

Open attacks on the judiciary began in 2007, when the government initiated several impeachment processes against members of the Supreme Court in response to rulings that supposedly benefited members of the opposition. Similar actions were followed in May and August 2009, immediately after the new constitution was ratified in a popular referendum. As regards the Constitutional Court and the Judicial Council, the government followed the strategy of inducing the exit of its members until both bodies were de facto unable to function (see Pérez-Liñán and Castagnola 2011). These actions paved the way for filling positions in these bodies with government allies after 2009. After being reelected in December 2009, the president also violated a key point in the constitutional agreement, namely the inability to run as presidential candidate for more than two periods. In 2013, the president's party passed a congressional law with the interpretation that the period initiated after the 2009 election was the president's first and not second term, so that he could be reelected again in 2014.

Although Bolivia continued to be an electoral democracy, its liberal dimension declined after the new constitution was adopted. According to Polity IV, Bolivia had a score of 7 in 2014, above the minimum of 6 to qualify as a democracy. Six years earlier in 2008, however, Bolivia had a higher level of democracy with a score of 8. According to V-DEM, in turn, the index of liberal democracy in Bolivia went from a score of 0.46 in 2008 to a score of 0.44 in 2014. The main factor that explains the lack of effective implementation of the institutional constraints on executive power created in 2009 lies in the rapid change of the initial balance of forces in favor of the incumbent government. In the 2009 election, the president was reelected and his party reached a qualified majority in both the lower and upper houses, sufficient to approve constitutional changes. The PODEMOS opposition alliance, one of the main actors during the constitution-making process, disappeared and was replaced by Plan de Progreso para Bolivia, which won less than 30 percent of the seats in both chambers of Congress. As the same imbalance has

---

[36] According to the CCP indexes, whereas the number of citizen rights after Bolivia's 2009 constitution went from 64 to 88, the power of the executive increased from 4 to 5 and the power of the legislature decreased from 0.38 to 0.33.

[37] On the consensual properties of this system, see Shugart and Carey (1992).

persisted since the incumbent president's reelection in 2014, the prospects for improving liberal democracy in Bolivia remained low.[38]

IV CONCLUSION

A long tradition in constitutional theory has emphasized the democratizing potential of participatory constitution making. An alternative perspective, relatively recent in constitutional studies but with roots in a well-established research agenda on democratization, stresses the critical role of elite accommodation during constitution writing for the inauguration and consolidation of democracy. I have argued that a focus on the actions of political elites provides the most promising starting point for understanding the link between constitution making and democratization in comparative perspective. In particular, I proposed that only cooperation among a plurality of elected political representatives at the constitution-making stage is likely to improve the liberal dimension of democracy after the enactment of the new constitution, at least in the short term. Analyzing the effects of citizen participation and elite cooperation during constitution making in the context of existing electoral democracies, this chapter has shown quantitative and qualitative evidence that is consistent with this hypothesis.

The arguments and findings of this chapter do not contradict the widely cherished idea that citizen participation is an essential principle of democratic constitution making or that it may be politically desirable when constitutional change is a response to popular demands. Yet they provide reasons to be skeptical about the democratizing effects of citizen involvement in constitution making, in isolation from the actions and decisions of political representatives at the elite level. Inclusive constitutional agreements among representative elites and the fragmentation of partisan power that makes them possible facilitate not only the formal creation of constraints on executive power and strong citizen rights but also their effective implementation.

It is important to note, however, that the democratizing effects of many elite constitutional agreements made in a context of distributive, ideological, or ethnic polarization are likely to be short-lived and last only as long as the balance of forces that prevailed at the constitution-making stage remains stable. This leads to the question of under what conditions elite agreements are genuinely consensual and signal a change in the norms of behavior so that regular compliance with the constitution becomes relatively immune to short-term shifts in the distribution of

[38] In 2016, the president lost a referendum to seek a third reelection in 2019 under the new constitution, but then managed to obtain from the Constitutional Tribunal a highly political ruling declaring unconstitutional the presidential term limit. As of the time of this writing (November 2019), Bolivia's democracy has been interrupted by a coup to oust president Evo Morales after his attempt to get reelected in an allegedly fraudulent election.

political power. The answer probably goes beyond the events that surround the relatively short period in which a constitution is drafted and lies in whether precedent transformations in the economy and in society induce the main political actors to prefer cooperation over confrontation in the long run.

REFERENCES

Alberts, Susan, Chris Warshaw, and Barry Weingast. 2010. "Democratization and Counter-majoritarian Institutions: Power and Constitutional Design" in *Self-Enforcing Democracy*. Tom Ginsburg (ed.) Cambridge: Cambridge University Press, 69–100.
Albertus, Michael, and Victor Menaldo. 2018. *Authoritarianism and the Elite Origins of Democracy*. Cambridge: Cambridge University Press.
Alesina, Alberto, et al. 2003. "Fractionalization." *Journal of Economic Growth* 8 (2): 155–194.
Arato, Andrew. 1995. "Forms of Constitution Making and Democracy." *Cardozo Law Review* 17(2): 191–232.
      2009. "Redeeming the Still Redeemable: Post Sovereign Constitution Making." *International Journal of Politics, Culture, and Society* 22(4): 427–443.
      2010. "Post Sovereign Constitution Making in Hungary: After Success, Partial Failure, and Now What?" *South African Journal of Human Rights* 26(1): 535–555.
      2016. *Post Sovereign Constitutional Making*. Oxford: Oxford University Press.
Banks, Angela M. 2008. "Expanding Participation in Constitution Making: Challenges and Opportunities." *William & Mary Law Review* 49(4): 1043–1069.
Bannon, Alicia. 2007. "Designing a Constitution-Drafting Process: Lessons from Kenya." *The Yale Law Journal* 116(8): 1824–1872.
Böhrt Irahola, Carlos. 2013. "El Proceso Constituyente Boliviano" in *Los Procesos Constituyentes Boliviano y Ecuatoriano: Análisis Comparativo y Prospectiva*. Carlos Böhrt Irahola and Norman Wray Reyes (eds.) Stockholm: IDEA International, 9–153.
Boix, Carles. 2003. *Democracy and Redistribution*. New York: Cambridge University Press.
Burton, Michael, Richard Gunther, and John Higley. 1992. "Introduction: Elite Transformations and Democratic Regimes" in *Elites and Democratic Consolidation in Latin America and Southern Europe*. John Higley and Richard Gunther (eds.) Cambridge: Cambridge University Press, 1–37.
Carey, John. 2009. "Does It Matter How a Constitution Is Created?" in *Is Democracy Exportable?*. Zoltan Barany and Robert G. Moser (eds.) Cambridge: Cambridge University Press.
Collier, Ruth. 1999. *Paths Toward Democracy: The Working Class and Elites in Western Europe and South America*. New York: Cambridge University Press.
Colón-Ríos, Joel. 2012. *Constitutionalism: Democratic Legitimacy and the Question of Constituent Power*. London: Routledge.
Committee of Experts on Constitutional Review. 2010. Final Report of the Committee of Experts on Constitutional Review. Nairobi, Kenya.
Coppedge, Michael, and John Gerring, et al. 2011. "Conceptualizing and Measuring Democracy: A New Approach". *Perspectives on Politics* 9 (2): 247–267.
Coppedge, Michael, et al. 2016. V-Dem Country-Year Dataset v6. *Varieties of Democracy (V-Dem) Project*.
Eisenstadt, Todd A., A. Carl LeVan, and Tofigh Mabboudi. 2015. "When Talk Trumps Text: The Democratizing Effects of Deliberation during Constitution-Making." *American Political Science Review* 109(3): 592–612.
      2017. *Constituents before Assembly*. Cambridge: Cambridge University Press.

Eisenstadt, Todd A., and Tofigh Maboudi. 2019. "Being There Is Half the Battle: Group Inclusion, Constitution Writing, and Democracy." *Comparative Political Studies* 52(13–14): 2135–2170.

Elkins, Zachary, Tom Ginsburg, and Justine Blount. 2008. "The Citizen As Founder: Public Participation in Constitutional Approval." *Temple Law Review* 81(2): 361–382.

Elkins, Zachary, Tom Ginsburg, and James Melton. 2009. *The Endurance of National Constitutions*. Cambridge: Cambridge University Press.

2017. Characteristics of National Constitutions [v.2.0]. Retrieved at comparativeconstitutionsproject.org.

Escudero, Maria Cristina. 2017. "Determinantes del Éxito de los Procesos Constituyentes Latinoamericanos." Unpublished dissertation, Pontificia Universidad Católica de Chile.

Fishkin, James. 2011. "Deliberative Democracy and Constitutions." *Social Philosophy and Policy* 28(1): 242–260.

Gargarella, Roberto. 2013. *Latin American Constitutionalism: 1810–2010*. Cambridge: Cambridge University Press.

Gerring, John. 2006. *Case Study Research: Principles and Practices*. Cambridge: Cambridge University Press.

Ginsburg, Tom, Zachary Elkins, and Justine Blount. 2009. "Does the Process of Constitution-Making Matter?" *American Review of Law and Society* 5: 201–223.

Haggard, Stephan, and Robert R. Kaufman. 2017. *Dictators and Democrats: Masses, Elites, and Regime Change*. New Haven: Princeton University Press.

Hart, Vivien. 2010. "Constitution Making and the Right to Take Part in a Public Affair" in *Framing the States in Times of Transition: Case Studies in Constitution Making*. Laurel E. Miller (ed.) Washington, DC: US Institute of Peace Press, 20–54.

Held, David. 1987. *Models of Democracy*. Redwood City: Stanford University Press.

Higley, John, and Michael Burton. 2006. *Elite Foundations of Liberal Democracy*. New York: Rowman & Littlefield.

Holmes, Stephen, and Cass Sustein. 1995. "The Politics of Constitutional Revision in Eastern Europe" in *Reponding to Imperfection: The Theory and Practice of Constitutional Amendment*. Sanford Levinson (ed.) Princeton: Princeton University Press, 275–306.

Horowitz, Donald. 2013. *Constitutional Change and Democracy in Indonesia*. Cambridge: Cambridge University Press.

Jung, Courtney, and Ian Shapiro. 1995. "South Africa's Negotiated Transition: Democracy, Opposition, and the New Constitutional Order." *Politics & Society* 23(3): 269–308.

Kalyvas, Andreas. 2005. "Popular Sovereignty, Democracy, and the Constituent Power." *Constellations* 12(2): 223–244.

Kirby, Coel, and Christina Murray. 2016. "Constitution-Making in Anglophone Africa: We the People?" in *Growing Democracy in Africa: Elections, Accountable Governance, and Political Economy*. Muna Ndulo and Mamoudou Gazibo (eds.) Cambridge: Cambridge Scholars Publishing, 102–106.

Loughlin, Martin. 2003. *The Idea of Public Law*. Oxford: Oxford University Press.

Maddison Project Database, version 2018. Bolt, Jutta, Robert Inklaar, Herman de Jong and Jan Luiten van Zanden (2018), "Rebasing 'Maddison': new income comparisons and the shape of long-run economic development", Maddison Project Working paper 10.

Manin, Bernard. 1997. *The Principles of Representative Government*. Cambridge: Cambridge University Press.

Marshall, Monty G., Ted R. Gurr, and Keith Jaggers. 2019. *Polity IV Project: Political Regime Characteristics and Transitions, 1800–2008*.

Miller, Laurel E. 2011. "Designing Constitution-Making Processes: Lessons from the Past, Questions for the Future" in *Framing the States in Times of Transition: Case Studies in Constitution Making*. Laurel E. Miller (ed.) Washington, DC: US Institute of Peace Press, 601–666.

Negretto, Gabriel L. 2016. "Constitution Making in Democratic Constitutional Orders: The Challenge of Citizen Participation" in *Let the People Rule? Direct Democracy in the Twenty-First Century*. Saskia Ruth-Lovell, Yanina Welp, and Laurence Whitehead (eds.) Colchester: ECPR Press, 21–40.

2017. "Constitution Making in Comparative Perspective" in *Oxford Research Encyclopedia of Politics*. William R. Thompson (ed.) Oxford: Oxford University Press.

Negretto, Gabriel L., and Mariano Sánchez-Talanquer. 2019. "Constitutional Origins and Liberal Democracy: A Global Analysis." Paper presented at the 2019 ICON conference, Santiago de Chile, July 1–3, 2019.

O'Donnell, Guillermo, and Philippe Shmitter. 1986. *Transitions from Authoritarian Rule: Tentative Conclusions about Uncertain Democracies*. Baltimore: Johns Hopkins University Press.

Paine, Thomas. [1791] 1995. "The Rights of Man" in *Thomas Paine: Collected Writings*. New York: Library of America, 124–230.

Pérez-Liñán, Anibal, and Andrea Castagnola. 2011. "Bolivia: The Rise (and Fall) of Judicial Review" in *Courts in Latin America*. Gretchen Helmke and Julio Ríos-Figueroa (eds.) Cambridge: Cambridge University Press, 278–305.

Preuss, Ulrich K. 1995. *Constitutional Revolution: The Link between Constitutionalism and Progress*. London: Humanities Press International.

Przeworski, Adam. 1988. "Democracy As a Contingent Outcome of Conflicts" in *Constitutionalism and Democracy*. Jon Elster and Rune Slagstad (eds.) Cambridge: Cambridge University Press, 59–80.

Sartori, Giovanni. 1962. "Constitutionalism: A Preliminary Discussion." *American Political Science Review* 56(4): 853–864.

Shugart, Matthew S., and John Carey. 1992. *Presidents and Assemblies: Constitutional Design and Electoral Dynamics*. Cambridge: Cambridge University Press.

Tierney, Stephen. 2012. *Constitutional Referendums: The Theory and Practice of Republican Deliberation*. Oxford: Oxford University Press.

Voigt, Stephan. 2004. "The Consequences of Popular Participation in Constitutional Choice: Towards a Comparative Analysis" in *Deliberation and Decision: Economics, Constitutional Theory and Deliberative Democracy*. Anne van Aaken, Christian List, and Christoph Luetge (eds.) Hants: Ashgate, 199–229.

Weingast, Barry, 1997. "The Political Foundations of Democracy and the Rule of Law," *American Political Science Review* 91(2): 245–263.

2004. "Constructing Self-Democracy in Spain" in *Politics from Anarchy to Democracy: Rational Choice in Political Science*. Irwin L. Morris, Joe Oppenheimer, and Karol Edward Soltan (eds.) Redwood City: Stanford University Press, 161–195.

Widner, Jennifer. 2008. "Constitution Writing in Post-Conflict Settings: Overview." *William and Mary Law Review* 49(4): 1513–1554.

PART II

Case Studies

6

The Difference Power Diffusion Makes

Explaining Divergent Outcomes in Colombia (1990–1991) and Venezuela (1998–1999)

Ana María Bejarano and Renata Segura[*]

People around the globe have been busy writing constitutions in the past three decades. Latin America has been no stranger to this trend: since 1978, all countries in this region have either drafted a new constitution or modified the existing one in substantial ways (Negretto 2012). In the Andean region, in particular, every single country carried out a complete overhaul of their constitutional framework between 1991 and 2009. Most of these reform processes have not gone through the regular channels in the legislature, but have instead been the result of popularly elected assemblies, charged with the task of drafting an entirely new constitution.

According to many scholars (see Hart 2003; Chambers 2004; Moehler 2008; Elkins, Ginsburg, and Melton 2009; Nolte and Schilling-Vacaflor 2012) as well as some international organizations such as IDEA, Interpeace, and USIP, participatory constitution-making processes should yield more inclusive and legitimate constitutions which, in turn, should have better prospects of being implemented and enduring over time. We share this enthusiasm for processes of institutional reform that incorporate previously excluded political and social sectors (see Segura and Bejarano 2004). However, our own examination of the Andean constitution-making exercises leads to more mixed conclusions: for even if they have contributed to widening democracy by creating broader channels of participation in collective decision-making while also expanding bills of rights and freedoms, it is also true that – with very few exceptions – most of the new Andean constitutions have reinforced a presidential tradition that is inimical to competition, contestation, and accountability.

Following Robert Dahl (1971), we believe that although inclusion and participation are indeed a fundamental component of liberal democracies, they must also

[*] An earlier version of this chapter was written for the conference "Constitution Making in Democratic Constitutional Orders: Theoretical and Comparative Perspectives," Mexico City, August 11–12, 2016. We thank all the participants at this conference and the editor of this volume for their comments. We also want to thank Todd Eisenstadt, Carl LeVan, Robert Albro, and Matthew Taylor for their feedback and suggestions.

include an opposition/contestation dimension. We thus claim that a constitutional framework advances the cause of democracy to the extent that it: (a) opens up numerous and more accessible avenues for inclusion; at the same time that it, (b) offers plenty of opportunities for the representation of the diverse interests present in society, for contestation of government policies, and for the full exercise of political rights and civil liberties on the part of the opposition.

Under what conditions, then, does participatory constitution redrafting lead to democratic deepening? Our main argument is that participatory constitution redrafting generally results in constitutions that widen democracy through the introduction of novel participatory mechanisms and expansive bills of rights, allowing for the inclusion of new actors, interests, and demands. However, they don't always result in institutional architectures that are favorable to competition, dissent, and accountability. The latter only happens when a variety of political forces present in the constitution-making body participate in a centripetal dynamic of negotiation and bargaining that results in a consensual and balanced constitutional text that disperses power. By contrast, constitution redrafting processes characterized by the presence of a dominant force or coalition that does not need to engage in negotiations with other actors present in the assembly tend to produce institutional arrangements that concentrate power in the executive at the expense of those institutions that place limits on the use of power, thereby reducing opportunities for dissent and the possibility of accountable governments.

In this chapter, we study the cases of Colombia and Venezuela, which illustrate quite clearly the contrast between two different constitution-drafting dynamics leading to divergent political outcomes. In both cases, the new constitution was made with high levels of direct citizen involvement. However, whereas in Colombia the constitution was designed and approved by a consensual agreement among a plurality of political representatives, in Venezuela the incumbent executive and his party imposed the new text. This, in turn, led to a constitution whose institutions facilitated the deepening of democracy in Colombia but deteriorated it in Venezuela. Our analysis thus complements from the point of view of constitutional design Negretto's emphasis in Chapter 5 on the importance of inclusive constitutional agreements for the improvement of the liberal dimension of democracy after the implementation of the new constitution. It also illustrates Partlett's argument (Chapter 3) about the democratic risk of constitution-making processes that place a unilateral emphasis on the use of majoritarian mechanisms to break the veto power of political minorities.

I CONSTITUTION DRAFTING AS A POLITICAL PROCESS

The constitution drafting process is made of a series of interlocking stages, events, and decisions that, together, constitute the causal chain leading from process to constitutional choice. We argue that the resulting text will be shaped by: (a) the degree of inclusion of social and political actors in the constitution drafting body, and their capacity to represent broad sectors of society; (b) the distribution of power and degree of symmetry or asymmetry between the different actors and coalitions present in the constitution drafting body; and finally, (c) the resulting dynamics within the assembly.

The degree of pluralism and diversity of the assembly is of great importance in determining if and how the constitution rewriting process is perceived by the general public as a tool to promote inclusion.[1] Following Bonime-Blanc (1987), we see party ideologies as central to explaining the drafters' behavior and capacity for coalition building. We also follow Negretto (1999; 2009a; 2013), by keeping in mind that parties' behavior is also crucially affected by their present electoral strength and future expectations. Thus, individual, party, and institutional ideas and interests, as well as electoral calculations and strategies, help explain the constitution makers' behavior and the potential for coalition formation.

A second key factor is, of course, the distribution or balance of power among the different coalitions that may form within the assembly.[2] A relatively even (or symmetrical) distribution of power may lead to a dynamic of negotiation, therefore yielding more balanced outcomes, favorable to all the parties involved. By contrast, a marked asymmetry in the distribution of power among the constitution drafters may lead to an unbalanced dynamic where the majoritarian coalition falls into the temptation of unilaterally imposing a constitutional text without regard to the interests and demands of the minority.

Depending on different combinations of these factors, we envision two main types of constitutional-drafting dynamics (routes or patterns), with some important variations within each category: negotiation or imposition of the new constitutional text. The negotiating route takes place when the assembly includes multiple political forces, and power is distributed relatively symmetrically among them. Bargaining may be based on ideological coincidences or on short-term strategic calculations. In situations where the different groups are not diametrically polarized in ideological terms, negotiations may follow a centripetal trend that is likely to result in a consensual document, where all actors see their preferences at least partially reflected.[3] However, if power is evenly distributed but actors are ideologically polarized, dynamics may take a centrifugal turn. In this case, conflict between two opposing coalitions risks producing a constitutional text that is incoherent and

---

[1] In the Andean nations, where politics has traditionally been in the hands of the elites and wide sectors of the population have been marginalized from decision-making, the visible participation of these sectors in constitution making has been a source of legitimacy both for the processes themselves, as well as for their results. See Segura and Bejarano (2004).

[2] We draw on Corrales (2018) for the notions of power symmetry and asymmetry.

[3] This scenario is clearly illustrated by the Colombian case (1991). See also Cepeda (1993a; 1993b; 2007).

contradictory, thereby offering a poor instrument to guide the post-constituent political process.[4]

Constitution drafting would follow the imposition pattern when the assembly is dominated by an actor or coalition that shares the same ideological project and believes that it will continue to be a majority in the short- and medium term. This dominant coalition does not need to negotiate with the minorities present in the assembly and can thus unilaterally impose their project of institutional reform. In this case, the minorities have two choices: they can stay in the assembly and express their disagreement,[5] or they can walk out and abandon the constitution-making effort to publicly denounce their marginalization.[6] If minorities do not offer any resistance, the approval of the constitution takes place without confrontation. If, on the contrary, the minority refuses to approve the text, the process can become mired in conflict.

II LINKING PROCESSES AND OUTCOMES

We claim that these different dynamics, patterns, or modes of constitution making lead to substantially different constitutional texts.[7] Our interest is to examine whether the new institutional arrangements are conducive to democratic deepening, defined as an expansion of both rights granted to all citizens, especially vulnerable minorities (inclusion), and institutional protections for the political opposition (contestation).

The enthusiasm surrounding recent episodes of constitutional change in the Andes owes, to a large extent, to their potential to create wider spaces for inclusion, thus reversing the region's historical tendency to exclude wide sectors of the population (Segura and Bejarano 2004). A crucial question is therefore whether these new constitutions open a permanent space for the incorporation of those previously excluded, or whether this inclusion proves to be ephemeral once the country returns to politics as usual. We therefore emphasize the creation of mechanisms that would foster the institutionalization of inclusion. It is in the expansion of rights that provide citizens with access to the political arena where constitutions can

---

4 Constitution making in Ecuador (1997–1998) nicely illustrates this scenario.
5 In Hirschman's terms (1970), this would be the "voice" option. This is the strategy adopted by the six members of the opposition during the 1999 constitution-making experience in Venezuela.
6 In Hirschman's terms (Hirschman 1970), these drafters would be taking the "exit" option. This is the strategy adopted by the Bolivian opposition when constitutional negotiations broke down in 2008.
7 For the purposes of this work we do not deal with the long-term downstream consequences of constitutional choice, because of three main reasons: one practical (the sheer size of the project), one empirical (discrepancy between the actual time elapsed since the constitution was approved in each case makes it difficult to compare the aftermath) and one theoretical (the difficulties associated with predicting the long-term consequences of major institutional overhauls), as pointed out by Elster (1988, 304 and 303–323 passim).

contribute most significantly to the advance of democracy: by creating the channels, mechanisms, and institutions through which diverse social sectors can make their demands visible and participate actively in the decision-making process.

However, given the difficulties associated with direct democracy, the institutional-ization of inclusion necessarily implies building more and better mechanisms of representation – that is, mechanisms that will provide for the regular participation of all sectors of society in the processes of selecting and holding accountable those representatives who participate (on their behalf) in collectively binding decision-making. As Castiglione puts it succinctly: "in all but directly democratic venues (and even sometimes then), the norm of democratic inclusion is achieved through representation" (Castiglione 2005, 5).

The second crucial dimension of democracy considered in our analysis concerns the need to guarantee a space for contestation, understood as the dimension of "a political system that allows for opposition, rivalry, or competition between a government and its opponents" (Dahl 1971, 1). To guarantee such space, besides the bills of rights included in the dogmatic part of the constitution, it is crucial to have an institutional architecture that reduces incumbency advantage (Widner 2013) and levels the playing field (Levitsky and Way 2010), thereby guaranteeing the rights and freedoms of those who oppose the government. The ultimate purpose of this complex institutional arrangement, as Charles Tilly once brilliantly put it, is to make "protected consultation" possible (2007, 13)

This (constitutional or liberal) dimension of democracy includes those institu-tions that contribute to a more even distribution of power: to the lessening of asymmetries between the government and the opposition (Hartlyn and Luna 2009); to the creation of a playing field that provides similar opportunities to all political forces thus preventing the "tyranny of the majority."[8] In the absence of an institutional architecture that fosters a balanced distribution of power, the expansion of rights and freedoms as well as the opportunities for further participation may indeed become dead letter.

Our main argument is that certain variations in the mode of constitution making will have recognizable consequences in the resulting constitutions. A cursory read-ing of recent constitution-making episodes in Latin America (starting with Brazil in 1988 up to the more recent one in Bolivia, 2006–2009), leads to the conclusion that participatory constitution making generally tends to widen the institutional avenues and channels for inclusion and participation. It is in the dimension of contestation (or opposition) where we found the most interesting variation. Colombia and Venezuela exemplify two polar opposites in this regard: in the former, the

---

[8] This dimension is operationalized through the analysis of those provisions that distribute power among the three branches, particularly the executive and the legislative, the judicial power and the agencies of horizontal control; it also includes the vertical distribution of power (or level of centralization or decentralization of the state).

constitution of 1991 created a better balance of powers, reducing previous presidential prerogatives and strengthening the role of congress and the courts while deepening the decentralization process initiated years before. In Venezuela, on the other hand, the 1999 constitution increased existing presidential powers, created a unicameral congress with a diminished capacity to exert political control over the executive, undermined judicial independence, and put a break on decentralization – all reforms which negatively affect the possibilities of contestation. Given that both of these assemblies were popularly elected, such variation in their results provides an excellent opportunity to conduct a comparative inquiry into the causes of their divergence.

Based on the analytical model outlined above, the following pages offer a paired contrast of these two cases that, while controlling for their many similarities, highlights variation in certain key aspects of the constitution-making process. It is in these specific variables (breadth of the pro-reform coalition, electoral system, distribution of power in the assembly, ideological polarization, and internal dynamics) that we find a plausible explanation for why, despite them both being highly participatory, these two constitution-making processes yielded such divergent outcomes in terms of the institutions selected.

III COLOMBIA: THE MAKING OF THE 1991 CONSTITUTION

Since its transition to democracy in 1958, Colombia's political regime suffered from restrictions that affected the competitive nature of elections. The National Front pacts[9] not only limited competition between the two main parties (Liberal and Conservative), but also excluded third parties from the electoral game for a period of sixteen years (1958–1974). The regime at the time was correctly described as semi-competitive, restricted, or limited. While most formal limitations were gradually lifted, many informal restrictions remained – a legacy of the strong constraints placed on the democratic game. Many have pointed to its exclusionary nature as the central flaw of Colombia's democracy.

A national debate on the need to introduce crucial political reforms started in the late 1970s, but efforts to pass them through Congress went nowhere.[10] Simultaneously, the need for deep institutional reforms was made evident by the peace negotiations between the government and several guerrilla groups – including the

---

[9] Seeking to end the decade-long conflict known as *La Violencia* (1948–1958), the Liberal and Conservative Parties signed these pacts, agreeing to alternate the presidency for sixteen years, to share all other positions of power, and to restrict third party access to elected office. See Hartlyn (1988) and Bejarano (2011).

[10] Efforts at constitutional reform by the Lopez (1974–1978) and Turbay (1978–1982) administrations were stopped by the Supreme Court. The Betancur administration (1982–1986) managed to pass a significant reform of local politics, including the popular election of mayors. Barco's government's (1986–1990) three attempts at reforming the constitution failed. See Valencia Villa (1989; 2010).

April 19 Movement (M-19), the Popular Liberation Army (EPL), the Revolutionary Workers' Party (PRT), and the Quintín Lame Armed Movement (MAQL), among others – since the early 1980s.[11] These peace negotiations played an important role in triggering the constitution-making process in 1991. In turn, once the door was open for the election of a constituent assembly, it became an important incentive for the insurgent groups to finalize those peace negotiations. A virtuous circle was engendered between the peace talks and the constituent assembly – which nonetheless was unable to entice all insurgent groups.[12]

The late 1980s witnessed some of the worst violence in Colombia's history: three presidential candidates were killed in little over six months, and random terrorist attacks marked the zenith of a violent campaign led by the drug dealers against the Colombian state. Together, these factors provide the backdrop against which one can better explain the fact that Colombia responded to the 1989–1990 crisis with a constitutional reform aimed at deepening its democracy: first, the protracted erosion of the institutional arrangement created in 1958, and the recognition, on the part of sectors of the political elite (among others), of the need to reform it; second, the ongoing negotiations with multiple guerrilla groups, which demanded political reform in exchange for their decision to lay down their arms and engage in the legal political game; and third, an increasingly obvious inability on the part of the State to respond adequately to the threat posed by violent actors of all stripes. In sum, the constituent assembly of 1991 must be interpreted as Colombia's imperative response to a serious crisis of institutional performance (Figueroa Garcia-Herreros 2012; Negretto 2013).

It was in this turbulent context that a student movement emerged to claim that a popularly elected constituent assembly (hereafter CCA) would provide a lasting solution to the crisis.[13] Thanks to wide coverage by the media, and the editorial support of the most important national and regional newspapers, the student movement managed to convene an informal consultation in the March 11, 1990, legislative elections, where approximately two million voters cast ballots in favor of summoning a constituent assembly (Dugas 2001, 809; see also Lemaitre 2009). Faced with this citizen-led push for a constitutional convention, which also gained the support of the main presidential candidates, on May 3, President Barco (1986–1990) issued a state of emergency decree (No. 927 of 1990) calling for an official referendum to decide if the assembly should meet. A ruling by the Supreme Court (issued on May 24, 1990) allowed the extra-constitutional referendum to take place – even though the existing constitution explicitly foreclosed such option – with the argument that there was an

---

[11] The EPL was the first one to argue, back in 1983, for the need to convene a constituent assembly. The M-19 also called in the early 1980s for an open and inclusive "National Dialogue."

[12] The National Liberation Army (ELN) and the Colombian Revolutionary Armed Forces (FARC) refused to take part in the assembly.

[13] On the student movement see Dugas (2001) and Lemaitre (2009, chapter 2).

TABLE 6.1 *Colombian constituent assembly (1991)*

Party or movement	Ideology	Number of seats	Percentage (of total seats)
Liberal Party, LP (including student movement)	Center-right	25	35,7
Alianza Democrática M-19 (ADM-19)	Left	19	27,1
Union Patriótica & Communist Party (UP-PCC)	Left	2	2,9
Indigenous movements	Left	2	2,9
Movimiento de Salvación Nacional (MSN)	Right	11	15,7
Social Conservative Party (PCS)	Right	5	7,1
Independent Conservatives (IC)	Right	4	5,7
Christian Union (UC)	Right	2	2,9
Appointed guerrilla representatives	Left	2	
Total		72	100

Source: Segura and Bejarano (2004, 220)

explicit connection between constitutional reform and the need to put an end to the violence (see Lemaitre 2009, 13–114). The consultation took place on May 27, 1990, simultaneously with the presidential election: 88.89 percent of the vote was in favor of the assembly, while 3.9 percent voted against it (Pinzón de Lewin 1991, 116–132).

Newly elected President Gaviria (Liberal Party) also used emergency powers and issued decree No. 1926 of 1990 to convene the CCA and call elections to choose its drafters on December 9, 1990. On October 9, the Supreme Court upheld this decree as well, arguing once again in favor of the connection between institutional reform and peace (Lemaitre 2009, 131)[14]. The electoral system was extremely proportional: the seventy delegates would be chosen from closed party lists competing in a single nationwide district; seats would be distributed to each list in proportion to their votes, following the Hare (or simple quota) system. Two additional seats were granted to the guerrilla groups involved in ongoing peace negotiations with the government, and two more were reserved for guerrilla groups who had declared their willingness to demobilize.[15] As shown in Table 6.1, the result was a diverse, pluralistic, and highly representative assembly.

III.A *Inside the Assembly*

The elected delegates represented an unprecedented diversity of social and political sectors, particularly when compared with the exclusionary and elitist composition of

[14] Though the Court supported the call for the CCA and the electoral system being proposed, it declared all limits on the matter under discussion, as contained in the decree, unconstitutional – based on the argument that the constituent power should not be subject to limits once convened. On this point, see also Landau (Chapter 4 of this volume).

[15] The latter had voice but no vote in the assembly.

the political world that prevailed in Colombia until then. The immediate consequence of this distribution was that no single party or movement could behave as a
dominant force, thereby imposing a new constitution single-handedly. This was a
pluralistic assembly, with representation from the traditional Liberal and Conservative parties, but also from an array of forces that had traditionally been left out of the
political arena. The very low level of asymmetry between the different forces present
in the assembly gave rise to an intense dynamic of negotiations, bargains and trade-
offs amongst its participants (Corrales 2018).

This dynamic of negotiation was also facilitated by the absence of a strong
ideological polarization in the assembly, something that came as a surprise considering that it was preceded by years of confrontation between the establishment and the
guerrillas. As the Table 6.1 indicates, the assembly had three main poles. The
Liberal Party had the largest plurality (twenty-five seats) but lacked the majorities,
internal coherence, and/or discipline necessary to play a dominant role. However,
both as a result of its internal fragmentation and also of its location at the center of
the ideological spectrum, it was able to negotiate with both the left and the right
playing a crucial role as pivot in the assembly.

On the other hand, the left – including the AD M-19, the Communist Party
(PCC), the Unión Patriótica (UP), and the indigenous representatives – obtained
an unprecedented level of electoral support and gained twenty-three seats, making
them a central actor in the assembly. Many Colombians voted for the AD M-19 as
a way of supporting their decision to leave the armed struggle; and the indigenous
parties had ample support among urban middle classes that recognized a historical
debt with these ethnic minorities. Arguably, the most significant coalition inside
the assembly was between progressive sectors of the Liberal Party and the left.
While not the only factor, the AD M-19's decision to enter an alliance with the
Liberal Party and to put forth a moderate agenda –seeking to appear as a force
committed to democracy and a feasible political alternative – was crucial in
determining the consensual mode of the process. Given its previous trajectory, it
could have brought radical proposals to the table that would have polarized the
assembly. However, in its attempt to reduce fears harbored by some that the CCA
would become the mechanism to institutionalize a failed armed revolution, the
AD M-19 ran a multi-party list and presented proposals that were far more moderate than expected.

Finally, parties classified as leaning toward the right gained twenty-two seats, and
were the third block in the assembly. The Movimiento de Salvación Nacional
(MSN), a bipartisan right-leaning dissidence led by Álvaro Gómez, obtained the
largest plurality of votes for the right. Gomez's caucus was willing to reach agreements with the other two blocks, and joined many of the majoritarian votes. Despite
disagreement on some issues, a conciliatory spirit prevailed in the assembly with
general agreement on some fundamental reforms. This led to the approval of most
decisions by near unanimous consensus: according to Cepeda, 74 percent of the

provisions were supported by the votes of forty-eight or more drafters, that is, by two-thirds or more of the assembly delegates (1991, xii). This strong centripetal tendency came from a shared sense of deep institutional crisis and the urgent need for reform to overcome it. This was reinforced by the relatively symmetric or even distribution of power within the assembly plus an increasing uncertainty about future elections (see Negretto 2013, 180).

III.B *Constitutional Outcomes*

The negotiated nature of the Colombian process had a direct impact on the outcomes. In terms of inclusion, there was an overall tendency to incorporate in the final text some modified version of the proposals brought by the diverse political actors. As is the case with most constitutions in the Andean region, the CCA enshrined a strong bill of rights, which includes civil, political, social, economic, cultural, and collective rights. Title II spans five chapters and a total of eighty-four articles. The identity-based recognition claims brought forward by the indigenous representatives found a good reception in the assembly, which created a nationwide electoral district exclusively for indigenous representatives, reserving two seats in the Senate and up to five seats in the House of Representatives for ethnic minorities (article 176), and designed the new indigenous territories known as Entidades Territoriales Indígenas (articles 286, 288, and 329).

The 1991 constitution also aimed at opening and widening the space for political participation and representation. The constitution states the rights of citizens to participate in the "creation, exercise, and control of political power" (Article 40) and creates an ample range of new mechanisms of citizens' participation including plebiscites, referenda, popular consultations, town meetings, legislative initiatives, and recall of elected officials (Articles 103, 104, 105, and 106). In the hopes of creating stronger links between the electorate and its representatives, the new constitution enshrined the "programmatic vote"[16] and the recall vote. It also opened spaces for citizen participation in national and local decision-making entities such as the National Planning Council (article 340) and the Local Administrative Juntas (JALs) (article 138). Fostering citizens' participation was, in the words of Manuel José Cepeda (the government's advisor for constitutional reform) "the core principle of the philosophy of institutional revolution promoted and headed by President César Gaviria" (Cepeda: interview with authors, Bogotá, April 2004).

There was broad consensus among the drafters regarding the importance of opening space for political parties that had been excluded in the past. Following an "incorporation logic" (Pizarro and Bejarano 2007), the CCA did not seek to increase the parties' capabilities to function as political intermediaries, but chose

---

[16] It requires candidates for mayorships and governorships to present a government program that they are obliged to fulfill if elected.

instead to increase the number of political parties and movements present in the political arena by easing the until-then stringent restrictions to run for public office (A. Ramírez Ocampo: Interview with authors, Bogotá, April 2004). The assembly voted by consensus in favor of loosening the requirements necessary to create a party or political movement: from then on (until 2003) 50,000 votes or signatures were enough for a movement to be recognized as a legal party by the National Electoral Council (Article 168).

Together with the electoral districts for the indigenous peoples (in the Senate) and other minorities (in the House of Representatives), the most significant reform aimed at enhancing political inclusion was the creation of a nationwide district for the Senate. This was one of the few issues that resulted in polarization among the drafters. Some members of the CCA hoped to break the clientelistic networks that dominated regional representation, while simultaneously favoring political and ethnic minorities that needed to pool votes from across the nation in order to be elected (Botero 1998). This reform faced opposition from many inside the CCA especially from the traditional Liberal and Conservative parties, which depended on strong local and regional clientelistic networks.[17] The National Constituent Assembly also created a runoff presidential election (if no candidate obtains an absolute majority in the first round) aimed at favoring smaller parties and promoting coalitions.

In terms of inclusion, a bill of rights incorporating numerous social and economic rights, innovations in terms of indigenous rights, and the creation of multiple channels for electoral and non-electoral participation meant a significant expansion of the political arena in Colombia after 1991. Indeed, by Elkins, Ginsburg, and Melton's measure "one of the most inclusive constitutions is Colombia's 1991 document, which includes six of the eight items on the scale" (2009, 99).

Regarding the dimension of democratic contestation, the constitution of 1991 placed constraints on "the discretion of the executive in most policy areas" (Archer and Shugart 1997, 118). It also aimed at creating a more balanced distribution of power, through strengthening Congress as well as various agencies of horizontal accountability and deepening decentralization. In spite of the prominent role that President Gaviria had during the constitution-making process, the CCA decided, with his acquiescence, to reduce the powers of the executive by eliminating the possibility of reelection, reducing its decree and legislative powers, and placing new limits to the president's emergency powers. On this issue, the assembly went beyond the proposal presented by the government, which established temporal limits to their use and restricted the legislative powers of the executive, but also contemplated a classification of states of exception that ranged from state of alarm to state of war.[18] In addition, Congress – which remained bicameral – recovered

---

[17] It passed with just forty-three votes out of seventy-two (Palacio Rudas 1994, 108).

[18] The assembly rejected this classification, as well as the government's proposal to have states of exception lasting forty-five days, which could be extended by government initiative. Instead, the

certain budgetary powers,[19] as well as the power to veto decisions made by the executive during periods of emergency.[20] The greatest innovation in terms of political control is the no-confidence motion against cabinet ministers.[21] While most of these initiatives came from proposals presented by the AD M19, usually in coalition with the MSN or the government and the Liberal Party, they were all approved by a majority of the drafters.

The new constitution also created new agencies of horizontal accountability. Particularly important was the creation of the "acción de tutela," which gives citizens recourse to the courts when public officials have violated, or failed to protect, their fundamental rights (defined in the constitution), and the setting up of a Constitutional Court (CC). The CC rules on the constitutionality of actions taken by the legislative and executive branches, making for a more balanced relationship among powers. Finally, the 1991 Constitution strengthened the institutions of horizontal accountability through assigning new and more precise functions to the offices of the inspector-attorney general (Procuraduría) and the comptroller (Contraloría), and the creation of the office of the ombudsman (Defensor del Pueblo). The new text also emphasized the independence of the National Electoral Council and the Central Bank.

The 1991 constitution also contributed to deepening the process of decentralization initiated since the mid-1980s. It made territorial entities uniform throughout the country (eliminating the previous *intendencias* and *comisarías*) and established the popular election of governors while ratifying that of mayors (instituted in 1986). This proposal obtained majority support within the CCA, except for the representatives of the conservative coalition, who opposed it. In terms of fiscal decentralization, the new charter went further than most in Latin America by constitutionally mandating that an increasing portion of national revenue be devolved to the departments and municipalities (Lora and Scartascini 2010).

Summing up, then, the CCA was elected through a proportional electoral system that yielded a greatly diverse body, in which bargaining and negotiation, rather than imposition, became the actors' dominant strategy. As a result of this centripetal consensual dynamic, the 1991 Constitution contributed to deepening Colombia's democracy through a series of complementary reforms: on the one hand, it opened and widened the channels for political participation and representation in the political system; on the other, it aimed at restoring the balance among the different branches of power. In addition, the Constitution of 1991 deepened the process of political and fiscal decentralization, devolving a significant measure of power to the

---

drafters decided on having emergency periods last ninety days and allowing these to be extended for two more periods total, the second of which required Senate approval. For more on this see Negretto (2013).

[19] Articles 345–354.

[20] Articles 212–215.

[21] Article 135.

regional and local levels of government, thus adding a new layer of control over the power vested at the center. These reforms came as the answer to a deep institutional crisis, where the political system's exclusionary restrictions rendered the state incapable of responding both to the demands of wide sectors of the population, and to the challenges of violent actors. While not without its flaws and shortcomings, since 1991, the new constitution has furthered symbolic and political inclusion and has fostered the emergence and growth of a political opposition – long lacking in the Colombian political landscape.

IV VENEZUELA: THE MAKING OF THE 1999 CONSTITUTION

Since the early 1980s, Venezuela saw the signs of a looming economic crisis – when the bust-cycle of oil prices coincided with the region's debt crisis. Devaluation of the Bolivar in 1993 signaled the end of prosperity and the beginning of a two-decade long decline in oil prices that ultimately had an impact on the state's and the parties' capacity to deliver, as well as on society – where increasing poverty rates led to a frustrated and angry electorate that put all the blame on the political class (Kornblith 1998; López Maya 2006). The 1989 neoliberal package was an attempt at addressing the structural sources of Venezuela's economic crisis, but it lacked political support and sparked momentous reactions – including the fateful urban riots of February 27 and 28, 1989, known as "el Caracazo." The crisis epitomized by "el Caracazo" revealed the incapacity on the part of the political parties to channel and control the people's reaction, as well as a poorly staffed, overburdened, and corrupted state that was increasingly unable to sustain even a limited version of the rule of law.

In 1992, two attempted military coups sent a clear message: Venezuela's democracy was at risk. The erosion of the political parties that had been the cornerstone of Venezuela's political system was irreversible. The two main parties, Acción Democrática (AD) and Comité Político Electoral Independiente (COPEI), had become centralized, and hierarchical to an extreme that led to a dramatic chasm between them and a rapidly changing society that grew resentful of the parties' inability to address the country's central ailments and finally disengaged. The first signs of a dramatic weakening of the parties came in the 1993 election. By 1998, the process of de-institutionalization and collapse of the party system was complete. In that year's electoral campaign, the banner of a fundamental change to the constitution was raised as the only possible way out of the crisis; a majority of the electorate supported it, together with the candidate who proposed it, ex-coup plotter Hugo Chávez.[22]

In contrast with other cases, in Venezuela there was no social or political movement explicitly organized around the demand for constitutional reform. By making it the centerpiece of his 1998 campaign, candidate Chávez spearheaded the

---

[22] Chávez, running as the candidate for a new party, Movimiento Quinta República (MVR) was elected in 1998 by 56.2 percent of the vote.

formation of a coalition against the incumbent regime made up of young military officers, a collection of small leftist parties, and the masses of Venezuela's urban poor. The promise of constitutional change took on a symbolic meaning: to "refound" the Republic, in Chávez's own words. On the day of his inauguration, February 2, 1999, President Chávez swore on the "dying" constitution of 1961 and immediately issued a decree calling for a referendum on the convening of a constituent assembly "aimed at transforming the state and creating a new legal order that allows the effective functioning of a social and participative democracy."[23]

The 1961 constitution did not provide for a constituent assembly as a mechanism for constitutional change. Private citizens brought to the Supreme Court a question about whether an extra-constitutional constituent assembly could be convened by way of a consultative referendum called by the president. After the December election, the Supreme Court came under pressure to decide in favor of Chávez's electoral promise and thus played, using Landau's classification of judicial interventions during democratic constitution making in this volume (Chapter 4), an "enabling" function. On January 19, 1999, two weeks before he took office, the Court issued two decisions that opened the gates for the convening of the assembly.[24] The referendum (which also included the electoral system to select the assembly delegates) took place on April 25, 1999, and was approved by close to 82 percent of those who participated.[25]

The electoral system was designed by the Presidential Commission for the Constituent Assembly[26] with little input or participation from other political forces. The assembly was to be composed of 131 members elected in 3 different ways: three members would be selected to represent the indigenous population of Venezuela, according to their "mores and customs,"[27] 104 members would be elected in 24 regional districts of different magnitude and the remaining 24 members were to be elected in a single nation-wide district. Candidates were to run individually (and not in lists). Each voter had the right to vote for as many candidates as there were

---

[23] Gaceta Oficial No. 36.634 (cited in Brewer-Carías 2010 b, 506).

[24] The winning argument, similar to that put forth by the Colombian Court, was that the original constituent power vested in the sovereign people, could always place itself above and beyond the existing constitution. See Brewer-Carías (2010 a; 2010b) for a critique of these decisions on the part of the Court.

[25] Turnout in this occasion was 39.1 percent. El Universal Digital, http://elecciones.eud.com/1999/04/25/250ac.html.

[26] The members of the Presidential Commission for the constituent assembly were directly appointed by President-elect Chávez in December 1998. (Ricardo Combellas, interview with authors, Caracas, February 2008).

[27] Combellas states that the three indigenous delegates were directly appointed by President Chávez who was a pioneer in opening the doors of the assembly to the indigenous peoples (see Interview, n. 26). Indigenous peoples represent less than 2 percent the total population of Venezuela and are thinly spread throughout the territory, except for the state of Zulia, which houses a large group of Wayuus. In part because of this geographic dispersion, the indigenous peoples of Venezuela had not achieved the degree of organization and visibility of the Colombian indigenous movement.

seats in the district, except in the nationwide district where voters were only allowed to choose ten candidates from all those who were running. The intention was to personalize the vote by allowing the electorate to vote for individual candidates rather than party lists.[28] It was not strictly a first-past-the-post system (because all districts had more than one seat), but it had the same majoritarian consequences.[29] Furthermore, it "did not include a proportional formula of any sort for the representation of the minorities" (Neuman and McCoy 2001, 28).

President Chávez got directly involved in the campaign to elect the delegates to the assembly promoting his unofficial lists (known as "las chuletas de Chávez," or Chávez's "cheat sheets"). By contrast, the opposition was extremely fragmented: fearing a reaction from the electorate who had so decisively shunned them in the 1998 election and trying to avoid party labels, instead of presenting "informal" lists to the electorate, it became dispersed in a myriad of hardly recognizable candidates running their own individual campaigns. The combination of this "atypical plurinominal electoral system" (Neuman and McCoy 2001, 17) with the electoral strategy and campaign tactics deployed both by Chávez and the opposition, yielded an extremely skewed result in the July 25, 1999, elections. As shown in Table 6.2, the pro-government candidates, who became part of the coalition known as Polo Patriótico, received 65.8 percent of the vote, but gained control of 93 percent of the seats (122) in the assembly.[30] All candidates who were supported by the president got elected, save one.

In dramatic contrast, the opposition received 34 percent of the vote but obtained only 4.6 percent of the seats (6). Four opposition delegates were elected in the nationwide district. The other two were elected in the states of Aragua and Nueva Esparta. This extremely asymmetric and lopsided electoral outcome left the opposition with an insignificant presence in the constitution-making body and "the Chávez government free of almost all obstacles to influence the decisions of the Constituent Assembly" (Neuman and McCoy 2001, 27).

Rather than a preexisting pro-reform coalition pushing for the convening of a constituent assembly and trying to shape the electoral system to translate its power into seats – as was the case in Colombia – what we see in Venezuela is the president, single-handedly, forming a pro-reform coalition, initially from his campaign quarters, and then, beginning in February 1999, from the Presidential Palace. Thanks to his electoral majorities, and the electoral system designed by his advisors, he was able to translate a majoritarian but vague and amorphous support into a dominant coalition (the Polo Patriótico) that controlled 93 percent of the seats and votes in the assembly.

---

[28] Combellas argues that the Presidential Commission (PCCA) decided on this system to honor the popular call for less party control and more citizen participation in the selection of their representatives (see Interview, n. 26).

[29] Regardless of the number of seats per district, those candidates with the most votes were selected until all seats were filled.

[30] Participation in this election was 46.3 percent of eligible voters.

TABLE 6.2 *Venezuelan constituent assembly (1999)*

Party or movement	Ideology/coalition	Number of seats	Percentage (of total seats)
MVR (Movimiento Quinta República)	Left/Polo Patriótico	53	40.46
Chavistas (running on individual basis)	Left/Polo Patriótico	36	27.48
MAS (Movimiento Al Socialismo)	Left/Polo Patriótico	12	9.15
PPT (Patria para Todos)	Left/Polo Patriótico	12	9.15
PCV (Partido Comunista de Venezuela)	Left/Polo Patriótico	2	1.53
27-N (Military)	Left/Polo Patriótico	2	1.53
Others	Left/Polo Patriótico	5	3.81
Opposition	Center-Right	6	4.6
Indigenous representatives (appointed)	Left/Polo Patriótico	3	2.29
Total		131	100

Source: authors

IV.A *Inside the Assembly*

The assembly met in Caracas on August 3, 1999. Five days later it approved its Operating Statutes.[31] In its first article, the assembly declared itself the depository of the popular will and expression of its sovereignty and thereby declared to have an "originary power" to reorganize the Venezuelan state and create a new juridical order.[32] This meant that all public powers were subordinate to the assembly, which "may limit or decide to cease the activities of the authorities which form public power."[33] Right after this declaration, the assembly embarked in a campaign to neutralize or eliminate all alternative sources of power, especially those located in the courts and the legislature.

On August 12, the assembly decreed the reorganization of all public powers.[34] It then declared a situation of "judicial emergency" and appointed a "Commission of Judicial Emergency" charged with evaluating the performance of the judiciary, proposing and executing a series of reforms, including the removal and replacement of "corrupt" or incompetent judges.[35] Immediately after, the assembly suspended the ordinary and extraordinary meetings of Congress, limited the number of areas in which Congress would be able to act independently, and otherwise subjected the legislative power to the permanent control and evaluation by the constituent

[31] Estatuto de Funcionamiento de la Asamblea Nacional Constituyente), *Gaceta Constituyente (Diario de Debates)*, Sesión Permanente, No. 4, sábado 7 de agosto de 1999 (hereafter *Estatuto...*).

[32] *Estatuto...*, p. 144.

[33] *Estatuto...*, p. 144.

[34] Decree of August 12, 1999, in *Gaceta Constituyente* No. 8, pp. 2–4.

[35] Decree of August 19, 1999, in *Gaceta Constituyente*, No. 10, pp. 17–22.

assembly – a decision akin to its dismissal.[36] This decree led to a violent confrontation between Congress and the assembly.[37] In the end, Congress backed down and "voluntarily" agreed to suspend its activities (Neuman and McCoy 2001, 31). All these decisions were challenged before the Supreme Court. However, contradicting its own previous rulings, the Supreme Court decided that the assembly had supra-constitutional power thereby signing its own death sentence. The President of the Supreme Court, Cecilia Sosa, resigned and the remaining members were sacked and replaced by the assembly on December 22, 1999 (see Brewer Carias 2010b).

One month into the assembly's proceedings, it became clear that the assembly, more than a forum for deliberating on a new institutional framework, had turned into the vehicle for building a new majority and replacing the old elites with the new ones who had erupted on scene just eight months before. The most tense and controversial situation during the deliberations of the assembly were not necessarily related to the drafting of the new constitution, but rather to its conflicts with the established powers, in particular with Congress (Combellas 2010, 155) – where the main opposition parties still held on to substantial power.[38] The opposition thus remained largely outside the assembly itself, in Congress and in the vestiges of the traditional parties (AD and COPEI) who had been mortally wounded during the presidential elections of December 1998; in this battle of wills with the constituent assembly, it was finally defeated.

The fact that the pro-government majority counted on 125/131 members of the assembly made their dominance in decision-making a foregone conclusion from the start. Deliberation on the new institutional framework started in September after the struggle with the established powers was over. Despite having five months left to conclude the task, President Chávez urged the assembly to finish drafting the new constitution, in order to submit it to approval via popular referendum by late November or early December 1999.

The timing imposed by President Chávez (and approved by the assembly's President, Luis Miquilena) was "the most important constraint during the drafting process" (Neuman and McCoy 2001, 32). After a month of discussions in the

---

[36] Decree of August 28, 1999, in *Gaceta Constituyente* No. 13. This same decree suspended the states' legislative assemblies. Another one (Decree of August 26, 1999 in Gaceta Constituyente 14) suspended municipal elections. (See Allan Brewer-Carías 2010b).

[37] "Un Congreso moribundo enfrenta a la constituyente de Hugo Chávez," El País de Madrid. www.pagina12.com.ar/1999/99-08/99-08-27/pag20.htm.

[38] After the congressional elections held in November 1998, the two traditional parties (AD and COPEI) together with CONVERGENCIA and Proyecto Venezuela, controlled 55.1 percent of the seats in the Lower Chamber and 60.39 percent of the seats in the Senate. On the other hand, the leftist coalition headed by Chávez and his Movimiento V República, which included Movimiento Al Socialismo, Patria Para Todos, La Causa R, the Partido Comunista de Venezuela, and Movimiento Electoral del Pueblo, controlled 38.9 percent of the seats in the Lower Chamber and 37.63 percent of the seats in the Senate. Data from Payne, Zovatto, and Mateo Díaz (2006: Appendix 3, Venezuela – Composición Cámara Baja). Data for the Senate from http://elecciones.eud.com/1998/12/conclusiones/resultados/199.htm.

Permanent Commissions behind closed doors, the Constitutional Commission integrated all proposals into a single constitutional draft containing 350 articles, which was submitted to the assembly on October 18, 1999.[39] At this time, the president urged the assembly again to wrap up its proceedings and finish the drafting process by November 15 in order to prepare for the referendum that would submit the new constitution to popular approval in December. The assembly thus had less than a month to carry out two rounds of discussion on the floor.

The first round took nineteen days (October 20–November 11) and provided the best opportunity for active deliberation on the part of the constituent delegates. The second round of discussion, however, occupied only three floor debates, from November 12 to 14, 1999, and was done in "blocks of chapters." This discussion "was hasty, given the regime's decision to carry out the referendum to ratify the text in December, and it used an iron-fist mechanism of decision making which curtailed the interventions, limiting the discussion to a few articles (having to do with freedom of the press, the discussion on bicameralism versus unicameralism, and presidential reelection) about which there was no consensus" (Ricardo Combellas, personal communication with authors, April 27, 2013).

Such a hurried process left little room for debate or public discussion, even less for the participation of civil society. It also signaled the absence of extensive bargaining and negotiation. With an overwhelming majority on the part of the pro-government coalition there was no need to engage in such negotiations. It also had an effect on the quality and consistency of the final text. Nevertheless, it achieved its goal – namely, to accelerate its approval: the final draft was completed on November 19, 1999, and submitted to a national referendum on December 15.[40] The members of the opposition, the Catholic Church, and the business umbrella organization, FEDECAMARAS, led the campaign for a "no" vote against the draft constitution. The traditional parties, disorganized and discredited, did not put up any concerted effort against it. President Chávez, on the other hand, campaigned intensively for the "yes" vote with resources drawn from the public treasury. As a result, voters approved the new constitution by 71.78 percent.[41]

---

[39] According to Neuman and McCoy, "the power attributed to the Constitutional Commission to reduce and change the content of the articles, in order to present a coherent version to the floor, was highly contested. Some members of the Constitutional Commission believed that it was necessary to modify the draft; others thought that the Commission did not have that authority. Conflict escalated to such heights that two key members resigned from the commission. The final draft that was presented to the floor for discussion had almost 400 articles, compared to the initial draft containing 800 articles" (2001, 32).

[40] In its final version, the new constitution had 350 articles, one derogatory provision, 18 transitory provisions and 1 final provision.

[41] With an abstention of 55.62 percent of registered voters (data from Consejo Nacional Electoral, www.cne.gov.ve/estadisticas/e010pdf). The new constitution was proclaimed by the National Constituent Assembly in Caracas on December 20, 1999 and published by the Gaceta Oficial de la República de Venezuela (No. 36860) on December 30, 1999, after which it entered into full force.

IV.B *Constitutional Outcomes*

In terms of outcomes, the 1999 constitution provides a prime example of a document that combines a decided effort to incorporate the excluded and widen the scope of participation on the one hand with, on the other, an unbalanced architecture of power that slants the institutional playing field in favor of the executive to the detriment of all other branches of government.

Other than the controversial renaming of the country as the "Bolivarian Republic of Venezuela," perhaps the most important provisions in terms of symbolic recognition are contained in Title III, chapter VIII, devoted to the rights of the indigenous peoples of Venezuela (Articles 119–126). The Venezuelan constitution of 1999 also includes a specific chapter devoted to delineating a long list of social and economic rights: to social security, to health care, to adequate housing, to education, to a safe and healthy environment, to just remuneration, to form or join trade unions, to rest and leisure, to strike, and to an adequate standard of living, among others (see Title III, chapters V and VII). Perhaps the most innovative feature in the Venezuelan constitution is not just the expanded list of socioeconomic rights, but also the fact that they are included in the constitution as "justiciable fundamental rights" (and not just as aspirational or "directive principles of state policy.")[42]

In terms of political inclusion, the new constitution puts forth a model of "participatory and protagonist democracy" that emphasizes the direct participation of the people in decision-making.[43] Articles 66, 70, 71, 72, and 233 offer a number of non-electoral participatory mechanisms (plebiscites, referenda, popular consultations, recall referendum, open town-hall meetings, legislative initiative, among others), which are meant to facilitate this. In terms of amendment procedures, the new constitution is ample and flexible: it provides three different mechanisms of revision, one of which allows for the convening of an "originary" (or sovereign) constituent assembly to replace the constitution (Article 347).

This emphasis on the direct participation of the people went hand in hand with an effort to reduce the role of political parties as vehicles for representation. Representative democracy was seen by many (not just the Chavista majority) as the crux of the problem in Venezuela – something that needed to be rooted out, rather than fixed. So the members of the assembly tried to overcome it by multiplying the number of mechanisms available for citizens to participate directly (see above); and secondly, by minimizing – in fact, marginalizing – the role of political parties. The 1999 charter is an anti-party constitution. The very expression "political party" practically disappeared from the text and was replaced by that of "association

---

[42] For definitions and the difference between these two types of rights, see the Toronto Initiative for Economic Rights. www.ties.org.

[43] This was also high on President Chávez's agenda who insisted on shifting from "representative democracy" to this new "participatory and protagonic" democracy.

(or alternatively, organization) with political ends." Article 67 expressly prohibits any sort of public funding of these associations. Furthermore, Article 201 states that the members of the National Assembly (the unicameral legislature) cannot be subject to any mandate or instruction other than their conscience, and that their vote is strictly personal, therefore precluding any attempt at imposing party discipline. In sum, alongside its participatory rhetoric, the 1999 constitution contains a series of strong disincentives to the formation of political parties.

As regards opportunities for contestation, a notorious feature of the 1999 constitution is the dramatic increase in the formal powers that presidents in Venezuela had in the past. The assembly extended the presidential term in office from five to six years while also allowing for the immediate reelection of the president for one consecutive term (Article 230).[44] Among other prerogatives the president also counts on enhanced powers to control the military – without having to pass through Congress to approve military promotions.[45] Part of the purpose was to "depoliticize" military appointments and promotions; however, the military went from being controlled by the parties (something they resented) to being controlled by one single individual: the president, with no congressional oversight. Additionally, the new constitution grants the right to vote to military personnel in active service, as well as an increased role for the military in national political life.

As for the legislature, the Venezuelan Congress was transformed from a two-chamber body to a unicameral assembly (the National Assembly) with its legislative powers greatly reduced in favor of the executive. The imbalance owes, to a great extent, to an increased ability, on the part of the assembly, to delegate its legislative powers to the president – the infamous enabling law (*"ley habilitante"*).[46] Among the many changes introduced by the new constitution, this is perhaps the most powerful instrument granted to the president by the Constitution of 1999. With the provisions allowing the president to call for the repeal of legislation through referendum, the "enabling powers" through which the National Assembly delegates unlimited decree powers to the president, and the elimination of congressional approval for military promotions, the new constitution gives the president "disproportionate powers to the other branches of government, particularly the legislature" (Neuman and McCoy 2001, 36–37). To cap it all off, the president has the power to dissolve the assembly if and when the National Assembly votes to remove the presidentially appointed vice-president three times.

---

[44] This provision was amended by referendum in 2009 to allow for the indefinite reelection of the president. The two provisions mentioned in text were among the priorities in President Chávez's agenda in 1999. On the powers of the president in Venezuela, see also Corrales and Penfold (2007).

[45] This was also part of President Chávez' original agenda.

[46] In fact, these "enabling powers" (*poderes habilitantes*), were used throughout Chávez's term in office (in 1999, in 2000, and in 2007) to legislate on all kind of matters and to push forth his "revolutionary" agenda without having to enter into negotiations or craft any kind of compromise with the various factions within the Chavista majority, much less with the opposition.

In terms of the decentralization process, the new charter respected the popular election of governors and mayors (introduced in 1989), but otherwise represents a setback in terms of fiscal decentralization. The Venezuelan state remains formally federal, and the constitution provides for a Federal Council of Government that is supposed to direct public policies related to the decentralization process (see Combellas 2010, 156). However, the Council is firmly in the hands of the executive and its control of fiscal transfers from the federal to the state and municipal levels signals a reversal in the process of fiscal decentralization. Additionally, the abolition of the Senate and the change from a bicameral to a unicameral congress eliminated the representation of states and regions at the federal level thus contradicting the (now only nominal) "federal" nature of Venezuela's political architecture.

In short, while the 1999 Venezuelan constitution broadened the definition of rights and responsibilities, and sought to expand political participation, it also allowed for an extreme concentration of power in the hands of the president while at the same time weakening the legislature, reducing the opportunities for horizontal accountability, and putting a break on the process of decentralization initiated in the late 1980s. There is no doubt that in this new institutional architecture "the cards were stacked in favor of the government and against the opposition" (Skidmore, Smith and Green 2010, 237–238).

V CONCLUSION

For decades, Colombia and Venezuela were considered exceptional in Latin America because of the duration and apparent stability of their democratic regimes. Starting in the late 1980s, they both entered a turbulent period, which sent their democracies spiraling into deep crises. In part as a response to these, the two countries sought to redesign their institutional arrangements through popularly elected assemblies: first, Colombia in 1991; and then, Venezuela in 1999.

Despite their apparent similarities, these two experiments in institutional engineering yielded different constitutional outcomes with divergent impacts on the prospects for further democratization of these two ailing democratic regimes. In Colombia, the drafters of the 1991 constitution wrote an expanded bill of rights, espoused inclusive electoral rules, introduced stronger limits on the government (particularly on the executive's emergency powers), strengthened the judiciary and other institutions of horizontal accountability (including more congressional oversight), and deepened fiscal and political decentralization. The new constitution, therefore, not only widened the avenues for political inclusion and participation, but also created a more balanced institutional architecture whereby the power of the executive would be tempered by the powers allocated to other (vertical and horizontal) institutions, thus guaranteeing a space for the emergence of the opposition and its right to contest government policy, therefore also enhancing accountability.

In Venezuela, by contrast, the institutional architecture that emerged from the 1999 constitution was heavily skewed in favor of the executive while reducing the oversight capacity of institutions such as the (unicameral) assembly, the judiciary, the national electoral council, the central bank, or the subnational levels of government. The new constitution, driven as it was by a new majority, was committed to deepening inclusion in its many forms: symbolically, in terms of economic redistribution and also politically, through the adoption of an expanded bill of rights and novel forms of participation. However, this emphasis on inclusion and participation was not accompanied by a parallel effort at limiting the ability of the executive to do as it wishes. Quite the contrary; precisely because the government and its popular head, President Chávez, represented a new majority, the new constitution added to the factors favoring the concentration of power in the hands of the executive thus reducing the opportunities and avenues for the opposition to contest the will of the majority.

As we have argued, whereas the diffusion of partisan power and absence of polarization in the Colombian process accounts for the power-sharing design of the new constitution, the concentration of partisan power and polarization observed in Venezuela explains a clear power-concentrating design. While we have not focused on the actual implementation of these different constitutional designs, it seems right to attribute to institutional arrangements an important degree of influence on subsequent levels of democracy. It is no mere coincidence that whereas Colombia improved its Polity IV score of democracy in the immediate years that followed the adoption of the new constitution, Venezuela saw a sharp decline. To be sure, constitutional provisions that disperse power may not be implemented in practice. Yet one can be reasonably confident that a constitution designed to concentrate power in the executive and the incumbent party will be detrimental to liberal democracy.

REFERENCES

Archer, Ronald, and Matthew S. Shugart. 1997. "The Unrealized Potential of Presidential Dominance in Colombia" in *Presidentialism and Democracy in Latin America.* Scott Mainwaring and Matthew Shugart (eds.) Cambridge: Cambridge University Press, 110–159.

Bejarano, Ana María. 2011. *Precarious Democracies: Understanding Regime Stability and Change in Colombia and Venezuela.* South Bend: University of Notre Dame Press.

Bonime-Blanc, Andrea. 1987. *Spain's Transition to Democracy: The Politics of Constitution Making.* New York: Westview Press.

Botero, Felipe. 1998. "El Senado que nunca fue: la circunscripción nacional después de tres elecciones" in *Elecciones y Democracia en Colombia 1997–1998.* Ana María Bejarano and Andrés Dávila (eds.) Bogotá: Fundación Social, Departamento de Ciencia Política, Universidad de los Andes, Veeduría Ciudadana a la Elección Presidencial, 285–335.

Brewer-Carías, Allan. 2010a. *Dismantling Democracy in Venezuela: The Chavez Authoritarian Experiment.* Cambridge: Cambridge University Press.

2010b. "The 1999 Venezuelan Constitution making Process as an Instrument for Framing the Development of an Authoritarian Political Regime" in *Framing the State in Times of*

Transition: Case Studies in Constitution Making. Laurel E. Miller (ed.) Washington, DC: United States Institute of Peace Press, 505–531.

Castiglione, Darío. 2005. "Representation Re-examined: A Conceptual and Theoretical Agenda." Paper presented at the New School for Social Research Work-in-Progress Series, April, 28 2005. Unpublished manuscript.

Cepeda Espinosa, Manuel José. 1993a. *Introducción a la Constitución de 1991. Hacia un Nuevo Constitucionalismo*. Bogotá: Presidencia de la República, Consejería para el Desarrollo de la Constitución.

1993b. *La Constituyente por Dentro. Mitos y Realidades*. Bogotá: Presidencia de la República, Consejería para el Desarrollo de la Constitución.

2007. *Polémicas Constitucionales*. Bogotá: Legis Editores, S.A.

Chambers, Simone. 2004. "Democracy, Popular Sovereignty, and Constitutional Legitimacy." *Constellations* 11(2): 153–173.

Combellas, Ricardo. 2010. "La Venezuela de la V República: la Reforma Política y sus Implicaciones Institucionales" in *Desafíos de la Gobernabilidad Democrática. Reformas Político-Institucionales y Movimientos Sociales en la Región Andina*. Martin Tanaka and Francine Jacome (eds.) Lima: Instiuto de Estudios Peruanos, International Development Research Centre, 149–172.

Corrales, Javier and Michael Penfold-Becerra. 2007. "Venezuela: Crowding Out the Opposition." *Journal of Democracy* 18(2): 99–113.

Corrales, Javier. 2018. *Fixing Democracy: Why Constitutional Change Often Fails to Enhance Democracy in Latin America*. Oxford: Oxford University Press.

Dahl, Robert A. 1971. *Polyarchy: Participation and Opposition*. New Haven: Yale University Press.

Dugas, John C. 2001. "The Origin, Impact and Demise of the 1989–1990 Colombian Student Movement: Insights from Social Movement Theory." *Journal of Latin American Studies* 33(4): 807–837.

Elkins, Zachary, Tom Ginsburg, and James Melton. 2009. *The Endurance of National Constitutions*. Cambridge: Cambridge University Press.

Elster, Jon, and Rune Slagstad. 1988. *Constitutionalism and Democracy*. Cambridge: Cambridge University Press, 1–45.

Figueroa García-Herreros, Nicolás. 2012. "Counter-Hegemonic Constitutionalism: The Case of Colombia." *Constellations* 19(2): 235–247.

Gargarella, Roberto, and Christian Courtis. 2009. "El nuevo constitucionalismo latinoamericano: promesas e interrogantes" in *Serie Políticas Sociales*. Santiago de Chile: CEPAL – Naciones Unidas, ASDI.

Hart, Vivien. 2003. "Democratic Constitution Making." Special Report, No. 107, United States Institute of Peace.

Hartlyn, Jonathan. 1988. *The Politics of Coalition Rule in Colombia*. Cambridge: Cambridge University Press.

Hartlyn, Jonathan, and Juan Pablo Luna. 2009. *Constitutional Reform in Contemporary Latin America: A Framework for Analysis*. Paper delivered at the meeting of the International Association of Political Science, IPSA, Santiago de Chile, July 12–16.

Hirschman, Albert O. 1970. *Exit, Voice and Loyalty: Responses to Decline in Firms, Organizations and States*. Boston: Harvard University Press.

Kornblith, Miriam. 1998. *Venezuela en los noventa: Las crisis de la democracia*. Caracas: UCV and Ediciones IESA.

Lemaitre Ripoll, Julieta. 2009. *El derecho como conjuro. Fetichismo legal, violencia y movimientos sociales*. Bogotá: Siglo del Hombre Editores – Universidad de los Andes.

Levitsky, Steven, and Lucan A. Way. 2010. "Why Democracy Needs a Level Playing Field." *Journal of Democracy* 21(1): 57–68.

López Maya, Margarita. 2006. *Del viernes negro al referendo revocatorio*. Caracas: Alfadil Ediciones.

Lora, Eduardo, and Carlos Scaartascini (eds.) 2010. *Consecuencias Imprevistas de la Constitucion de 1991: la influencia de la política en las políticas económicas*. Bogotá: Alfaomega Colombiana – Fedesarrollo.

Moehler, Devra. 2008. *Distrusting Democrats: Outcomes of Participatory Constitution Making*. Ann Arbor: University of Michigan Press.

Negretto, Gabriel. 1999. "Constitution Making and Institutional Design: The Transformation of Presidentialism in Argentina." *Archives Européens de Sociologie* XL(2): 193–232.

2009a. "Paradojas de la Reforma Constitucional en América Latina." *Journal of Democracy en Español* 1(1): 38–54.

2009b. "Political Parties and Institutional Design: Explaining Constitutional Choice in Latin America." *British Journal of Political Science* 31(1): 17–139.

2012. "Replacing and Amending Constitutions: The Logic of Constitutional Change in Latin America." *Law and Society Review* 46(4): 749–779.

2013. *Making Constitutions. Presidents, Parties, and Institutional Choice in Latin America*. New York: Cambridge University Press.

Neuman, Laura, and Jennifer McCoy. 2001. "Defining the 'Bolivarian Revolution': Hugo Chávez' Venezuela." *Current History* 100(643): 80–85.

Nolte, Detlef, and Almut Schilling-Vacaflor. 2012. *New Constitutionalism in Latin America. Promises and Practices*. Farnham: Ashgate Publishing Limited.

Palacio Rudas, Alfonso. 1994. *El Congreso en la Constitucion de 1991: del Edificio Fenix Al Centro de Convenciones*. Bogotá: Tercer Mundo Editores.

Payne, Mark, Daniel Zovatto, and Mercedes Mateo Diaz. 2006. Democracies in Development: Politics and Reform in Latin America. Washington D.C.:Inter-American Development Bank.

Pinzón de Lewin, Patricia. 1991. "Las elecciones de 1990" in *Los nuevos retos electorales. Colombia 1990: la antesala del cambio*. Ruben Sánchez David (ed.) Bogotá: CEREC – Universidad de Los Andes, 116–132.

Pizarro, Eduardo, and Ana María Bejarano. 2007. "Political Reform after 1991: What Still Needs to be Reformed?" in *Peace, Democracy, and Human Rights in Colombia*. Christopher Welna and Gustavo Gallón (eds.) South Bend: University of Notre Dame Press, 167–201.

Skidmore, Thomas, Peter Smith, and James Green. 2010. *Modern Latin America*. Oxford: Oxford University Press.

Segura, Renata, and Ana María Bejarano. 2004. "Ni una asamblea más sin nosotros! Exclusion, Inclusion, and the Politics of Constitution making in the Andes." *Constellations* 11 (2): 217–236.

Tilly, Charles. 2007. *Democracy*. Cambridge: Cambridge University Press.

Valencia Villa, Hernando. 1989. "De las guerras constitucionales en Colombia. Capitulo LXVIII: un informe sobre la reforma Barco." In *Análisis Político*, No. 6: 80–97.

2010. *Cartas de Batalla: una crítica del constitucionalismo colombiano*. Bogotá: Panamericana Editorial.

Widner, Jennifer A. 2013. *Constitutions and Consequences: Curbing Executive Abuse of Power*. Paper delivered at the LASA-Mellon Foundation workshop "The Gap from Parchment to Practice: Ambivalent Effects of Constitutions in Democratizing Countries," Washington, DC, May 28–29.

7

Democratic Constitutional Replacements and Majoritarian Politics

The Cases of Poland (1993–1997) and Hungary (2010–2011)

Gabriel L. Negretto and Solongo Wandan

The recent constitution-making processes in Poland and Hungary present an interesting contrast that can shed light on the role of majoritarian politics in democratic constitutional replacements and their impact on subsequent levels of democratization. Just as in Poland, in Hungary the new constitution was adopted after a sharp swing in electoral support from incumbent to challenger parties. In both countries, the newly elected governments had the formal capacity to control the process by excluding opposition interests. However, whereas in Poland the constitution was in the end the result of a compromise among a plurality of political interests, in Hungary the government unilaterally imposed the constitution with negative consequences for the future of democracy in the country. What explains these different outcomes?

In this chapter, we argue that a more consensual constitution-making process was possible in Poland because opposition forces, in spite of their meager results in terms of parliamentary representation, were able to exert influence over the process through extra-institutional and institutional means. In contrast to Hungary, where opposition groups were extremely weak or discredited, in Poland extra-parliamentary opposition maintained significant support among voters and functioned as an effective *political* constraint on dominant parties. Thanks to their strength outside formal political institutions, opposition forces in Poland were able to induce incumbents to make changes in the constitution-making procedures that allowed them to have some clout in the drafting of the constitution. Moreover, due to these contrasting interactions at the elite level, although mechanisms of direct citizen participation were implemented in both cases, only in Poland did they reinforce and complement channels of representation as part of a democratic articulation of citizen preferences into the process.

We begin the chapter by discussing the political and procedural challenges of replacing constitutions in regularly elected parliaments. Absent any specific and clear regulations of a constitutional nature, these bodies would make decisions concerning the constitution according to regular parliamentary procedures. As the Hungarian example in Section II shows, when power is unevenly distributed, dominant parties can exploit these rules to justify excluding the opposition, and control the process. However, the case of Poland analyzed in Section III shows that a seemingly comparable balance-of-power shift may result in different outcomes if the opposition maintains sufficient social support outside formal representative channels. Section IV discusses how the dynamics of each process at the elite level had a spillover effect on the nature and impact of the mechanisms of direct popular participation that were implemented. We conclude by summarizing the implications of the comparative analysis for understanding constitutional replacements in democratic orders.

I INTRA-DEMOCRATIC CONSTITUTIONAL REPLACEMENTS THROUGH CONSTITUENT LEGISLATURES

As noted in Chapter 1, constitutional replacements within democratic regimes have a different nature from similar events that occur during revolutions and democratic transitions. Whereas in revolutions and democratic transitions constitution making aims at creating new institutional structures that are radically opposed to, or negate those of the old regime, the goal during intra-democratic constitutional change is usually the deepening of representative institutions and the strengthening of accountability mechanisms. Constitutional replacements in democratic regimes also face specific constraints when it comes to determining the procedural rules of the drafting process.

During successful revolutions, drafting rules are dictated by new power holders and decided under the exclusion of members of the old elite. In a transition to democracy, the influence of authoritarian elites may vary. They may be displaced, as in a revolution, when the authoritarian regime collapses, or, if the democratic opposition is too weak, authoritarian elites may even have a dominant role in determining the rules of the drafting process. In negotiated transitions, procedural rules may be the result of compromises between government and opposition members. In all cases of transition, however, institutions of the old regime, even if they played a role in the initial stages of the drafting process, must at some point be dissolved and relinquish power.

The situation is different in a democratic regime. Here, established parties and political elites, even if discredited, have emerged out of free and fair elections, and thus have a legitimate claim to be involved in the drafting of a new constitution. Parliaments and popularly elected presidents, and even constitutional courts, cannot be fully excluded from the process if they make decisions under the indirect or direct authorization of the voters. This diversity of legitimate claims to political power in democratic regimes should result in plural and cooperative rules for replacing the constitution through an inclusive process at both the elite and citizen level.

However, claims to such plural involvement during constitution making based on popular vote share can also have the opposite effect. If elections result in highly uneven outcomes that lead to a radical shift in the balance of power, governing parties can exploit electoral results as a popular mandate to adopt a new constitution. This is precisely how Fidesz-KDNP in Hungary justified its decision to adopt a new constitution; namely, translating the "revolution in the voting booth" into a constitutional revolution to complete the unfulfilled promise of the 1989 transition (see Scheppele 2011; Brodsky 2015; Szilágyi and Bozóki 2015). In such a situation, constitution making can easily turn into a strategy to capture state power in favor of a particular group.

The risk of such an outcome is high when the constitution is written by a special convention. Although election of an independent convention may allow for a stricter separation between ordinary and constitutional rule making, placing higher standards of consensus for the latter, history shows that these bodies often transgress the legal limits of their mandate and base their supposedly higher democratic legitimacy on contingent electoral majorities (see Negretto 2018). Constituent legislatures are often seen as "constituted" bodies and thus less likely to invoke sovereign power and claim the right to intervene in the functions of the other branches of government. From this perspective, it is easier to subject their mission to preexisting regulations stipulating, for instance, more consensual procedures than those of ordinary lawmaking.[1] As we will see, however, even in the presence of such procedures constituent legislatures can also fall prey of majoritarian political groups if large swings in electoral support provide these groups with the capacity to activate a constitution-making process and manipulate its rules on their behalf.

An ordinary legislature would always follow regular house rules and proceedings as a fallback option to reach constitutional decisions. For example, the drafting of the 1992 Small Constitution in Poland was undertaken in a committee created by parties in the 1991–1993 parliament, the "Extraordinary Committee on the Draft of the Constitutional Act on the Appointment and Dismissal of Government and Other Changes to the Highest State Organs" (Chruściak and Osiatyński 2001, 338, our translation). Similarly, the decision on the distribution of seats and leadership roles during the drafting of a constitution would be made, as in the case of regular law-making, on the basis of the balance of power between parties in parliament – that is, their concrete share of the vote. In the 1993 Polish parliament, the leader of the party with the highest vote share, Aleksander Kwasniewski, also led the parliamentary Constitutional Committee (see Chruściak and Osiatyński 2001, 222).

Following a similar logic, if constitutional regulations do not prescribe a different requirement, a political force that was previously excluded from government and

---

[1] This expectation holds in practice. Although most constitution-making bodies in the world make decisions by majority rule, those that have passed new constitutions by qualified majority are more often constituent legislatures than special conventions. See Negretto (2017).

wins a parliamentary election with substantial electoral support can interpret this result as a mandate not only to change the legislative status quo but also to reshape constitutional structures. As the 2010–2011 process in Hungary shows, parliamentary elections can be exploited and manipulated in this way. In Hungary, a new government pushed through the new constitution utilizing regular parliamentary procedures and forums, due to their landslide electoral victory and the extraordinary share of parliamentary seats it obtained from it. The subsequent comparison with the drafting of the 1997 Polish Constitution shows that a less drastic shift in electoral support for challenger parties, a more divided government coalition, and a stronger social support enjoyed by opposition forces in Poland made possible a more cooperative and pluralistic process in spite of the formal control that the government coalition could have over it.

II UNCONSTRAINED MAJORITARIAN POLITICS IN CONSTITUTION MAKING: HUNGARY (2010–2011)

Since transitioning to democracy in 1989/90, Hungary has built a stable multi-party democracy with a unicameral parliamentary system checked by a strong and respected Constitutional Court. Its post-transition constitutional framework did not result from a legal break or rupture but from a series of negotiated amendments to the 1949 Communist Constitution. Representatives of government and opposition met in the Round Table Talks of 1989 and decided to postpone the adoption of a new constitution while using the amendment procedure of the old constitution to fundamentally transform Hungary's political system (see Szikinger 2001). What the amended constitution lacked in democratic legitimation – its drafters were not elected and the constitutional settlement was never put to a popular referendum – it provided in functionality. In fact, it proved so successful that in democratic Hungary there was simply no systemic need to go through a costly constitutional drafting process (see Kis 2012; Scheppele 2014).

Thus, at the time of the 2010 parliamentary election, Hungary was facing no system-threatening political or constitutional crisis and the adoption of a new constitution was not an important social demand. Hungarian voters were, however, clearly ready for political change. Tired of the political scandals and ineptitude of the previous left-wing governing coalition, a clear electoral majority expressed their dissatisfaction at the voting booth by supporting the conservative Fidesz (Hungarian Civic Alliance), which ran on a joint list with the Christian Democratic People's Party (KDNP) (see Gorondi 2006; Szilágyi and Bozóki 2015). The popular vote for Fidesz–KDNP thus must be understood as much as a vote *against* the status quo as a vote *for* its political platform.

However we interpret the outcome, the shift in electoral preferences was quite significant and it had a substantial impact in the distribution of institutional resources across the two main political forces at the time, the Hungarian Socialist

TABLE 7.1 *Hungary's shift in electoral support and institutional resources across the main parties, 2006–2010*

Party/coalition	L-R[a]	Percentage of votes		Percentage of seats	
		2006	2010	2006	2010
Hungarian Socialist Party (MSZP)	2.9	43.2	19.3 (−23.9)	49.2	15.3 (−33.9)
Fidesz + KDNP	6.5	42	52.7 (+10.7)	42.5	68.1 (+25.6)
Alliance of Free Democrats (SzDSz)	4.0	6.5	0.25 (−6.25)	5.2	0 (−5.2)
Hungarian Democratic Forum (MDF)	6.5	5	2.2 (−2.8)	2.8	0 (−2.8)
Jobbik Movement	8.8	2	16.7 (+14.7)	0	12.2 (+12.2)
Politics can be Different (LMP)	2.5	–	7.5	–	4.1

[a] Left-Right position on a continuous scale ranging from 1 (extreme left) to 10 (extreme right).
Source: authors, based on Parliaments and Governments Database (www.parlgov.org)

Party (MSZP) and Fidesz-KDNP (Fidesz). As shown in Table 7.1, between the 2006 and 2010 elections, the electoral support of MSZP went from 43.2 to 19.3 percent, which in turn translated in a decline in its share of parliamentary seats from 49.2 to 15.3 percent. Fidesz, in turn, went from 42 to 52.7 percent in electoral support, and from 42.5 to 68.1 percent in its share of parliamentary seats.

Shortly after the election, Fidesz swiftly took action to institutionally protect and consolidate its electoral victory. To this end, the new government issued a series of constitutional amendments and legislative acts to weaken key institutional checks and balances, and, in a parallel process, sought to entrench its hold on power in a new constitution in 2011. The justification for a constitution-making process could be found in the failure of previous efforts to adopt a new constitution, particularly during the 1994–1998 legislature (see Szikinger 2001). Yet the most immediate factor was that, as a result of the election and a highly disproportional electoral system, Fidez gained control of 68 percent of legislative seats – that is, more than the two-thirds required by the existing constitution to introduce amendments.

It has been argued that this outcome was primarily the result of "mistakes of constitutional design" rather than specific political dynamics (see Bánkuti, Halmai, and Scheppele 2012, 138). Particularly problematic in this view was the continued use of the amendment procedure of the revised 1949 constitution, which required a single two-thirds vote in parliament to change any of its provisions (Bánkuti, Halmai, and Scheppele 2012, 139). This rule continued to exist even after the government elected in 1994 established a four-fifths "super" supermajority to decide the rules of a future process of constitutional replacement in a consensual manner (see Arato 2011a).[2]

It is clear that when formal rules are ambiguous or subject to alternative interpretations, their effective implementation would depend on the actual distribution

---

[2] See also Arato's "Constitution Making in Hungary and the 4/5 Rule." www.iconnectblog.com/2011/04/arato-on-constitution-making-in-hungary-and-the-45-rule.

of political power. The coexistence of a lightly entrenched constitution with a replacement rule that itself was not placed out of the reach of elected majorities is unproblematic as long as power is shared among a plurality of parties in parliament (see Scheppele 2014, 62). In this case, parties in parliament have to compromise and cooperate to muster the required constitutional majorities, thus ensuring that a broad range of interests are considered in the adoption of constitutional amendments, as well as in the activation and implementation of a new drafting process. What legislators in 1994 did not foresee, however, are the effects of regular political dynamics on constitutional procedures when power in parliament is concentrated instead of diffused.

When the Fidesz–KDNP party coalition rose to power with control over two-thirds of parliamentary seats in April 2010, it was able to realize its constitutional project by utilizing and manipulating regular parliamentary procedures. Shortly after gaining office, the new government established an Ad Hoc Parliamentary Committee for the Preparation of the Constitution in June 2010, through Parliamentary Resolution 47/2010 (VI. 29) (see Tóth 2012, 458, 493). Membership in the Committee was decided on the basis of the distribution of seats in parliament, so that of the forty-five seats, the government held thirty and the opposition fifteen (see Tóth 2012, 459). The Committee's six thematic working groups had until December 31, 2010, so the Resolution stated, to develop a "concept paper" on the fundamental principles for the new constitution in parliament (Comments of Hungarian NGOs 2013, 2). The Committee's constitutional principles, developed through substantial input from civil society and, at least initially, opposition parties, were submitted to Parliament as a draft resolution on December 20, 2010 (Tóth 2012, 459).[3]

However, the impact of this "first stage" of constitution making on the second round of drafting in Parliament was severely limited. Parallel to the drafting process, which lasted until April 2011, the new government rushed through hundreds of new laws, including twelve amendments to the old constitution that together changed more than fifty individual provisions (Bánkuti et al. 2012, 6). Many of these amendments were meant to weaken or limit constraints on parliamentary power; for example, by changing the powers and composition of the Constitutional Court, and by abolishing the amendment that required a four-fifths threshold to adopt the procedural rules for a new drafting process (see Tóth 2012, 458). In this flurry of legislation, the new government emphasized speed over process; the constitutional and legislative initiatives were rushed through parliament by using the parliamentary procedure of a private member's bill (Bánkuti et al. 2012, 4).

---

[3] To protest the new government's barrage of constitutional amendments, particularly those aimed to limit the powers of the Constitutional Court, opposition parties, the Hungarian Socialist Party and LMP announced on October 26, 2010, that they would no longer participate in the work of the Ad Hoc Committee; the far-right wing party Jobbik followed suit on November 16, 2010. See Comments of Hungarian NGOs, 3.

Under the rules of parliamentary procedure in Hungary, a private member's bill can be used to streamline the legislative process by bypassing the consultation stage, during which civil society and opposition parties would have the chance to comment on proposed legislation. As a private member's bill, a new law could be introduced without any advance notice to parties that might oppose the law or be affected by it (Bánkuti, et al. 2012, 4). By utilizing this procedure, the government could take any of its legislative initiatives in parliament, including constitutional amendments or even the new constitution, from first proposal to full effect in a very short period of time, sometimes in a matter of days (Bánkuti et al. 2012, 4).

With crucial institutional checks out of the way or weakened, the new government could carry out the second stage of the drafting process without any challenges from opposition parties or institutions. Once parliament had received the constitutional principles in the form of a draft resolution, the review process was again expedited in order to minimize parliamentary debate around the draft. The first reading of the draft, which was a general debate that included all parties, was concluded within two days, and the second reading, meant as a debate about the details of the concept paper, lasted for less than five hours (Comments of Hungarian NGOs 2013, 3). Additionally, Fidesz MPs ensured that the content and scope of the draft Resolution would in practice be meaningless for the second round of drafting.

Substantively, the amended Resolution explicitly denied the constitutional principles any binding character by stating that Parliament could proceed "with or without taking into consideration" the work of the Ad Hoc Committee (Scheppele 2014, 16). Procedurally, the Resolution, passed on 7 March as Resolution 9/2011 on the Preparation for the Adoption of the New Constitution, restricted the time parliamentary groups had available to develop and submit constitutional proposals to only a few days (Scheppele 2014, 64). The week-long second round of constitutional drafting took place under complete secrecy; since there are no official records or reports, it is not clear who drafted or was consulted in the creation of the final constitutional text. On March 15, 2011, the new constitution was introduced to Parliament as an ordinary piece of legislation – as a private member's bill – by two Fidesz representatives. In this manner, the new constitution was adopted by the votes of the Fidesz–KDNP bloc in April 2011, and entered into force on January 1, 2012 (Scheppele 2014, 65).

III CONSTRAINED MAJORITARIAN POLITICS IN CONSTITUTION MAKING: POLAND (1993–1997)

The drafting of the Polish Constitution in 1993–1997 is usually studied as part of the country's transition to democracy that began in 1989, when government and opposition leaders negotiated a peaceful transition of power. In this view, the constitutional deliberations in the 1993–1997 parliament are just the final stage in a long and winding drafting process. In 1989, however, none of the participants intended that the completion of the constitution would take a total of eight years, through three parliamentary and two presidential elections. Polish drafters had initially hoped to adopt a new democratic constitution on May 3, 1991, the 200th anniversary of Poland's first Constitution (Garlicki and Garlicka 2010, 393). According to some observers, the reason why this symbolic completion date was not met lies in the unmediated influence that ordinary representative politics had on the constitution-making process (Osiatyński 1994).

In post-transition Poland, the outcomes of successive electoral processes had a clear impact on the development of the future constitution. After the first partly free election in June 1989, both houses of parliament set up Constitutional Committees in December 1989 to begin developing draft proposals (see Chruściak and Osiatyński 2001, 12, 38). Over the course of the following year, however, partisan as well as institutional conflicts between executive and legislative branches led to the dissolution of parliament, and with it, put an end to the constitution-making process (see Gortat 1993; Millard 1994; Wasilewski and Wnuk-Lipinski 1995).

The constitutional deliberations of the next parliament, elected in 1991, did not fare better. A highly proportional electoral law led to a hyper-fragmented parliament composed of twenty-nine parties that made the formation of stable coalitions nearly impossible (see Szczerbiak 2004). After several weak government coalitions and continued splits and defections in the party system, Parliament was again dissolved in 1993. In spite of this instability, political actors in Poland still had to find a way to adapt the existing constitution to new political conditions.

Up to 1993, adaptation of the old 1952 constitution to the democratic regime was undertaken in a way similar to Hungary's – that is, using the existing amendment rule, which also required a two-thirds vote in parliament to alter the constitutional text (see Chruściak and Osiatyński 2001, 38). The first parliament, from 1989 to 1991, utilized the amendment rule to change or delete key political, judicial, and economic provisions of the 1952 Constitution, and thus to create a legal basis for the democratization of institutions (Brzezinski 1991; Brzezinski 1993; Brzezinski and Garlicki 1995). One of the most important of these, a provision that stated that Poland is a "democratic state ruled by law," paved the way for new legislation to strengthen the independence of judges and grant more powers of oversight to the country's highest courts (Brzezinski 1991; Brzezinski and Garlicki 1995).[4] Particularly important were the reforms to the Constitutional Tribunal, a body of judicial review created in 1985 that gained significant powers to adjudicate the conformity of laws to the Constitution.[5]

---

[4] In a different translation, the amendment states that "Poland is a democratic legal State"; however, most Polish experts agree on "democratic state ruled by law." See Brzezisnki and Garlicki (1995, 108).

[5] Even though individuals were not able to access the court, it held considerable powers of abstract review. During 1990–1991, over two-thirds of the statutes reviewed by the Tribunal were held to be unconstitutional or were hastily modified by Parliament to avoid unfavorable Tribunal decisions. See Brzezisnki and Garlicki (1995, 32).

The next parliament, elected in 1991, continued these efforts by focusing on the institutional architecture in place to regulate the relations between the president and parliament. At the time of its creation in April 1989, the office of the president had been endowed with very broad yet undefined powers, which, in the climate of increasing political polarization and volatility in the party system, had led to unstable governments as well as legislative deadlock (Garlicki and Garlicka 2010, 403). An interim constitution, called the Small Constitution, adopted in October 1992 through the two-thirds amendment rule, addressed these problems by specifying and limiting the powers of the president (Osiatyński 1992). This means that even though up to 1993 the drafting of a new constitution had failed; Polish constituent legislators had nevertheless succeeded in creating a constitutional framework that safeguarded the democratic political process.

Only in the third parliament, 1993–1997, were political constellations stable enough to draft and adopt a new constitution (Sanford 2002; Szczerbiak 2004). However, the peculiar trait of the 1993–1997 parliament was that its representation was less encompassing and more biased than previous legislatures. Specifically, two left-wing parties, the Democratic Left Alliance (Sojusz Lewicy Demokratycznej, SLD) and the Polish People's (or Peasants') Party (Polskie Stronnictwo Ludowe, PSL), which later formed a government coalition, won the largest share of votes and reached a qualified majority of seats in parliament. By contrast, most parties of the right and center-right, including some that were part of the 1989 Round Table negotiations or close to the opposition forces that participated in it, were excluded from parliament. From an institutional point of view, then, the outcome of the 1993 elections placed Poland in a situation comparable to that of Hungary after the 2010 election. Although the previous parliament had issued a detailed set of rules in 1992 regulating the drafting and adoption of a new constitution, the Constitutional Law on the Procedure for Preparing and Enacting the Constitution, these rules coexisted with and were not exempt from being altered using the two-thirds amendment rule. Yet both the dynamics of the process and the outcome were radically different in Poland than in Hungary.

Whereas the government elected in Hungary in 2010 was confrontational and exclusionary as regards the creation of a new constitution, the new Polish government behaved in a consensual manner, basically in the spirit of the 1989 Round Table talks. Instead of exploiting their legislative advantage, majoritarian parties in Poland decided to increase representation in the drafting body by inviting opposition and popular constitutional proposals. They also included a larger number of actors in the reform coalition and made several concessions to the demands of the extra-parliamentary opposition. This explains why Hungary's 2011 constitution significantly weakened the previous democratic regime, while Poland's 1997 constitution not only preserved but further expanded the democratic provisions of the constitutional framework created by previous parliaments. Several factors account for these contrasting outcomes.

TABLE 7.2 *Poland's shift in electoral support and institutional resources across the main parties, 1991–1993[a]*

Party/coalition	L-R[c]	Percentage of votes		Percentage of seats	
		1991	1993	1991	1993
Democratic Left Alliance (SLD)	2.8	12	20.4 (+8.4)	13	37.2 (+ 24.2)
Polish People's Party (PSL)	4.2	8.7	15.4 (+6.7)	10.4	28.7 (+18.3)
Democratic Union (UD)	5.2	12.3	10.6 (−1.7)	13.5	16.1 (+2.6)
Labor Union (UP)[b]	2.0	2.1	7.3 (+5.2)	0.9	8.9 (+8.0)
Non-party block (BBWR)	6.2	–	5.4	–	3.5
Confederation for Independent Poland (KPN)	5.8	7.5	5.8 (−1.7)	10	4.8 (−5.2)
Christian National Union (ZchN)	7.4	8.7	6.4 (−2.3)	10.7	0 (−10.7)
Solidarity Citizens' Committee (KOS)	3.3	5.1	4.9 (−0.2)	5.9	0 (−5.9)
Centre Agreement (PC)	5.6	8.7	4.4 (−4.3)	9.6	0 (−9.6)
Liberal Democratic Congress (KLD)	5.3	7.5	4.0 (−3.5)	8.0	0 (−8.0)
Other parties	–	27.4	15.4	18	0 (−18)

[a] Lower chamber (Sejm).
[b] Labor solidarity in 1991.
[c] Left-Right position on a continuous scale ranging from 1 (extreme left) to 10 (extreme right)
Source: authors, based on Parliaments and Governments Database (www.parlgov.org)

In the first place, if we look at the distribution of votes rather than seats and assume that the former reflects the actual level of societal support of parties, it seems clear that the shift in voter preferences in Poland was much less dramatic than in Hungary. As shown in Table 7.2, although the SLD and PSL, the two largest parties that formed a government coalition after the 1993 election, increased their popular support compared to the previous election, they obtained together only 35 percent of the vote in the Sejm election. In addition, although the two government parties were ideologically close and together won 303 of 460 seats (65.9 percent), they were not supported by voters as a single electoral alliance with a homogenous political program. It should also be noted that although the success of the left was clear, a party with historical links with Solidarność, the centrist Democratic Union (UD), suffered a very small decline of in its electoral support (less than 2 percent) and it actually increased its share of parliamentary seats from 13.5 to 16.1 percent. Finally, a political group created by Lech Wałęsa for this election (the Non-party block or BBWR) was able to reach a small share of votes and seats.

The most significant and observable fact in this election is not so much a radical swing in the mood of the electorate as the disproportionality between votes and seats. Whereas about a third of the total electorate in Poland was left without parliamentary representation, the SLD and PSL together obtained control over virtually two-thirds of parliament with just a minority of the popular vote. As several authors have pointed out, the two main variables that explain this result were the new electoral system and the failure of the right to coalesce in response to the rules of electoral competition (see Millard 1993; Kaminski, Lissowski, and Swistak 1998; Szczerbiak 2004).

In 1991, a highly proportional electoral law had created a hyper-fragmented parliament of 29 parties, in which the largest party (Democratic Union) won only 12.3 percent of the vote and 62 (out of 460) seats (see Szczerbiak 2004). To increase stability for the September 1993 election, a new electoral law set higher voting thresholds for parties and party coalitions, smaller district magnitudes, and a d'Hondt formula that favored larger parties (see Grzymala-Busse 2002, 214). These more restrictive provisions were particularly consequential for center-right parties, which, unable to build an electoral coalition and overcome fragmentation, failed to reach the minimum share of votes required by law and were thus excluded from the 1993–1997 parliament.

After many trials and tribulations involving dissolved and polarized parliaments, most parties in Poland agreed to adopt an electoral law that would facilitate stable governing coalitions by reducing the number of parties represented in Parliament. This stability, however, came at a price because a large percentage of all votes cast were left without parliamentary representation, and thus without agents to influence the work of the Constitutional Committee (see Herold and Wandan 2014; Wandan 2015).

The 1992 Constitutional Law on the Procedure for Preparing and Enacting the Constitution held that the Constitutional Committee of the National Assembly (both houses of parliament combined) would be composed of 10 percent of the members of each house of parliament, Sejm and Senate, in accordance with their share in seats. Its task was to prepare constitutional principles, and after submitting these for a general debate in the Sejm, to prepare a consolidated draft of the constitution (Garlicki and Garlicka 2010, 394–395). The consolidated draft had to undergo several readings in the National Assembly, during which the text could be further amended and changed. The final version of the constitution was to be approved by two-thirds of the vote of both Houses of Parliament, and adopted by a popular referendum (Garlicki and Garlicka 2010, 394).

For several center-right political groups with origins in Solidarność, the 1993 election resulted in a situation in which they not only were excluded from legislative and constitutional decision-making processes but also, more critically, in which both were dominated by successor parties of the former communist regime. In spite of the presence of UD (transformed into Freedom Union or UW in 1994, after an alliance with the Liberal Democratic Congress party) and BBWR in parliament, the drafting of Poland's new democratic constitution was now primarily in the hands of the post-communist SLD and PSL. Therefore, right from the start, the work of the parties represented in the Constitutional Committee had to contend with accusations of its unrepresentative and therefore illegitimate character by excluded parties and their affiliate organizations (Herold and Wandan 2014; Wandan 2015).

This critique soon turned into concrete political action intended to show the level of social support enjoyed by the extra-parliamentary opposition. At the end of 1993, only a few months after the work of the official Committee had begun, Marian Krzaklewski, then leader of the Solidarność trade union, initiated a separate constitution-making process. To this end he invited legal scholars and trade union members to draft an alternative "citizen constitution," the Citizens' Constitutional Project Solidarność (Obywatelski Projekt Konstytucji Solidarności) (Wandan 2015). In this drafting process, representatives of the "nation," as opposed to a mere electorate, were supposed to realize the values and ideals of those that were not represented in Parliament. The mobilization around this draft and the support the initiative received from key Polish institutions such as the Catholic Church and center-right parties forced the government to introduce important procedural changes to the 1992 law (Herold and Wandan 2014).

In April 1994, as a response to mounting extra-parliamentary opposition, Parliament amended the 1992 Constitutional Law on the Procedure for Preparing and Enacting the Constitution. To increase the level of representation in the Committee, all drafts submitted in the previous parliament could be re-submitted. Additionally, and most importantly, the amendment made it possible for the Committee to consider popular drafts submitted with the support of at least 500,000 signatures. In reaction to this reform, within only one month, in May 1994, the Solidarność citizen draft had collected 900,000 signatures and was thus accepted by the Committee for consideration. While these significant procedural concessions were meant to reestablish Parliament as a central drafting forum and increase representation, they nevertheless were not able to stifle the critique of opposition parties outside (Herold and Wandan 2014).

In 1996, when the drafting process was almost completed, Krzaklewski described the work of the Committee as a "postcommunist conspiracy" against the Polish nation, the consequences of which would be no less grave than the "onslaught of the Bolshevik Red Army in 1920" (Brier 2006, 89). In November 1995, center-right parties had had to stomach another no less symbolically charged electoral result. Aleksander Kwasniewski, SLD party leader and head of the Constitutional Committee, won the presidential election against incumbent and Solidarność's most charismatic leader, Lech Wałęsa. As a result, post-communist parties controlled Poland's central political institutions, the presidency, Parliament, and with it the Constitutional Committee; therefore, claims of a "conspiracy" and "a resurgence of communist oppression" continued to effectively mobilize Krzaklewski's supporters.

In a speech in front of both Houses of Parliament on February 25, 1997, Krzaklewski proposed that in the concluding popular referendum, citizens should be able to vote on two constitutions, the official draft as well as the "citizen constitution" (Krzaklewski 1997). By then, the Solidarność draft had garnered a staggering two million signatures and was supported by the formation of a new party, the Solidarity

Electoral Action (Akcja Wyborcza Solidarność, AWS).[6] Created in 1996 by Krzaklewski, AWS united over thirty center-right parties to effectively compete in the upcoming parliamentary election, scheduled for September 1997 (Szczerbiak 2004, 64). Although the government did not accept the proposal of submitting the two proposals to popular vote, the extra-institutional and increasingly institutionalized contestation from opposition forces had an impact on the content of deliberations in the official Constitutional Committee. In particular, several changes to the content of the preamble and rights provisions of the draft constitution were adopted as a concession to outside demands (Herold and Wandan 2014; Wandan 2014).

Finally, it is crucial to emphasize that in spite of the fact that the SLD and the PSL had formal power to control the process, the government coalition was not monolithic in its conception of the new constitution. Although both parties had a leftist platform and had collaborated in the past, the parliamentary groups that represented these parties had different ideological and economic visions on issues such as the Christian character of Polish society, the method of privatization, and state support for agriculture (see Wyrzykowski 2001). Moreover, besides making concessions to the views of the extra-parliamentary opposition, the government coalition also sought to incorporate other parties in the parliamentary reform coalition in order to increase support in the final vote to pass the constitution before submitting it to a popular referendum. In this respect, representatives of the Labor Union (UP) and the Freedom Union (UW) were part of the constitutional coalition in the final stages of the process (Garlicki and Garlicka 2010).

In sum, in Poland extra-parliamentary opposition effectively constrained the actions of an otherwise unconstrained government. As stated earlier, no rule, constitutional or otherwise, prevented the SLD-PSL coalition from dominating the constitution-making process; on the contrary, formally it controlled all relevant political institutions. Successful extra-parliamentary opposition, however, functioned as *political* constraint on majoritarian decision making, with the result that procedural rules were altered to increase rather than diminish plural representation in the drafting body. In Hungary, this crucial element was missing. Within parliament, opposition parties were too weak or too inexperienced to effectively respond to Fidesz–KDNP's barrage of constitutional changes after the election. Outside parliament, their social support was meager. While some of the government constitutional strategies and measures were met with outspoken protest from opposition parties and segments of the public, in comparison to Poland, the opposition was too ideologically divided or socially delegitimized to mobilize effectively against Fidesz's constitutional reform project from within or outside of parliament (Kis 2012, 13; Lembcke and Boulanger 2012, 284).

Representative mechanisms and channels of direct citizen participation are often considered as different dimensions of the same phenomenon of "inclusion" or

---

[6] On this, see Herold and Wandan (2014).

"popular participation" in constitution making (see Elkins, Ginsburg, and Melton 2009; Eisenstadt, LeVan, and Maboudi 2017). The cases of Hungary and Poland show that representation and participation are neither manifestations of the same phenomenon nor completely independent events. In particular, the comparison illustrates how the dynamics of cooperation at the elite level determine whether public input is simply a strategy aimed at masking an essentially centralized and exclusionary process or a complement that reinforces representative pluralism in democratic constitution making.

IV THE LINKS BETWEEN REPRESENTATION AND PARTICIPATION IN HUNGARY AND POLAND

As Negretto argues in Chapter 5 and Bejarano and Segura illustrate with the comparative analysis of Colombia and Venezuela in Chapter 6, when power is sufficiently diffused among parties, the drafting process is likely to allow for plural representation and compromise. By contrast, when power is concentrated without any effective contestation, the resulting procedural rules are likely to give an advantage to parties in power and exclude the opposition. The Hungarian and Polish processes suggest that these factors have a similar impact on the rules governing citizen participation in constitution making. Just as it was able to control and contain the input from opposition parties, Fidesz–KDNP's uncontested majority position in the constituent legislature also allowed it to severely limit the influence of citizens. In comparison, effective contestation against majority parties in the Polish parliament led to both the inclusion of opposition forces and an expansion of opportunities for genuine and active citizen participation. In other words, whereas in Hungary citizen participation worked as an instrument for the self-legitimation of the incumbent government, in Poland it provided a venue through which citizens and opposition forces without institutional representation were able to have a say in the drafting of the new constitution.

The two stages of Hungary's constitutional replacement process described earlier featured different forms of direct public consultation. In the first stage, the Ad Hoc Parliamentary Committee for the Preparation of the Constitution, a body composed of government and, initially, opposition parties, had the task of developing a draft of constitutional principles for Hungary's new constitution. The committee's proceedings were formally open to the public and broadly accessible. According to governmental self-assessment, several hundred written comments were received from "specialist individuals, state organs, and civil society organizations" (Comments of Hungarian NGOs, 2). The comments were made publicly available on the committee's website. Additionally, the Ad Hoc Committee also organized public hearings for stakeholder groups such as trade unions and churches (Comments of Hungarian NGOs, 2).

As discussed earlier, the draft constitutional principles that emerged out of this participatory first stage had no binding or constraining effects on the actual drafting process in the second stage. Up to the point when the draft principles were discussed and approved by parliament, they could still be amended and altered. Once the Ad Hoc Committee had submitted its draft principles to Parliament in December 2010, Fidesz MPs ensured that the content of the constitutional principles, and with it the input from the public, would in practice be meaningless for the drafting of the constitution. According to Resolution 9/2011 on the Preparation for the Adoption of the new Constitution, passed on March 7, Parliament could proceed "with or without taking into consideration" the work of the Ad Hoc Committee. As a result, the participatory first stage "was entirely disconnected from the second, secret stage of the constitutional drafting process" (Scheppele 2014, 65).

It is also questionable whether the second government initiative to directly involve citizens in the drafting process had any meaningful impact on constitutional deliberations in Parliament. In late February and early March 2011, the government conducted what it called a "social consultation" with the Hungarian public to solicit voter preferences on the content of the new constitution. To this end, a questionnaire consisting of twelve questions on "some of the national issues that were undecided at that point" was sent out to voters (Scheppele 2013). However, as scholars and independent observers such as the Hungarian Helsinki Committee have pointed out, the questions were more a "populist wish-list" on social and economic issues than meaningful queries to elucidate public opinion on constitutional design or the drafting process.

Whatever loose connection the questionnaire may have had with the drafting process, it is impossible to know whether or not its results affected constitutional deliberations. On the one hand, the questionnaires were sent out before the government's constitutional draft was submitted and they were returned before, during, and after the short one-month window between the time the constitution was introduced to Parliament on March 14 and its adoption in April 2011 (Scheppele 2013). Therefore, they cannot be viewed as an endorsement of the result. An actual ratification of the final constitutional text by popular vote was rejected by the governing parties, despite broad support for that option amongst citizens (see Tóth 2012, 459–460). On the other hand, since the drafting process in Parliament was secret, and since the government has not made the results of the social consultation public, it is impossible to compare the content of the final constitution with citizen preferences expressed in the questionnaires (Scheppele 2013).

In Hungary, the two episodes illustrate a more general problem of citizen participation during constitutional replacements in democratic regimes. When constitutional reform is initiated because of a radical shift in the balance of power, new governing parties can exploit their legislative dominance not only to marginalize the opposition, but also to manipulate participatory channels into window-dressing forms of democratic legitimation. Governments frequently use social consultations of the type utilized during the drafting process in Hungary to claim that their decisions derive from a democratic mandate rather than to seek meaningful citizen input.

Most of the procedural rules governing the drafting of the final 1997 constitution in Poland were the product of the previous constituent legislature. The 1992 Constitutional Law on the Procedure for Preparing and Enacting the Constitution included detailed provisions on the composition of the drafting body, voting procedures, and thresholds for decision-making as well as the various deliberative stages of the drafting process in parliament. In terms of citizen participation, the 1992 law held that the final constitutional text, after adoption in parliament, had to be ratified through a popular referendum. Mechanisms of participation were, however, strengthened by governing parties in the 1993–1997 parliament.

As we have already discussed, governing parties amended existing procedural rules to increase opportunities for direct citizen participation through the submission of reform proposals backed by citizen signatures. At the same time, some chairs of thematic committees invited members of nongovernmental organizations (NGO) to sit in on the meetings in order to increase transparency and public engagement (Wandan 2014). These openings of the process enabled civil society organizations to mobilize around the constitution-making process and formulate their own draft proposals. In addition to the Solidarność trade union and its affiliated groups, other civil society organizations also took advantage of this new mechanism.

For instance, a variety of environmental groups and think tanks in cooperation with green parliamentarians decided to organize "a process with the people," to develop constitutional provisions on environmental protection (Wandan 2014). To this end, a societal committee was established called "Ekologja w Konstytucji" (Ecology in the Constitution) in which representatives of grassroots environmental organizations were invited to participate. Even though the campaign ultimately failed to collect the necessary 500,000 signatures to make a formal submission, the constitutional proposal and the coalitions between green parliamentarians and civil society groups that were built in the process had a lasting effect on constitutional deliberations in parliament. As Wandan (2014) has described, through lobbying and informal contacts with members in the Constitutional Committee of the Parliament, in the end the proposal was considered during constitutional deliberations.

Although the impact of direct forms of citizen participation, such as consultation processes and referendums, on the drafting process is generally difficult to ascertain, it is clear that in the case of Poland, citizen input was more genuine and consequential than in Hungary. Not only were citizens who were deprived from representation in parliament able to use the mechanism of proposal submission to provide an alternative draft of the constitution in Poland (the "citizen constitution"), but as some observers have noted, this draft had a visible impact on the final writing of the constitution (see Wyrzykowski 2001). Moreover, the ratification of the constitution in a referendum only reinforced this effect due to the need of incumbents to satisfy opposition demands in order to reduce the number of votes against the new constitution.

What the comparison between the cases of Hungary and Poland suggests, in line with Bejarano and Segura's argument in Chapter 6, is that looking at direct participatory indicators alone may prove insufficient to ascertain the democratic qualities of a constitution-making process. The interaction between cooperation at the elite level and participation at the citizen level, on the one hand, and the interaction between informal and formal mechanisms of interest mediation, on the other, provide superior insights about this issue. As we have argued, it was the higher degree of collaboration among political elites combined with the stronger social support of extra-parliamentary opposition that made a democratic constitution-making process possible in Poland that exhibited better democratic qualities than a formally similar procedure in Hungary.

V CONCLUSIONS

Hungary's "constitutional coup" illustrates the complex set of challenges democracies face when constitutions are replaced as the result of a radical balance-of-power shift in representative institutions. When one party or a coalition of parties achieves a disproportionate share of the popular vote, the resulting dominance in the legislative process can be exploited to justify a majoritarian drafting process. With control over a supermajority of seats in parliament, the new government in Hungary was able to sidestep existing procedural constraints, as well as to manipulate regular parliamentary proceedings to realize its constitutional project. It single-handedly activated *and* set the rules for the drafting process. The outcome was a secretive, exclusionary drafting process that ignored opposition and popular voices, and resulted in a constitution specifically designed to preserve the power of the existing government.

The drafting of the 1997 constitution in Poland presents an interesting contrast. Although before the approval of the new constitution electoral support in parliament shifted to left-wing parties whose government was able to control the constitution-making process, the Polish constitution was, in the end, the result of a compromise among a plurality of political interests. As we have shown in this chapter, this outcome was possible mainly due to the support that opposition forces were able to retain in society and use to exert extra-institutional influence over the process. In Hungary, by contrast, opposition forces declined in both institutional and social support, thus paving the way for the government party's interpretation of the 2010 election as a mandate to unilaterally replace the constitution.

The claim of the Fidesz–KDNP government to have a broad "democratic mandate" for constitutional overhaul, and thus to dominate the drafting process as the most popular party was clearly questionable. As an established party that had been instrumental in shaping, and in fact consolidating, the post-1989 Hungarian constitutional framework, there is no doubt that Fidesz was aware of earlier debates over the adoption of a new constitution. It was certainly involved in the 1994–1995 attempt to regulate the drafting of a new constitution (Scheppele 2013). At the same time, however, the writing of a new constitution was not part of its party platform during the 2010 election campaign, or for that matter, of the platform of any other party competing in the election. By all accounts, after the important revisions introduced in 1989, Hungary's 1949 constitution provided for a stable, functioning political process. The new governing parties called for constitutional overhaul only *after* they were already firmly in power. Thus, the constitutional replacement process in Hungary amounts to the type of self-authorized, "revolutionary constitution making that all too easily steps over the threshold of dictatorship" (Arato 2009, 428).

The same problem did not occur during the drafting of the 1997 Polish constitution. In the lead-up to the 1993 parliamentary election, the Polish public knew that the constitution-making process that had failed in previous parliaments would again be restarted in the new parliament. Elected drafters, despite the vagaries of electoral laws, thus could legitimately claim to represent their constituents not only in the ordinary legislative process but also in important constitutional decisions. The significance and impact of such a "constitutional mandate" is illustrated in the subsequent mobilization and debate over legitimate representation in the drafting process. Political conflicts among parties over plural legitimate claims to exercise an electorally granted constitutional mandate generated effective political constraints on the drafting process. As a result, citizens in Poland indirectly and directly participated in the beginning, during, and after the conclusion of the drafting process.

The consequences of these contrasting processes were visible in the democratic regime that followed the enactment of the new constitution. Immediately after adopting the 2011 constitution, Hungary became one of the most troubled democracies in Europe while Poland remained, at least until the rise of the conservative Law and Justice Party after 2015, a typical case of democratic consolidation. According to V-DEM indicators, the index of liberal democracy declined in Hungary from 0.72 in 2010 to 0.64 in 2012. In Poland, however, it went up from 0.79 in 1996 to 0.80 in 1998. Although features of constitutional origins do not cancel out the impact of preceding long-term structural and historical variables, nor prevent future shifts in the course of democratization, they certainly matter in the short term to keep a country within a democratic path or derail it from such a path.

REFERENCES

Arato, Andrew. 2009. "Redeeming the Still Redeemable: Post Sovereign Constitution Making." *International Journal of Politics, Culture, and Society* 22(August): 427–443.
2011a. "Orbán's (Counter-)Revolution of the Voting Booth and How It Was Made Possible." *Verfassungsblog*, April 16. http://verfassungsblog.de/orbns-counter-revolution-voting-booth.
2011b. "Constitution Making in Hungary and the 4/5 Rule." http://www.iconnectblog.com/2011/04/arato-on-constitution-making-in-hungary-and-the-45-rule/
Bartory, Agnes. 2010. "Election Briefing No 51: Europe and the Hungarian Parliamentary Elections of April 2010." www.sussex.ac.uk/sei/documents/epern-election-briefing-no-51.pdf.
Bánkuti, Miklós et al. 2012. "Opinion on Hungary's New Constitutional Order: Amicus Brief for the Venice Commission on the Transitional Provisions of the Fundamental Law and the Key Cardinal Laws." http://lapa.princeton.edu/hosteddocs/hungary/Amicus_Cardinal_Laws_final.pdf.

Bánkuti, Miklós, Gábor Halmai, and Kim Lane Scheppele. 2012. "Disabling the Consti-
tution." *Journal of Democracy* 23(3): 138–146.
Brier, Robert. 2006. "The Constitutional Politics of Culture. Symbols, Interests, and
Constitution-Drafting in Poland's Third Republic." PhD diss., Europa-Universität Via-
drian Frankfurt (Oder).
Brodsky, Clava. 2015. "Hungary's Dangerous Constitution." *Columbia Journal of Trans-
national Law*. http://jtl.columbia.edu/hungarys-dangerous-constitution.
Brzezinski, Mark F. 1991. "Constitutional Heritage and Renewal: The Case of Poland."
Virginia Law Review 77(1): 49–112.
    1993. "The Emergence of Judicial Review in Eastern Europe: The Case of Poland."
American Journal of Comparative Law 41(2): 153–200.
Brzezinski, Mark F., and Leszek Garlicki. 1995. "Judicial Review in Post-Communist Poland:
The Emergence of a Rechtsstaat?" *Stanford Journal of International Law* 31(1): 13–60.
Comments of Hungarian NGOs on the Draft Report on the Situation of Fundamental Rights:
Standards and Practices in Hungary and on the Position of the Hungarian Government.
2013. http://tasz.hu/files/tasz/imce/tavares_gov_ngos_comments_20130523.pdf.
Chruściak, Ryszard, and Wiktor, Osiatyński. 2001. *Tworzenie Konstytucji W Polsce W Latach
1989–1997*. Warszawa: Instytut Spraw Publicznych.
Eisenstadt, Todd, A. Carl LeVan, and Tofigh Maboudi. 2017. *Constituents Before Assembly:
Participation, Deliberation, and Representation in the Crafting of New Constitutions.*
New York: Cambridge University Press.
Elkins, Zachary, Tom Ginsburg, and James Melton. 2009. *The Endurance of National
Constitutions*. New York: Cambridge University Press.
Elster, Jon. 2006. "Legislatures As Constituent Assemblies" in *The Least Examined Branch the
Role of Legislatures in the Constitutional State*. Richard W. Bauman and Tsvi Kahana
(eds.) Cambridge: Cambridge University Press, 181–197.
Garlicki, Lech, and Zofia A. Garlicki. 2010. "Constitution Making, Peace Building, and
National Reconciliation: The Experience of Poland" in *Framing the State in Times of
Transition: Case Studies in Constitution Making*. Laurel E. Miller (ed.) Washington,
DC: US Institute of Peace Press, 391–416.
Gortat, Radzisława. 1993. "The Feud within Solidarity's Offspring." *The Journal of Commun-
ist Studies* 9(4): 116–124.
Gorondi, Pablo. 2006. "Hungary's Prime Minister in Trouble over Leaked Recording."
Washington Post, September 18. www.washingtonpost.com/wpdyn/content/article/2006/
09/18/AR2006091800616.html.
Grzymała-Busse, Anna. 2002. *Redeeming the Communist Past: The Regeneration of Commun-
ist Parties in East Central Europe*. Cambridge: Cambridge University Press.
Herold, Maik, and Solongo Wandan. 2014. "Verfassung Jenseits Der Konstituante: Solidarność
Und Die Politische Mobilisierung in Polen 1993–1997" in *Die Verfassung Des Politischen
Festschrift Für Hans Vorländer*. André Brodocz, Dietrich Herrmann, Rainer Schmidt,
Daniel Schulz, and Julia Schulze Wessel (eds.) Berlin: Springer, 271–286.
The Hungarian Helsinki Committee. "Documents Submitted to the EP by the Hungarian
Government concerning the Draft Constitution Are Misleading." www.helsinki.hu/en/
documents-submitted-to-the-ep-by-the-hungarian-government-concerning-the-draft-con
stitution-are-misleading.
Kaminski, Marek, G. Lissowski, and P. Swistak. 1998. "The Revival of Communism or the Effect
of Institutions?: The 1992 Polish Parliamentary Elections." *Public Choice* 97(3): 429–449.
Kis, János. 2012. "Introduction: From the 1989 Constitution to the 2011 Fundamental Law" in
Constitution for a Disunited Nation: On Hungary's 2011 Fundamental Law. Gábor Attila
Tóth (ed.) Budapest: Central European University Press, 1–24.

Krzaklewski, Marian. 1997. Speech given in the National Assembly on February 25, available at www.niedziela.pl/zaw/archiwalne_strony_www/n10/n10_krza.htm.

Lembcke, Oliver W., and Christian Boulanger. 2012. "Between Revolution and Constitution: The Role of the Hungarian Constitutional Court" in *Constitution for a Disunited Nation: On Hungary's 2011 Fundamental Law*. Gábor Attila Tóth (ed.) Budapest: Central European University Press, 269–301.

Millard, Frances. 1993. "The 1993 Polish Parliamentary Election." *Representation* 32(117): 15–18.

  1994. *The Anatomy of New Poland: Post-Communist Politics in Its First Phase*. Aldershot: Edward Elgar.

Negretto, Gabriel L. 2017. "Constitution Making in Comparative Perspective" in *Oxford Research Encyclopedia of Politics*. William R. Thompson (ed.). Oxford University Press.

  2018. "Democratic Constitution-Making Bodies: The Perils of a Partisan Convention," *International Journal of Constitutional Law* 16(1): 254–279.

Osiatyński, Wiktor. 1992. "A Bill of Rights for Poland." *East European Constitutional Review* 1(3): 29–32.

  1994. "Poland's Constitutional Ordeal." *East European Constitutional Review* 3(2): 42–45.

Sanford, George. 2002. *Democractic Government in Poland: Constitutional Politics Since 1989*. London: Palgrave Macmillan.

Scheppele, Kim Lane. 2011. "Hungary's Constitutional Revolution." *The New York Times*, December 19, 2011. http://krugman.blogs.nytimes.com/2011/12/19/hungarys-constitutional-revolution.

  2013. "Guest Post: Hungary, the Public Relations Offensive." *The New York Times*, April 8, 2013. https://krugman.blogs.nytimes.com/2013/04/08/guest-post-hungary-the-public-relations-offensive/.

  2014. "Constitutional Coups and Judicial Review: How Transnational Institutions Can Strengthen Peak Courts at Times of Crisis (with Special Reference to Hungary)." *Transnational Law & Contemporary Problems* 23(1): 51–117.

Szczerbiak, Aleks. 2004. "The Polish Centre-Right's (Last?) Best Hope: The Rise and Fall of Solidarity Electoral Action." *Journal of Communist Studies and Transition Politics* 20(3): 55–79.

Szikinger, István. 2001. "Hungary's Pliable Constitution" in *Democratic Consolidation in Eastern Europe. Volume I: Institutional Engineering*. Jan Zielonka (ed.). New York: Oxford University Press, 406–430.

Szilágyi, Anna, and András Bozóki. 2015. "Playing It Again in Post-Communism: The Revolutionary Rhetoric of Viktor Orbán in Hungary." *Advances in the History of Rhetoric* 18(1): 153–166.

Tóth, Gábor Attila (ed.). 2012. *Constitution for a Disunited Nation: On Hungary's 2011 Fundamental Law*. Budapest: Central European University Press.

Wandan, Solongo. 2014. Making New Rights: Constitutional Agenda-Setting in the Transitions of Poland (1989–1997) and South Africa (1990–1994 [1996]). PhD diss. The New School for Social Research.

  2015. "Nothing Out of the Ordinary: Constitution Making As Representative Politics." *Constellations* 221(1): 44–58.

Wasilewski, Jacek, and Edmund Wnuk-Lipinski. 1995. "Poland: Winding Road from the Communist to the Post-Solidarity Elite." *Theory and Society* 24(July): 669–696.

Wyrzykowski, Miroslaw. 2001. "Legitimacy: The Price of a Delayed Constitution in Poland" in *Democratic Consolidation in Eastern Europe, Vol. 1: Institutional Engineering*. Jan Zielonka (ed.). New York: Oxford University Press.

8

Thailand's Democratic Moment

The Constitution of 1997

Tom Ginsburg

Modern Thai constitutional and political history is stable only in its instability. Since the country became a constitutional monarchy, Thailand has had twenty constitutions (the most recent adopted in early August 2016), somewhere between seventeen and twenty-four coups and coup attempts, and nearly sixty governments.[1] Democracy, when it has been attempted, is shallow and fleeting; but dictatorship has also been impermanent, as each coup-leader follows a pattern of announcing a set of reforms to lay the groundwork for a return to elected government. Relative to its Southeast Asian neighbors, dictatorships are relatively mild: there is no history of genocidal violence such as found in Cambodia, Myanmar, or Indonesia. But democratic periods are also weakly institutionalized, and characterized by a lack of retrospective accountability for the prior dictators.[2]

The 1997 (B.E. 2540) Constitution was a watershed in Thai political history. Recently described by the *Economist* as "Thailand's best" it was the first constitution to reflect genuine and deep public participation.[3] Interestingly, its very success in facilitating mass public participation led to counter-reaction, and a cycle of instability culminating in a coup in 2006. The decade since then has witnessed a brief period in which the democratic forces aligned with exiled populist billionaire Thaksin Shinawatra have governed, followed by a coup. At this writing, a return to weak democracy looks like a possibility, though not a certainty.

The collective project of this volume considers a constitution to be "democratic" if it occurs within more than five years after the (re-)introduction of democracy

---

[1] The dates of the country's constitutions include 1932 (two documents were promulgated that year), 1946, 1947 (interim), 1949, 1952 (revisions of the 1932 constitution), 1957, 1968, 1972 (temporary), 1974, 1976, 1977, 1978, 1991 (two documents), 1997, 2006 (interim), 2007, and 2014 (interim). The last constitution was approved in a referendum on August 7, 2016.

[2] Tyrell Haberkorn, "Without Account: A History of Coup Amnesties in Thailand," manuscript on file with author.

[3] "The Generals Who Hid Behind the Throne," *The Economist*, July 23, 2016, pp. 8–9.

(see Negretto, Chapter 1). In the case of Thailand, such a coding is delicate and sensitive to slight differences in periodization, given the tenuous state of the country's political institutions at any one time. Cross-national codings characterize Thailand as a democracy for some periods before 1997, including the late 1980s. However, given the brief interruption of democracy in the form of a coup d'etat in 1991, Thailand's 1997 constitution is both intra-democratic and the result of a transition to democracy that began in late 1992. As will be described below, the 1991 coup-makers' attempt to translate their power to civilian form failed miserably, and created a reaction that ultimately led to the 1997 Constitution. Such is the nature of Thailand's political cycles that it will always appear to be in some sort of transition.

This chapter describes the drafting of the 1997 Constitution and its impact on Thai democracy. It first provides some context of Thai political history. Next, it explains the forces that converged to produce the 1997 constitution-making process, the first to ever involve an elected drafting assembly. While the life of the constitution was tumultuous, culminating in its death at the age of nine in 2006, it has had a profound afterlife (Ginsburg 2009) with significant effects on Thai democracy, and institutional legacies that have survived even in the unambiguously authoritarian periods of 2006–2007 and 2014–2016. It thus shows how a democratic constitution-making process can have important institutional effects beyond its formal legal operation. At the same time, the transition to a new monarch in 2016 marks a major shift in the trajectory of the country, with negative implications for its democratic future.

I BACKGROUND

Modern Thai history begins in the late nineteenth century, with a set of modernizing reforms under the great King Chulalongkorn (1868–1910), which put into place a European model of state and law. He built a powerful centralized bureaucracy under an absolute monarch, and kept the country free from foreign domination or colonial rule. Chulalongkorn's heirs were not made of the same strong stuff, and in 1932, a group of young officers and bureaucrats led a reform establishing a constitutional monarchy. Since that time, Thailand has been ruled by a succession of military leaders with episodic democratic interventions, all under the shadow of a monarchy that gradually cemented its position as the ultimate arbiter of political authority (Handley 2006). The central political forces were a deep state, the military, the monarch, and a Bangkok-based business community. It was a highly elitist arrangement, though as mentioned above relatively un-repressive in comparison with its neighbors.

One of the interesting things about Thai constitutional history is that military regimes insist on using constitutional form. As Engel (1975) puts it, this reflects "almost mystical faith that the promulgation of modern codes, statutes and constitutions would somehow produce a modern Thailand." But there is also ambivalence about both constitutions and democracy that stems from the very top. The universally revered late King Bhumibol Adulyadej emphasized that Western notions of democracy may not work in Thailand and that constitutions are impermanent human creations, in contrast with the enduring monarchy or Buddhist law (Handley 2006, 344, 434). In doing so, he drew on Buddhist ideas of impermanence. History, in this view, is one of cycles, rather than a linear progression toward a stable social and political order.

Since 1932, Thailand's political history has involved contestation and cycling between military dictatorships and more or less corrupt civilian governments, with neither providing a universally legitimate and accepted basis for the polity. Reflecting the cycle of coup and counter-coup, the pattern of constitution making has involved rotation among a relatively small number of institutional variants. The primary indicator of whether a constitution has been drafted in a democratic or authoritarian period is the method of selecting the upper house or Senate. In democratic periods, this body is typically elected; in authoritarian periods it tends to be appointed by the government, military, or king, and immunized from political parties. Another crucial axis is constraints on executive power. Military constitutions, predictably, tend to involve fewer constraints on the executive, and often allow unelected premiers, whereas democratic constitutions do not.[4]

The proximate background to the 1997 Constitution can be said to date to the Bangkok student uprisings of 1973 and 1976, which marked the first time in Thai history that a mass political movement asked for a change in leadership. The student movement, though reflecting elites, demanded greater public participation. The 1973 movement led to a civilian government, but the 1976 protests were met by brutal repression by the police, leading the military to step in. Many of the students fled to the mountains to avoid arrest. This model of confrontation and violent repression was a new phenomenon, and in some sense marked a shock to the system. While it foreshadowed developments in 1992, it also provided an antimodel in which constitutional breakdown was a real threat.

A new constitution was written in 1978 to provide a return to democracy. Stepping back from the brink, the 1980s marked a period of gradual and contested democratization in Thailand. Former general and future privy councilor Prem Tinsulanonda was the dominant figure of the era, running the country as premier despite never contesting an election. In the 1988 general election, former general (and Prem associate) Chatichai Choonhavan of the Chart Thai party took the premiership as a civilian. Chatichai's era was marked by an economic boom but also widespread corruption.

---

[4] It is interesting to note that a referendum that took place in August 2016 asked the public not only whether it approved a military-drafted constitution, but also whether the constitution should allow an unelected premier.

In February 1991, Generals Sunthorn Kongsompong and Suchinda Kraprayoon led a coup deposing Chatichai, nominally over issues of corruption. Establishing a so-called National Peace Keeping Council to run the country, they promptly abrogated the 1978 constitution and replaced it with an interim document. The coup went against the global trend of the time toward democratization, and the military leaders sought legitimacy by appointing a widely respected technocrat, former diplomat Anand Panyarachun, as interim premier. Anand's government received high marks for its independence and competence, and led the process of drafting a new constitution, which was completed that December. After elections in March 1992 in which no party won a majority, General Suchinda assumed the premiership despite having promised never to do so a few months before. However, this prompted massive protest, and as in 1973 and 1976, the authorities responded with violence. When soldiers fired on unarmed demonstrators in May (the so-called Black May Incident), killing an unknown number of people, the King intervened, calling Suchinda and the civilian protest leader to the palace, and, in a televised audience, publicly reprimanded both. This led to Suchinda resigning, and after a short time, being replaced again by Anand. Elections in September 1992 led to the victory of the Democrat Party, and Chuan Leekpai took power. Some consider his administration to be the first to assume power without the active backing of either military or monarchy. Thai democracy seemed to be getting off the ground at last.

II THE POLITICS OF DRAFTING THE 1997 CONSTITUTION

The aftermath of the 1991 coup and the 1992 violence led to the gradual emergence of a powerful reform movement. Democracy was in the air globally, and political instability seemed to be keeping the country down. In 1994, an activist named Chalat Worachat launched a hunger strike in front of parliament to call for a new constitution and direct elections. Others launched public calls for reform. The democratic political forces proved responsive, initially seeking to amend the constitution, and setting up new special committees in the House of Representatives to generate ideas. These bodies worked with academics to put together a wide-ranging set of recommendations to cement democratization. A well-known academic, Prawase Wasi, also organized a series of public consultations around the country, trying to focus on key issues. At one point, he suggested that a new constitution was needed to prevent political violence should the king pass away; this highly sensitive statement was not reported in the media (McCargo 1997).

The reform coalition included not only civil society, but also establishment figures like Anand who was an advocate of good governance, as well as rural leaders who sought more participation in the highly centralized Thai state. Broadly speaking, the goals of the reformers included putting an end to the cycle of coup and counter-coup that had dominated Thai politics: the cleaning up of the political process, which was characterized by rampant vote-buying and impunity for corruption; the end of unstable coalition governments; and a broader agenda of "good governance."

A negative view of politics pervaded the public discourse (Tamada 2008), and when 1995 elections produced a government led by an old-style politician, Banharn Silpa-Archa, demands for a completely new constitution picked up steam. Gradually, all the political parties coalesced around the idea, but they were following public demand rather than leading it. In addition, distrust of the legislature as embodying "politics as usual" gave impetus to the idea of a specially elected constitutional drafting body. However, the existing legislature and Banharn's party resisted the idea, and sought to have constitutional reform proceed entirely through the parliament. A breakthrough occurred in 1996, when the reform advocates along with technocrats around Anand prevailed over the traditional parties. At this point, the Constitution was again amended to provide for a specially elected Constitution Drafting Assembly (CDA) (Uwanno and Burns n.d.). This was the first time in Thai history that constitution making would proceed through this modality.

III PROCESS

As mentioned in Chapter 1 of this volume, continuity between the old and the new constitutional order is a common trait of intra-democratic constitution making. It is notable, but not surprising in the Thai context, that the drafting of the 1997 Constitution sought to preserve legal continuity (Arato 2009). Despite (or perhaps because of) its tremendous instability at the level of high politics, Thailand has a legalistic bureaucratic culture, and there is a norm of following procedural rules within the periods of democratic governance. Having just recently staved off a military challenge, civilian leaders wanted to ensure that the new Constitution was produced in an orderly fashion that was consistent with prior legality. Previous constitutions produced after transitions from military rule tended to follow promulgation processes defined in coup-leaders' constitutions as well.

The CDA was to include seventy-six elected members, one from each *jangwat* (province), along with twenty-three experts in public law, political science, and public administration selected by the parliament. MPs were prohibited from participating. The provincial members were to be selected by parliament from lists of ten put forward by direct election in each province; this process took place in December 1996 and the CDA was formed in early January 1997. Former Speaker of the House Uthai Phimchaichon, who had been a powerful advocate for the CDA, was elected the chair, and the body set up various committees, including one to coordinate public input (Tawada 2008, 131). The process required the CDA to draft the constitution within 240 days and send it to the National Assembly for approval; should the National Assembly reject it, the draft would go to public referendum, which would have been a first in Thai history. This itself had been a compromise: whereas activists had sought a referendum in any case, traditional elites had resisted it.

Perhaps the fact that the country is a monarchy meant that there was little sense that the public *had* to bless the product as an exercise of the *pouvoir constituent* (constituent power). (Indeed, when a referendum was held in 2016 to approve the current, military-drafted Constitution, the King demanded and obtained minor amendments after the public vote but before promulgation, clearly indicating the true locus of sovereignty.) Law Professor Borwornsak Uwanno became the secretary-general of the CDA, and led the process of completing a first draft by May of 1997. The CDA then held public consultations throughout the country to gather information and feedback. A second draft reflecting the results of these consultations was presented within the CDA in early July, and a final draft later that month. In mid-August the CDA voted overwhelmingly to approve the draft and send it to the National Assembly.

Forces mobilized for and against the new Constitution; supporters wore green T-shirts while opponents wore yellow. The chief lines of opposition came from smaller parties concerned about the system of proportional representation, and decentralization provisions that would have reduced the role of village headmen. In the end, the referendum was unnecessary because of overwhelming approval in the National Assembly in September 1997: the final vote was 574 in favor, 16 opposed, and 17 abstentions, and the Constitution was promulgated on October 11, 1997. One critical factor in the successful adoption may have been the Asian financial crisis, which unfolded in Thailand in July of 1997, and created an urgent sense of the need for reform.

In short, the drafting process of the 1997 Constitution proceeded with legal continuity, under amendments to the 1992 constitution. Those amendments set up the CDA, while also placing outer boundaries on reform by stipulating that the democratic system with the king as head of state would be maintained. Institutionally, the process involved a number of far-reaching innovations, including the somewhat odd two-stage selection process with direct election mediated through parliament, the broad public consultations, and the introduction of the possibility of a popular referendum to approve the Constitution. While it did not involve the judiciary in any way, the role of citizens was unprecedented. As the introduction to this volume points out (Chapter 1), the making of the Constitution was an almost textbook illustration of a balance between a broad elite consensus and input from ordinary citizens.

IV DESIGN

The 1997 Constitution was massive, comprising 336 articles and 142 pages in English translation. This alone was far longer than any predecessor. The content reflected a large number of innovations, and a desire to stabilize democratic politics while controlling its excesses. I have called the approach post-political, in that it reflects a strong Thai tradition of distrusting elected authorities, yet also seeks to be democratic (Ginsburg 2009).

The key innovations were several. In the Thai context, the document included many more rights than had any previous constitution, including rights to information, access to the media, and social and economic rights like health care and education. This likely reflected the desire among reformers to tame the Thai state. The draft also sought to reform electoral politics. It made voting compulsory. The House of Representatives was to be elected with a mixed system of single-member districts and proportional representation, in an effort to strengthen parties. House members were required to belong to political parties, and the constitution provided that expulsion from a party required giving up one's seat.[5] This innovation, along with the fact that one-fifth of the seats were to be selected using proportional representation, was designed to give party leaders control over their members and to encourage party discipline. It also was designed to overcome chronic problems of party-switching that had prevented the emergence of stable parties, as candidates would move around depending on which party made the best offer.[6] Reflecting an elitist strand in Thai thinking, MPs had to have a bachelor's degree. But the Constitution also introduced popular initiative in lawmaking. 50,000 voters could now submit a draft bill to parliament or petition to remove government officials.

The Senate was to be elected in single-vote, multimember districts, and its members were to be nonpartisan. Candidates were restricted from campaigning and could not run for reelection. The thought was that the Senate would attract local personalities who already had grassroots support, and hence were unlikely to be corrupted by the process of formal campaigning, in a reflection of the distrust of party politics. In fact, the system led to the rise of so-called husband and wife constituencies in which a spouse of an elected MP would run for the Senate. Relative to earlier constitutions, however, the very fact that the Senate was elected was of great importance.

The creation in 1997 of a system of administrative courts to allow citizens to challenge government action was an enormous innovation.[7] Another set of innovations was the establishment of a whole plethora of independent institutions to check government. These included the Election Commission, Audit Commission, Human Rights Commission, Ombudsman, Supreme Court (which included a special Criminal Division for Persons Holding Political Office), Supreme Administrative Court, Constitutional Court, and National Counter-Corruption Commission

---

[5] Constitution of 1997 § 118. The constitution also contained some paternalistic elements. MPs were required to have a bachelor's degree, an undemocratic requirement that Harding believes was nevertheless widely supported. (Harding 2001, 241) One effect of this restriction was to strengthen urbanites relative to traditional bosses in the countryside.

[6] One politician I spoke with recalled being asked to give a substantial amount of money to the party for a seat on the party list. Presumably the rule preventing party-switching strengthened party bosses relative to candidates, and would increase the price paid to parties, as opposed to parties paying candidates to join them.

[7] 1997 Const., §§ 276–279.

(NCCC). These were constituted by a complex set of nested selection committees defined in the constitution itself, and subject to Senate approval. For example, the NCCC was to be nominated by a fifteen-member selection committee, including the presidents of the Supreme, Constitutional, and Supreme Administrative courts, which submitted a list of names to be selected by the Senate. The Election Commission nominees were to be chosen by supermajority of a special ten-member selection committee that included the presidents of the Constitutional and Supreme Administrative Courts, four rectors of universities elected by their fellow rectors, and four representatives of political parties that held seats in the House.

Under the 1997 Constitution, the Constitutional Court had a central role in policing the other independent bodies. The Court was composed of a president and fourteen judges appointed by the king on the advice of the Senate. It included five justices of the Supreme Court, two from the Supreme Administrative Court, five other lawyers, and three persons with political science degrees. Nominations for the latter two categories came from the selection committee, which included four deans of law and four of political science faculties, four MPs and the president of the Supreme Court. This committee nominated ten persons with law degrees and six with political science degrees; the Senate then elected five law degree holders and three political science degree holders from this list to serve on the Court.[8]

The NCCC was to collect reports on assets from politicians and senior bureaucrats to ensure no mysterious increases accrued during their period of public service. Those who failed to report assets could be barred from office, subject to approval by the new Constitutional Court.

In addition to interpreting the constitution and resolving jurisdictional disputes among governmental authorities, the Constitutional Court exercised a broad array of ancillary powers. It could confirm findings of and evaluate disclosures submitted to the NCCC, review whether any appropriations bill would lead to involvement of an elected official in the expenditure of funds, determine whether an emergency decree was warranted by a true emergency, determine whether election commissioners should be disqualified, and decide whether political party regulations violate the constitution or fundamental principles of Thai governance.[9] The Constitutional Court was thus a lynchpin institution in the constitutional scheme.

In short, the Constitution sought to enhance political parties while at the same time limiting the space for their decision-making through a broad set of institutional watchdogs and a nonpartisan Senate. Participation, good governance, and the process of adoption led its proponents to refer to it as the "People's Constitution."

---

[8] 1997 Const., § 255–257.
[9] 1997 Const., § 180 (appropriations bills); § 219 (emergency); § 142, *referring to* §§ 137 and 139 (election commission); § 47, para. 3 (party regulations).

V PERFORMANCE

Thinking about the various goals of the 1997 Constitution allows us to provide an assessment of its performance and a postmortem. In doing so, we can simply use the stated goals of its proponents as a kind of internal benchmark (Ginsburg and Huq 2016). Start with the great success of the 1997 Constitution, the set of independent institutions and courts it set up. These institutions reflect the idea that democratic politics ought to be constrained and that the political process cannot be trusted to ensure clean politics. Instantiating these ideas in new institutions can be considered an enduring success, as every subsequent constitution has included them, even if not all the institutions functioned effectively even during the 1997–2006 period.

How did they work in practice? The Constitutional Court had a very central role. Early on, the Constitutional Court took up several high-profile cases involving government corruption and malfeasance. Sanan Kachornprasart, the Minister of Interior and Deputy Prime Minister, was found to have deliberately submitted a false statement of his assets to the NCCC. In August 2000, the Constitutional Court unanimously confirmed the report of the NCCC, leading to a five-year ban from office for the prominent politician.[10] By the end of 2000, the Court had confirmed NCCC decisions in seventeen cases, suggesting that the institutions were supporting each other in the effort to clean up politics. The Election Commission powers were extensive: it could annul election results, order new elections, and investigate fraud allegations. It used these powers extensively during Senate elections in 2000 and 2001, disqualifying seventy-eight candidates.

The NCCC was celebrated by some as being particularly effective, but came under severe attack in 2005, when it awarded itself a significant salary increase without parliamentary scrutiny. The Criminal Division of the Supreme Court ruled that the nine commissioners violated the law, and removed them from office. New appointments were not forthcoming, so the commission became dormant. All in all, the general perception was that the independent agencies did not function as they should have as the period went on, though they had some early successes.

Another goal of the Constitution was to resolve problems of fragmented party politics, and in this it was arguably too successful. The Constitution changed the electoral system from a multimember constituency model toward a mixed system with 400 single seat constituencies and 100 party list seats, the latter with a 5 percent threshold requirement. A provision against party-switching was designed to stop the practice of politicians trading their affiliation for cash, which had contributed to coalition instability. In addition, it strengthened the prime minister by forcing MPs to resign seats should they become ministers. As Hicken (2006) argues, this indeed contributed to the consolidation of political party system.

---

[10] Constitutional Court Decision 31/2543 (2000).

When former policeman and telecoms billionaire Thaksin Shinawatra ran for office in the general election of 2001, his Thai Rak Thai party developed a populist platform, a switch from the earlier clientelism that had dominated Thai electoral politics. Once he won office, he implemented many of these proposals, benefiting, as Hicken (2006, 397) notes, from the enhanced power of the prime minister. Thaksin's political program was decidedly populist, featuring cash handouts to the poor and cheap medical care. He gave voice to a long-neglected rural population based in the north and northeast of the country. This powerful electoral base, along with his strong-arm tactics, engendered opposition from the Bangkok elite.

Incidentally, Thaksin was accused by the NCCC of having violated campaign rules by registering some of his assets in the name of associates and staff. The Constitutional Court was called on to ban him for five years, but in a bizarre decision, decided that Thaksin should be allowed to take office and not serve a five-year ban from politics. By merging several parties with his own, Thaksin was then able to form Thailand's first-ever majority government in 2001; his own party won 248 out of 500 seats, nearly double that of Chuan Leekpai's Democrat Party. Thaksin then used this position to try to stack, intimidate, and influence the various independent institutions, including the Senate. He won another large victory in January 2005, and stepped up the attempts to reach into every corner of government.

In early 2006, Thaksin sold his company to Temasek, the Singapore sovereign wealth investment fund, without paying taxes. A case went to the Constitutional Court but was rejected as Thaksin had already captured the institution. Large demonstrations ensued in Bangkok, and Thaksin called an election to resolve the crisis. However, the opposition boycotted the election, and Thaksin's party won 80 percent of the seats. This led the king to meet with the heads of the various courts to tell them they had to come up with a solution, quite a bit of pressure for relatively young judicial institutions. The Constitutional Court responded by annulling the election; three Election Commissioners were jailed, on the grounds that the time allowed for the campaign had been too brief and that some polling booths had been positioned to allow others to view the ballots as they were cast. A new election was scheduled for November, but before that, Thaksin began to interfere with the military hierarchy, promoting his own associates over those associated with Privy Counselor Prem. As public demonstrations both supporting and opposing Thaksin intensified, the military staged a coup on September 19, 2006, while the prime minister was at the United Nations General Assembly. Thaksin fled to London and has not returned to his homeland since.

The military junta dissolved parliament and the Constitutional Court, banned the Thai Rak Thai party, and prohibited its executives from running for office for five years. Meanwhile, the government adopted an interim Constitution and initiated a process of drafting a new permanent Constitution. That process involved a large constitutional commission, and a thirty-five–member drafting committee. There were some public discussions, and the Constitution was put to the people for a referendum in August

2007, passing with support of 56 percent of the population. Elections followed in December 2007, and a new attempt to create democratic governance began.

VI AFTERMATH

While elections were restored in late 2007, Thailand's democracy did not stabilize. Thaksin's allies reorganized his party into the People's Power Party, and won the 2007 election. Premier Samak Sundaravej took office, but opposition street protests accused him of being a stooge for Thaksin. Meanwhile, the courts began to bring charges against several leaders of the party for various failings, personal and political. Samak remained in office, even as protests intensified, but in September, the Constitutional Court ordered him removed from office as he had violated his duty to do no private sector work. Samak had apparently been serving as an emcee of a cooking show while prime minister, hardly a lucrative position or particularly corrupt act by Thai standards. After Samak stepped down, Thaksin's brother-in-law Somchai Wongsawat became prime minister. But he too was removed after a short while, on the grounds that he had wrongfully suspended a corruption investigation while at the Ministry of Justice some years earlier. In a parallel proceeding, the Constitutional Court decided to disband the PPP.

With Thaksin's allies under attack, the opposition Democrat Party was able to form a government, under Abhisit Vejajiva. But this change in power did not bring peace. In April 2009, Thaksin broadcast a video accusing Abhisit of being a stooge of the military, and hundreds of thousands of his "red-shirt" supporters descended on Bangkok, under the rubric of the United Front of Democracy against Dictatorship (UDD). This led to a state of emergency. Massive demonstrations and counter-demonstrations lasted more than another year, until an agreement was announced to hold elections in July 2011. These were again won by the Thaksin-associated Pheu Thai Party, and his sister Yingluck Shinawatra became the first female prime minister in Thai history. In late 2013, however, her party passed a highly contentious amnesty bill that would have provided amnesty to both sides for political crimes committed after 2004. It was widely perceived as allowing Thaksin himself to return to Thailand without facing charges filed in 2006. This too led to anti-government protests, culminating in yet another military coup d'etat in May 2014, led by current Prime Minister Prayuth Chan-Ocha.

The 2014 coup was arguably different from earlier ones in some respects (Soprazetti 2016). While in accordance with the unwritten rules of coup-making, a new constitution-making process was undertaken and completed with a referendum in 2016, repression has been fairly severe, and the coup-leader has drawn on traditional idioms of paternalistic guidance of the people. Claims of "Thai-style democracy" are euphemisms for authoritarian guidance, even if elections have returned as of 2019. State-sponsored violence against activists and repression of free speech has been a constant since the 2014 coup, and the referendum of 2016 was held under conditions in which criticism of the draft was not allowed. Any pretext of balance between the people and elites is long gone. Furthermore, unlike General Suchinda two decades earlier, Prayuth was able to translate his power into an electoral victory in 2019. Meanwhile in 2019, a new monarch was crowned as Rama X. He has taken an active role in certain aspects of governance, but is not yet as popular as his beloved father.

The introduction to this volume (Chapter 1) notes that many instances of redrafting constitutions in democratic orders do not lead to improvements in governance. If one takes the five-year before-and-after period offered there, Thailand is a counter-example, as the country was surely more democratic at the end of 2002 than it was at the beginning of 1992 when General Suchinda still held sway.[11] A longer window, say between 1987 and 2007, suggests that the Constitution did not have an enduring positive impact on democratization, at least using standard measures. But a qualitative assessment of its legacies is more nuanced.

VII AFTERLIFE

The Constitution of 1997 died at the age of nine years old; it was the longest lasting democratic constitution in Thailand's history, and second only to Sarit Thanarat's 1959 repressive interim charter, which lasted a bit past its ninth birthday. Despite its short lifespan, it remains a lynchpin in Thai political history and has had what I have elsewhere called an "afterlife" (Ginsburg 2009). The political forces it unleashed, indirectly, continue to dominate the landscape and have exposed previously latent cleavages in Thai society. And its institutional legacies are significant. We divide our discussion into the political and institutional.

Let us first begin with an assessment of the political legacies. Much, of course, depends on an understanding of what constitutions can – and cannot – do (Ginsburg and Huq 2016). We must be cautious in attributing every negative outcome of Thai politics to the Constitution itself. The Constitution merely provided a framework for governance, including both incentives for the emergence of majoritarian coalitions, and institutions to check the vagaries or excesses thereof. The first emerged quickly, in the first general election following the adoption of the Constitution. The second showed real promise in its early years. The institutions were established and showed some gumption.

The failures of the institutions to check the rise of Thaksin is hardly to be laid at the feet of the Constitution itself but must be blamed primarily on Thaksin for not observing basic democratic rules, and his supporters for tolerating his bullying and

---

[11] This assessment, of course, may vary in different cross-national democracy indicators. As noted in Table 1.3 in Chapter 1, Thailand's democracy improved during the first five years after the enactment of the 1997 constitution according to the V-DEM liberal democracy index, but maintained the same level of democratization if one uses the polity score of the Polity IV database.

vote-buying. Pieces of paper are not self-enforcing. Institutional checks on power are perhaps best characterized as speed bumps, raising the price of consolidating or abusing power. From this perspective, the watchdog institutions of 1997 may have slowed the rise of a megalomaniac intent on dominating an entire country, but it could not stop it.

Perhaps the best analogue to Thaksin is Recip Tayyip Erdogan, the current president of Turkey. Like Erdogan, Shinawatra came to power on the basis of a newly mobilized, long-excluded segment of the country; in both cases democracy led to inclusion. And in both cases, once in power, the leaders sought to dismantle any truly independent institutions. In Thaksin's case, the techniques no doubt included bribery. He first targeted the independent constitutional watchdogs, and later moved to the media and the military. Whereas Erdogan has succeeded in his blatant purges of these institutions, Thailand's political culture is less tolerant of mass purges of the bureaucracy, which is a conservative political force in its own right. And the military has strong internal norms for promotion and rotation that no strongman has been able to completely ignore, at least over the last three decades. So Thaksin was less successful than Erdogan, as evidenced by his exile since 2006. Still the two are analogous in their basic lack of respect for democracy, and their deployment of populist rhetoric to justify their rule.

The sequence of events also led to increasing polarization in Thai society. The phenomenon of demonstrators wearing competing colors – green and yellow in the case of the constitution, yellow and red in the demonstrations of the 2000s – seems here to stay. Political violence in modern Thai history has chiefly come from the state, quashing demonstrators as in 1973, 1976, and 1992. But the last few years have seen confrontations in which violence is used from below, with limited violent demonstrations and counterdemonstrations. A significant cleavage is part of the legacy of 1997, even if it is currently under deep suppression by military rule.

At the same time, the 1997 Constitution established the basic institutional structure for what future constitutions are expected to include. All subsequent constitutions have retained most of the independent watchdog institutions, even if they were not completely effective in 1997–2006. The current Constitution of 2017 produced under strict military dominance retains the National Human Rights Commission, National Anti-Corruption Commission, Constitutional Court and Ombudsmen. Each of these various institutions has developed, since 1997, internal procedures, norms, and precedents for how to behave. So there is a substantial institutional legacy.

There has also been some learning and refinement of constitutional structures. The 2007 and 2017 Constitutions simplify the selection committee structure for the institutions; instead of a specially constituted committee for each institution, nominations are now made by a core group consisting of the presidents of the Supreme Court and Supreme Administrative Court, the president of the House and leader of the Opposition, along with appointees of the independent organs. The courts thus have a role in guarding the guardian institutions. Another change introduced in the 2007 document, adopted to correct problems that emerged under Thaksin, was to prevent parties from merging when they have seats in the house, and to limit aisle-crossing. The 2017 Constitution went further in introducing an electoral system designed to fragment power. In this sense, a future Thaksin will have a harder time consolidating power, but democratic politics are disabled and designed to be ineffectual.

Another institutional legacy is the partially elected Senate. Neither of the subsequent military-produced constitutions (of 2007 and 2017) adopted the old model of a completely appointed Senate.[12] The 2007 Constitution included the requirement of Senators having a bachelor's degree (and had the same requirement for ministers and election commissioners) although this was removed in 2017. But neither allowed Senators to have any connections with political parties.

A final legacy is the rhetoric of reform. Unlike some of his predecessors, Prime Minister Prayuth has sought to constrain policy in the name of "reform" (Soprazetti 2016). The eternal quest for a clean politics hides a good deal of dirt underneath. But the co-optation of that language in the production of the 2017 Constitution reflects its rhetorical dominance.

In short, the Constitution of 1997 has had a significant afterlife: it should get credit for mobilizing a public, for establishing the basic institutional structure of Thailand's governance, and for increasing baseline expectations about public participation. It is perhaps no accident that the chief line of criticism for the constitution approved by referendum in August 2016 was not its substance so much as the fact that it has been produced in a completely nontransparent manner. Although produced under military rule, the final draft emerged only after one failed drafting process in which public criticism may have made a difference. In Thailand's peculiar political history, the 1997 Constitution was a turning point in introducing the norm of public involvement, even if that has gone by the wayside in practice.

VIII CONCLUSION

We should, however, conclude on a note of serious caution. Between 2001 and 2014, the political forces associated with Thaksin Shinawatra won every major election on the national scene. Even in the highly constrained 2019 election, Pheu Thai finished second behind the military leader's Palang Pracharat Party. The excesses of its leader notwithstanding, Pheu Thai is a political force that will not go away. The Democrat Party, which was for most of the period a leading contender, has not expanded its base from the south and Bangkok to compete effectively in the north and northeast. Without policies that benefit these long-excluded regions, Thai democracy is likely to be affected by Thaksin's legacy for some time even if he

[12] Thail. Const. 2007, §§ 111–113 [hereinafter 2007 Const.]

never sets foot in the country again. While the terrain is tough, there is no doubt that the exposure of this cleavage is attributable to 1997. The failure to close it, on the other hand, lies in the decisions of Thailand's political class. The prospects of redemocratization will depend on how the party system develops, and whether it responds to the political demands of all sides. A failure of channels to express their grievances properly could drive people to the streets yet again. The only permanent feature of Thai politics is impermanence.

REFERENCES

Arato, Andrew. 2009. *Constitution Making under Occupation: The Politics of Imposed Revolution in Iraq.* New York: Columbia University Press.

Chambers, Paul. 2002. "Good Governance, Political Stability and Constitutionalism in Thailand." Bangkok: King Prajadhipok's Institute Occasional Paper (August 10, 2002).

Crouch, Melissa, and Tom Ginsburg. 2016. "Between Endurance and Change in Southeast Asia: Military and Constitutional Reform in Myanmar and Thailand" in *Annual Review of Constitution-Making.* Stockholm: International IDEA, 67–84.

Engel, David. 1975. "Law and Kingship in Thailand during the Reign of King Chulalongkorn." Michigan Papers on South and Southeast Asia. Vol. 9. Center for South & Southeast Asian Studies, University of Michigan.

Ginsburg, Tom. 2009. "Constitutional Afterlife: The Continuing Impact of Thailand's Post-Political Constitution." *International Journal of Constitutional Law* 7(1): 83–105.

Ginsburg, Tom, and Aziz Huq. 2016. "Assessing Constitutional Performance" in *Assessing Constitutional Performance.* Tom Ginsburg and Aziz Huq (eds.) Cambridge: Cambridge University Press, 3–26.

Handley, Paul. 2006. *The King Never Smiles: A Biography of Thailand's Bhumibol Adulyadej.* New Haven: Yale University Press.

Harding, Andrew. 2001. "May There Be Virtue: 'New Asian Constitutionalism' in Thailand." *Australian Journal of Asian Law* 3(3): 236–269.

Hicken, Allen. 2006. "Party Fabrication: Constitutional Reform and the Rise of Thai Rak Thai," *Journal of East Asian Studies* 6(3): 381–407.

Ivarsson, Søren (ed.) 2010. *Saying the Unsayable: Monarchy and Democracy in Thailand.* Copenhagen: Nordic Institute of Asian Studies.

McCargo, Duncan. 2002. *Reforming Thai Politics.* Copenhagen: Nordic Institute of Asian Studies.
  2007. "A Hollow Crown: Review of Paul Handley's *The King Never Smiles.*" *New Left Review* 43: 135–144.

McDorman, Ted L. 1998. "Constitutional Change and Continuity in Thailand in the Aftermath of the 1991 Coup" in *Asia-Pacific Legal Development.* Douglas A. Johnson and Gerry Ferguson (eds.) Vancouver: University of British Columbia Press.

Suwannathat-Pian, Kobkua. 2003. *Kings, Country and Constitutions: Thailand's Political Development 1932–2000.* London: Routledge Curzon.

Sopranzetti, Claudio. 2016. "Thailand's Relapse: The Implications of the May 2014 Coup." *Journal of Asian Studies* 75(2): 299–316.

Tamada, Yoshifumi. 2008. *Myths and Realities: The Democratization of Thai Politics.* Kyoto: Trans-Pacific Press.

Uwanno, Borwornsak, and Wayne D. Burns. N.d. "The Thai Constitution of 1997: Sources and Process." *Thailand Law Forum.* www.thailawforum.com/articles/constburns1.html.

9

Political Elites and the People

Kenya's Decade-Long Constitution-Making Process

Christina Murray

Kenya adopted a new constitution in 2010 after a long and difficult journey. It was the result of two processes, involving different bodies, different decision-making rules, and each under significantly different political conditions. The first process started when the government could no longer ignore demands for constitutional change by opposition parties and civil society. It ended in 2005 when a draft constitution was rejected at a referendum. The second process followed the 2008 peace deal that brought an end to the deadly conflict after the 2007 general elections. This chapter describes these linked processes, exploring why the first failed and the second led to the adoption of a new constitution. There is, of course, no simple or single answer to this question but, as the chapter shows, a central difference between them was the different ways in which they dealt with elites and ordinary citizens. In short, insisting on a "people-driven" process and failing to secure elite buy-in was fatal for the first process; requiring consensus among the elite, along with a degree of public involvement, was key to bringing the second process to a successful conclusion.

The achievement of elite consensus and the acceptance by the general public of a reduced role in the second process was a result of a complex set of circumstances, dominated by the impact of the unprecedented ethnic violence of early 2008. The more receptive political atmosphere post-2008 was complemented by the hard-headed design of the second process: it strategically avoided the stumbling blocks of the first, demanding elite consensus while meeting the public's or, at least, organized civil society's expectation of participation. As a result, Kenya may provide an object lesson for Negretto's argument in Chapter 5 that some level of elite agreement (and compromise) is essential if a constitution is to be a framework for a stronger democracy. In Kenya, public participation in constitution making may have enhanced the legitimacy of the constitution and surely did lead to a better constitution, but constitutional change could not be achieved without elite buy-in. However, as the chapter concludes, whether or not that argument about the effects of its constitution-making processes is right, more is needed in Kenya to bring about the fundamental political, social, and economic change necessary for a more just and democratic society.

I THE FIRST PROCESS: THE CONSTITUTION OF KENYA REVIEW COMMISSION, THE NATIONAL CONSTITUTIONAL CONFERENCE, PARLIAMENT, AND A REFERENDUM

By the time that the process of constitution review formally started in Kenya in 2001, it was long overdue. The old constitution is commonly referred to as the Independence Constitution but it had been amended significantly since independence in 1963 to concentrate power in the national executive. It provided minimal protection for human rights, largely because the judiciary was complicit in the government's widespread abuse of power, and provided little resistance to rampant corruption and privatized use of force. However, by the late 1980s, the Kenyan political landscape was shifting. In particular, pressure, mainly from elites who had been maneuvered out of formal politics, was growing and, post-cold war, there was increased pressure from the international community. These factors, together with the political turmoil of the third wave of democratization elsewhere in Africa, combined to persuade President Daniel Arap Moi to repeal the constitutional provision that declared Kenya a one-party state and, in 1992, to permit the first multiparty elections since 1969.

The introduction of multiparty politics eased some pressures but President Moi, a born survivor who had held office since 1978, won the first and second multiparty elections and continued to wield enormous power despite considerable popular opposition to his rule. Many Kenyans had hoped that the reforms of the early 1990s would rapidly bring fundamental change. Instead, in the 1990s, cronyism and corruption deepened, inequalities and the neglect of large sections of the population continued to grow, and political mobilization along tribal lines increased. Kenyans who had struggled for social justice came to believe that more fundamental constitutional change was necessary to address these problems.

The first constitution-making process was governed by the provisions in the existing constitution governing its alteration and the Constitution of Kenya Review Act 13 of 1997. Fraught negotiations involving the government, opposition parties, and civil society led to three amendments of the Review Act between its initial adoption in 1997 and the start of the process. By 2001, the Act supplemented the minimalist constitutional provisions by setting up an ambitious and idealistic three-stage process which was to be "people-driven" (Kiplagat Report 2006, para 62). First, the Constitution of Kenya Review Commission (CKRC) was to consult the people of Kenya and draft a bill to alter the existing constitution. Second, a large National Constitutional Conference (NCC), consisting of politicians from national and district level, and representatives of other interest groups, was to meet to consider the CKRC's draft and approve a version to submit to Parliament. Finally, Parliament was to adopt the draft constitution as approved by the NCC and the president to sign it into law. As this highly participatory process unfolded, it was supplemented by the requirement that any new constitution was to be approved in a referendum before becoming effective.

I.A *Constitution of Kenya Review Commission (CKRC)*

The CKRC ultimately had twenty-nine members, of which the Moi-controlled government selected fifteen. Later, when political and civil society opposition threatened to derail the process, fourteen additional members were added, primarily drawn from civil society to increase the Commission's legitimacy. As noted above, the CKRC's task was to prepare proposals for "altering" the existing constitution but, despite the reference to "alteration" alone, it was generally expected that the CKRC would prepare a new constitution, which it duly did. The Review Act set out the functions of the CKRC in detail, reflecting – and securing – the agenda that had emerged from the preceding years of political and civil society mobilization. It emphasized public participation and detailed the forums and processes that the CKRC was to use in public education and consultation. As a result, the CKRC conducted what is probably still Africa's most participatory process.[1]

The inclusion of civil society members on the CKRC satisfied the demands of those who had campaigned for the process but, whatever unity civil society had found in demanding a constitution-making process broke down in decision-making on the CKRC: many of the newly added civil society representatives were as partisan as the original government appointees, signaling the complicated role that civil society was to play throughout the process. Nonetheless, despite deep rifts among commissioners and accusations and counter-accusations of political interference (Kiplagat Report 2006, 21), the CKRC concluded its work in September 2002 with the publication of an imaginative draft constitution, which reflected both local concerns and the many developments in international understanding of constitutionalism over the past half century.

I.B *National Constitutional Conference (NCC)*

The second step in the process was deliberation on the draft by the NCC. Like the CKRC, the NCC was designed to be inclusive but, in contrast to the CKRC, it was huge, with 629 members. No one was directly elected, instead, representativeness was secured by including people from diverse sectors: The 223 members of the National Assembly (Parliament) were members; each of the 70 councils of the

---

[1] See Section III in this chapter for a short description of the program of public education and consultation.

administrative districts in Kenya elected three representatives, one of whom was required to be a woman; 41 members represented the registered political parties (in addition to the MPs); and 126 members represented religious, professional and women's groups, trade unions and NGOs.[2] The twenty-nine CKRC members made up the total but did not have voting rights (Review Act 1997, section 27(2)).[3] The outcome, as Cottrell and Ghai (2004, 7) say, was that "the NCC was the most representative body ever assembled in Kenya and was set up to reflect public concerns." The NCC was probably also the first body in Anglophone Africa representing diverse sectors of society with significant constitution-making powers (Kirkby and Murray 2016). Although, drawing on French history, countries in Francophone Africa had established national conferences for constitution making, the custom in Anglophone Africa has been for constitution making to be firmly located with politicians. In some cases, a government-appointed commission has provided initial contributions but the rest of the process has typically been in the hands of the executive and parliament (or the military). Significantly, elected politicians were a minority on the NCC (293 of 600 voting members).

The NCC was intended to be established as soon as the CKRC's draft was ready but was delayed by the 2002 elections. These elections transformed the political landscape. They brought the first change of government since independence and saw Mwai Kibaki elected as president rather than President Moi's choice, Uhuru Kenyatta, a transition made possible by the introduction of presidential term limits in 1992 and cooperation among opposition parties that had been elusive in the preceding two multiparty elections. A key element in forging the opposition coalition was an agreement among opposition parties that had, at its core, a deal that if Kibaki, a Kikuyu, won the elections, Raila Odinga, a Luo and prominent political leader, would be given a to-be-created position of prime minister. Cabinet positions would be shared among the participating parties.

The change in government had a direct impact on the constitution-making process. For many, constitutional reform had been a tactic to dislodge President Moi. Now, with Moi and his chosen successor gone, a new constitution was no longer needed for that. The interests of those who supported constitutional reform as a means to access power shifted to ensuring that it helped them to retain power. Nonetheless, the NCC was convened at a time when, buoyed by the elections, Kenyans were more optimistic than ever before. Although the NCC was governed by the Review Act, its mandate was open-ended: it was to be convened for the "discussion, debate, amendment and adoption" of the Commission's draft (section 27(2)); questions were usually to be settled by consensus but, in case of disagreement

---

[2] Unusually, election procedures in the county councils and the mechanism for choosing the 126 representatives of civil society were determined by the CKRC within a broad framework set in the Review Act.

[3] The Act limited the number of representatives of civil society to not more than 25 percent of the other members of the Conference combined.

on a proposed provision of the constitution, a two-thirds majority was required. The Act also provided for a referendum in certain cases of disagreement but this process was not used. Regulations, prepared by the CKRC, set out stages for the work of the NCC and other procedural matters.

Spurred by the change and pervasive optimism of the time, the NCC members engaged energetically with the issues. Decisions were taken in the plenary but much of the work was done in smaller groups, as CKRC members guided NCC representatives through the draft. But, again, there were divisions, deepened by Kenya's rapidly changing politics: the coalition on which President Kibaki had won the election was not functioning well and the pre-election agreement to create the position of prime minister for Odinga had not been fulfilled. Moreover, there were endless attempts to derail the process – through filibustering, litigation, increasing the number of sittings of Parliament that required the NCC to adjourn to allow MPs to fulfill their parliamentary duties, sudden amendments to the agenda that required delays for preparation, and so on. Despite all this, agreement was reached on many important issues.

However, two key matters seemed intractable: the system of government and devolution of power, the two issues that would determine how power was exercised in Kenya and, mostly likely, who would hold it. Eventually, differences on these matters precipitated the withdrawal from the NCC of President Kibaki's supporters and thus a substantial segment of the government (Chege 2008). Still quorate, the NCC concluded its work and, on March 23, 2004, adopted an idealistic draft constitution that, in its many mechanisms to secure accountability and to limit and disperse power, was a strong response to decades of abuse of power. However, now in power, and skeptical of such limitations on governmental power, in particular, devolution and the creation of a parliamentary system, Kibaki-aligned politicians boycotted the ongoing process, thus removing support for the new draft of a significant section of the governing elite.

I.C *Parliament*

Reflecting the political agreement of 2000 and the demand that constitutional review should not be in the hands of politicians, the Review Act originally required the attorney general to deliver the NCC's draft constitution to Parliament for an "up-down" vote: no amendments were permitted. But this process was changed in two profound ways. First, after the 2002 elections, Parliament amended the Review Act to permit it to amend any draft presented to it with a simple majority. Second, a 2004 decision of the Kenyan High Court, delivered after the NCC approved the draft (Timothy Njoya 2004), held that the Kenyan Constitution could not be replaced without a referendum because, among other things, section 47 of the existing constitution allowed for the amendment of parts of the existing constitution and their repeal, but not its complete replacement: "alter" does not mean "replace" and a new constitution requires an exercise of constituent power by the people. This judgment was followed by another that ordered all activities of the NCC to be suspended until other issues concerning its validity were settled (Njuguna Michael Kung'u 2004) leaving a lacuna: the first case required a draft constitution to be put to a referendum but the second case suspended the process by which a draft was to be adopted by the NCC.

The combination of these changes and the absence of political consensus was fatal to the process. Before Parliament voted on the draft, a series of political meetings were held to try to reach agreement on the contentious issues but, if anything, rather than parties drawing closer together, political disagreement increased. Finally, a draft was "agreed" upon at a meeting boycotted by opposition groups. On July 21, 2005, a deeply divided Parliament agreed to a fundamentally different draft to that approved by the NCC. This new draft was a temporary victory for the government group that had walked out of the NCC.

Two changes from the NCC draft were particularly significant. First, the NCC proposals on the system of government were replaced by provisions that concentrated power in a president and which, in essence, created a hyper-presidential system. (In addition, the draft had been meticulously edited to remove many of the checks on executive power in the NCC draft.) Second, the multilevel system of government supported by a Senate in the NCC draft, which was intended to disperse power and grant some autonomy to communities outside Nairobi, was largely undone. There was no Senate in the "Proposed New Constitution," and the powers of districts were subject to national law. As a result, the constitution put to the people in the 2005 referendum was very different from the one agreed at the NCC (Whitaker and Giersch 2009). Moreover, as the Kiplagat Commission, appointed by the government to review the process after the failed referendum, noted, by now "the political climate was ... intractably poisoned" (Kiplagat Report 2006, para 28). The way in which the NCC ended and certain actions of the president that were seen to undermine the coalition agreement, among other things, had built up political animosity, which inevitably infected the referendum.

I.D *The Referendum*

The Proposed New Constitution was rejected by 58 percent of the voters in the 2005 referendum.[4] The referendum was preceded by campaigns that, in the words of a Kenyan academic, were "waged on outright lies, misuse of state power, and nativist appeals to tribal hysteria" (Mutua 2008, 228). They were also sometimes violent. The erstwhile partners in the 2002 election campaign, Kibaki and Odinga, competed against one another as leaders of the "Yes and No" campaigns respectively although Odinga still served in Kibaki's cabinet. Kenyans rallied behind their

---

4 The turnout was 53 percent.

ethnic leaders and, finally, ethnic mobilization dominated the campaigns and voting was largely along ethnic lines (Andreassen and Tostensen 2006; Whitaker and Giersch 2009).

I.E *Consensus and Conflict in the First Process*

Like many constitution-making processes, many of those who had fought for a process of constitutional change had intended that, in part at least, it should be an exercise in nation-building. It was to demonstrate to Kenyans that they could come together and determine a future together. This ideal was captured in the 1997 Review Act that set out as the first principle of the process that "all Kenyans shall ... recognize the importance of confidence building, engendering trust and developing a national consensus for the review process" (Review Act Schedule 3 (i)). In addition, the Act stated that the outcome of the review was to be revisions to the Constitution that enabled "Kenyans to resolve national issues on the basis of consensus" (section 3(k)). Neither was achieved. Many attempts were made to reconcile differences and achieve consensus along the way. For example, the CKRC's extraordinary public engagement program was aimed at building agreement; when the NCC broke down, various committees were established to try to mediate differences; and, after the High Court judgments seemed to block the process entirely, politicians met in various configurations to try to overcome the legal impediments. Through all of this, political divisions became more pronounced rather than overcome.[5] Finally, as many observers concluded, the vicious referendum campaigns exacerbated already existing tensions and paved the way for the violence that followed the 2007 elections.

As already noted, the main areas of substantive disagreement were those most directly related to political and thus economic power in Kenya: the system of government and devolution. Here, as in Kenyan politics for decades, ethnic calculations dominated. Although ethnicity did not determine every vote in the 2005 referendum, it explains most. Even those issues not directly related to political power, such as religion, and particularly religious courts, gender, and citizenship, also played a role and were used aggressively by politicians to mobilize support for one side or the other. Later, discussing the failed process and its management of contentious issues and using diplomatic language that underplays the intensity of the conflict, the Kiplagat Commission reported that:

---

[5]   The Kiplagat Report (2006) puts a positive gloss on the difficulty in reaching consensus, noting that "attention to these [political and self-interested] concerns was inevitable and not in the least surprising. After all, constitution-making, it has been said, is the continuation of politics by other means." It adds that "many of these issues were managed with far less acrimony than what many delegates had anticipated." The Report also describes the complex and, it suggests, largely successful procedures adopted by the Conference to secure consensus.

What made issues contentious was not so much the propriety or constitutional value of proposals made in the Draft Bill, but rather their implications and consequences in contemporary Kenyan politics. For example, some delegates were clearly apprehensive about the radical changes proposed in the Draft regarding the overall system of Government (legislature, executive, judiciary) since these had profound implications for existing power arrangements. Yet others were unable to extricate themselves from deep-seated cultural and religious loyalties when it came to debate on the corpus of Kenyan law or the structure of the Courts. The debate on the Kadhi's Courts thus drew such loyalties from all religions.

It was apparent that debate on proposals to restructure the legislature and the role of legislators were more often hampered by fears of loss of status and privilege currently enjoyed by sitting members of Parliament than by strict constitutional principles.

(Kiplagat Report 2006, paras 81–82)

Indeed, as Whitaker and Giersch (2009, 8) put it, "much of the [referendum] debate was really about three Ps: process, politics, and positioning." On process, the struggle was about control. By the time the campaigns for the referendum began, large parts of the population felt betrayed by what they saw as a politically opportunistic use of the process and the "No" campaign took advantage of this dissatisfaction. On politics and positioning, the sides taken by political leaders at each stage were based both on old political grievances and on calculations about future political fortunes. Deep and long-standing grievances including over land, marginalization of certain groups and corruption, fueled the divisions further. The optimistic people-driven process that started in 2001 foundered on long-standing political and ethnic divisions.

I.F *Between the Two Processes: Disaster*

The failed constitution-making process, the divisive 2005 referendum, and increasing awareness of large-scale corruption throughout government provided the immediate background to Kenya's general elections in December 2007. Again, as in the referendum, the major partners of the winning 2002 coalition, Mwai Kibaki and Raila Odinga, competed against one another, this time for the presidency, each backed by a tribal alliance. The elections were hotly contested and polls suggested that the race was very close (Mueller 2008; 2011; Throup 2008). Also, as Cheeseman demonstrates, "contrary to the general depiction of the sequencing of the 2007 election, violence was one of the themes that ran right through the whole campaign" (2008, 170). Violence was present throughout the campaigning, but intensified dramatically when Kibaki was announced winner of the presidential race and, in stark contrast to the public celebrations of 2002, was sworn in in secrecy at night. The official results of the parliamentary election were that Odinga's Orange Democratic Movement (ODM) won convincingly, securing 105 of 197 seats. Kibaki's Party of National Unity (PNU) came second with 46 seats and the rest were shared among smaller parties. But, the Electoral Commission of Kenya announced, Kibaki had won the presidential election with 47 percent of the vote to Odinga's 44 percent. Suspicion that these results were rigged was compounded by an admission by the chair of the Electoral Commission that he had been coerced by officials from both major parties to release the results prematurely and did not know whether Kibaki had indeed won or not.[6]

The violence triggered by these events was unprecedented in Kenya. It spread rapidly and, in the words of the Report of the Commission of Inquiry into Post Election Violence, involved "systematic attacks on Kenyans based on their ethnicity and their political leanings" (Waki Report 2008, viii). Over 1,100 people died and, on a conservative estimate, about 350,000 people were displaced. The security forces, through incompetence or maliciousness, did nothing to mitigate the harm and, in many cases, cracked down brutally, contributing to the violence.

The mediation of the crisis has been well documented (Cohen 2008; Annan and Griffiths 2009; Juma 2009; Lindenmeyer and Kay 2009; Office of the AU Panel 2014). In summary, after a regional initiative contained the violence temporarily, Kofi Annan arrived in Nairobi to lead a group of eminent Africans who were to carry the process further. The mediation process was based on an agenda agreed to relatively quickly. It was headed by three urgent items to be addressed immediately: the violence and breaches of rights, the humanitarian crisis, and the political crisis. Agenda Item Four listed longer-term problems on which proposals were to be made within a year. Item Four was based on a recognition, spelled out in the Accord, that "poverty, the inequitable distribution of resources and perceptions of historical injustices and exclusion on the part of segments of Kenyan society constituted the underlying causes of the prevailing social tensions, instability and cycle of violence" (Kenya National Dialogue and Reconciliation 2008). Constitutional, legal, and institutional reforms were on the list.

By early March 2008, Kibaki and Odinga's parties had agreed not to rerun the presidential elections (clearly there was no realistic prospect of doing so in the face of the disarray of the Electoral Commission among other things) and had concluded a power-sharing agreement including a grand coalition government. Incorporation of the Accord in the Constitution was a central element of the deal. The Constitution was duly amended (Act 3 of 2008) and Parliament passed the National Accord and Reconciliation Act 4 of 2008 (Accord Act) to formalize arrangements in terms of which (1) Kibaki would retain the presidency, (2) Odinga would be prime minister, (3) each side would appoint a deputy prime minister, and (4) government would be through a coalition. The Cabinet was to be constituted in a manner that reflected

[6] The commission subsequently appointed to review the elections reported corruption in both the presidential and parliamentary elections (Kriegler Report 2008).

the representation of each party in Parliament and ministers from coalition parties were to be chosen by leaders of the parties.

II THE SECOND PROCESS: BUILDING IN POLITICAL DECISION-MAKING

Just days after the power-sharing arrangements were settled, four additional agreements were concluded, setting out frameworks for a commission to investigate the elections, a commission on the post-electoral violence, a "truth, justice and reconciliation" commission, and a process to draft and adopt a new constitution. The constitutional review agreement was brief, envisaging a law that would establish a five-stage process, with a draft to be approved by Parliament and adopted in a referendum.

The agreement set a year to complete the constitutional review, but government under the power-sharing arrangements was not smooth and it was almost a year before a new Constitution of Kenya Review Act (2008) and a complementary constitutional amendment were adopted. By then, although time had been lost, the process had been refined considerably from the roadmap set out in the original agreement. It was carefully sequenced and, most importantly, learning from the lessons of the first process, it included mechanisms to secure political buy-in and make obstruction more difficult.

The four aspects of the new process that distinguished it from its predecessor (and from the usual processes for constitutional review in Commonwealth Africa) worked to achieve a balance between a process in which the public had a say and elite decision-making. First, the issues on the table were to be limited by an independent committee – the Committee of Experts (CoE), whose members were to be chosen by Parliament. The CoE was mandated to start the review process by identifying the "contentious issues" (generally understood to be the issues that had occasioned the government walk out of the National Conference) and only those issues were to be the subject of a political settlement. Thus, many of the proposals from the earlier process were to be retained but those that had divided the country were up for discussion. Second, settling the contentious issues was placed firmly in the hands of the politicians or, more precisely, the partners in the coalition, rather than a more popularly composed body like the NCC. However, again to avoid deadlock, inability of the politicians to reach agreement would not be fatal because, in that case, the CoE's draft would prevail.

Third, although Parliament retained its traditional right to approve the new constitution, an amendment to the existing constitution limited its ability to change any draft presented to it (1963 Constitution of Kenya, Article 47A): changes to the draft constitution tabled in Parliament required a 65 percent majority. Fourth, to avoid the process being derailed by tactical litigation before the untrusted judiciary as had been happened before, a special court, the Interim Independent

Constitutional Dispute Resolution Court, was established to hear matters related to the constitutional review. Its nine judges were specially appointed by Parliament and included three foreigners. This too was secured in the existing constitution (1963 Constitution of Kenya, Article 60A). In addition, the entire process and many of its individual steps were subject to precise time limits and, as already noted, a new constitution was to be approved in a referendum.

The new process was centered on political agreement and clearly departed from the idea of a "people-driven constitution" that had dominated Kenyan constitutional discourse for more than a decade. The main mechanisms for securing legitimacy in the first process were inclusiveness and the participation of the people. Inclusiveness was particularly visible in the inclusion of representatives of civil society in the CKRC and in the large NCC. Broader participation was achieved in a massive public education and consultation program. For some, the idea underpinning that process was that elite interests could be overwhelmed by popular demand for limited and accountable government. In the new process, legitimacy was to be secured primarily through the credibility of the CoE and decision-making by the coalition partners. However, the emphasis on a people-driven constitution in the preceding years had built expectations that made a constitutional settlement reached by a small group of political elites impossible. To address the expectation of inclusiveness and public participation without endangering political control, the new process relied primarily on two things: (1) a diverse membership in the key decision-making bodies (the CoE and the main political body, the Parliamentary Select Committee [PSC]) and (2) linking the new process tightly to the old, thus allowing some of the popular legitimacy of the first to be transferred to the second. The link was most strongly expressed in the requirement that, on all but the contentious issues, the CoE was merely to "harmonize" the drafts produced in that hugely participatory process.

The CoE was also required to draw upon the views presented by the public in the previous process (Review Act 2008, section 29). In this way, the outcomes of the earlier process were to be carried through to the new one and the public was assured that views expressed and decisions made earlier would not be ignored. In addition, perhaps intending to meet the public halfway, provision was made for limited and targeted public engagement by the CoE and a special mechanism for a form of elite civil society engagement was devised: the 2008 Review Act required the CoE to consult a "Reference Group" of representatives of civil society organizations.

Overall then, the new process demanded that politicians decide the major contentious issues and acknowledged the importance of public engagement but limited it. As explained below, it was also cleverly structured to make it politically costly for the politicians to fail to agree at the crucial parliamentary committee stage. Nonetheless, the fact that the support of the governing coalition was necessary for the process to conclude successfully was a major departure from the first process. The goal was that Kenyans would not vote in another constitutional referendum in which the major factions of the political elite were on opposite sides.

II.A *The Committee of Experts (CoE)*

The clear intention in the 2008 Review Act was to depoliticize the CoE as much as possible. It was to be independent; its members were required to have "knowledge of and experience in" certain prescribed matters (section 10); and, unusually, three of the nine voting members were to be foreigners. The latter requirement, which mirrored the arrangements for the commissions set up under the Accord and the special court for matters arising in the process, was presumably to address the fear that, rather than acting as a more technical, expert body seeking principled solutions, like so many other Kenyan institutions and the CKRC before it, the CoE would be riven along ethnic and partisan lines and driven by old disagreements. The foreigners, a South African, a Ugandan, and a Zambian, were to add an element of neutrality. The selection of the members of the CoE by Parliament was also relevant symbolically as it removed it from the domain of the presidency, and politically as the ODM, Odinga's party, dominated Parliament.

The CoE started by reviewing the three principal draft constitutions that had been produced between 2000 and 2005. After public consultation on what issues should be identified as contentious (which was loosely understood as "not agreed" by the political actors),[7] the CoE identified three: (1) the structure of the state (not whether there should be devolution as that was provided for in all the earlier drafts, but what form it should take); (2) the system of government; and (3) transition in the judiciary. The first two were obvious because they had defined the main opposing positions taken for the referendum in 2005. The last may have been a surprise, however, by this point problems with the judiciary were ubiquitous and its inclusion was not contested. Pushing against the limited nature of this process, some Kenyans argued for other issues such as land and religious courts to be categorized as contentious but they were not because the three earlier drafts did not differ materially in their treatment. The CoE conducted further public consultations on the identified contentious issues, and held meetings with politicians and experts.

Things moved slowly. As before, a number of legal challenges to the process were launched (none successful) and sectors of the media took delight in belittling the CoE and deriding the process. The first clear indication that the process was on track was in November 2009 when the CoE released a draft constitution to the public for the brief month of consultations provided for in the Review Act. It then amended the draft in response to the public's views, most importantly by removing the proposed regional (middle) level of government and revising the number of

---

[7] The CoE's decision to consult the public on this was controversial in some circles. The 2008 Review Act required it to identify those issues and did not require it to consult. However, alert to public sensitivities about the diminished role of the public and the expanded role of politicians in the process, the CoE nonetheless consulted on the issue. This decision may have assisted the CoE in building much needed credibility.

units that were now to be the only subnational level. Early in 2010, it handed the revised draft to the politicians.

II.B *The Parliamentary Select Committee (PSC)*

The Review Act gave the twenty-seven–member PSC twenty-one days to deliberate on the CoE's draft, reach consensus on the issues that had been identified as contentious, and then return it to the CoE to incorporate the "achieved consensus" (section 33). Issues not identified as contentious by the CoE were, formally at least, out of bounds for the politicians. It was at the PSC stage, with the key political actors at the table, that the major political agreements had to be hammered out. But, as already noted, there was an implicit deadlock-breaking mechanism in the unstated assumption that, if the PSC could not agree, the CoE draft stood.

After difficult negotiations behind closed doors, the PSC produced a revised draft with changes to many sections, including provisions that clearly fell outside those identified as contentious. For example, it amended the electoral system, replacing the CoE's proposal with provisions agreed in the 2008 mediation: it revised the structure of the police, reduced provisions laying down strict integrity criteria for public officials, removed a number of the many independent commissions in the CoE draft, and slimmed down the Bill of Rights. A good number of these changes removed provisions that had been included in response to public submissions and they were later reversed by the CoE. At the same time, the politicians did not remove various provisions that they were known to dislike, such as a public right to recall elected representatives and controls on their salaries, presumably because of the downstream constraint of a referendum and memories of the previous process.

But the PSC also amended provisions concerning each of the three contentious issues. It rejected the parliamentary system proposed by the CoE in favor of an "American style" presidential system; it softened the CoE's proposals for devolved government; and it deleted a transitional provision requiring all judges to be "vetted" if they wished to continue serving on the bench. The agreement to adopt a presidential system appeared to be a huge concession by the Odinga wing of the coalition and Kenyans remain unsure what prompted it. Some suggest that it was agreed upon in exchange for a strengthening of the system of devolved government. But, if that was the case, the deal was not honored and the ODM was simply outsmarted. Others think that a presidential system suited the ODM now that it believed (wrongly it turned out) that it would win a presidential election. Many pin responsibility on Machiavellian maneuvers of William Ruto (now vice president) who, in a calculation relating to his political future, abandoned Odinga's side on the issue of the system of government and joined up with the Kibaki wing. What was clear to all was that the political consensus was fragile. Indeed, before the draft was handed over to Parliament, an unsuccessful attempt was made to convene a cross-party group that could reach a new agreement.

The CoE adapted the draft to incorporate many of the PSC's proposals. Sensitive to the tension among the politicians (or fearful of the ability of disgruntled politicians to derail the entire process), it not only accepted the PSC's decisions on contentious issues as the Review Act required, but also incorporated a considerable number of PSC amendments on matters outside the three contentious areas. This may be considered a lesson learned from the previous failed process. Nonetheless, the CoE resisted some of the PSC proposals, sometimes by simply retaining provisions that the PSC had rejected and sometimes by revising its original proposal to chart a middle way between its initial proposal and the PSC's position. Significantly, the CoE reinstated that requirement that judges should be vetted.

II.C *Parliament*

Tensions were high when the revised draft reached Parliament. Over 100 amendments were proposed but none had cross-party support and none received anywhere near the 65 percent majority required to pass. In the absence of a provision stipulating the majority required to adopt the constitution, the Speaker ruled that the usual requirement of a simple majority applied. On April 1, 2010, Parliament approved the draft submitted by the CoE without amendment. It was published, and a period of public education preceded the referendum.

II.D *The Referendum*

Now two political hurdles had been overcome – agreement in the PSC and approval in Parliament – but the underlying reluctance of the agreement made the third, the referendum, formidable. Disputes continued up to voting day. Ruto, who had "defected" from the Odinga camp during the meetings of the PSC to support the adoption of a presidential system, led an energetic "No" campaign focused on allegations that the new constitution would undermine land rights in the Rift Valley. Churches joined in, claiming that the constitution permitted abortion and gay marriage and provided unacceptable recognition of Muslim communities in its protection of Kadhis' courts.[8] But, critically, in one of the clearest public demonstrations of a partnership since the power-sharing agreement was concluded, President Kibaki and Raila Odinga campaigned jointly for the "Yes" vote, appearing together at rallies often enough to be persuasive. Although party structures were weak, Kibaki and Odinga's joint campaign drew in four of the five major ethnic groups. By and large, the less enthusiastic among their colleagues toed the line.

---

[8] Kadhis' courts were included in the Kenyan Constitution since independence because, in the international agreement through which parts of the present Kenya that then belonged to the Sultan of Oman were ceded to Kenya, Kenya undertook to protect the Kadhis' court system (Committee of Experts on Constitutional Review 2010, 58).

August 5, 2010 was referendum day. It passed peacefully and the Constitution was approved by over 67 percent of the voters. The promulgation of the Constitution on August 27 brought a huge crowd to Uhuru Park in celebration once again. Despite its sometimes vicious campaign, the "No" camp conceded gracefully and thousands enthusiastically celebrated the "rebirth" of Kenya and the beginning of the "second republic." In Odinga's words, "today we close a long chapter in our history. . . . We have opened a clean, new page in our book. On that page we begin to write the story of an equal and just society" (Odinga 2013). But the compromised nature of the transition was no secret and the promulgation event itself provided evidence of the hold of the past and challenges ahead. It was dominated by a parade of military force, a general stood beside President Kibaki when he signed the new Constitution and held it up to the crowd, and among the guests was International Criminal Court indictee, Sudan's President Bashir, invited in flagrant breach of Kenya's international obligations "because he [was] a neighbor."

II.E *Shallow Consensus*

The second process secured the elite consensus that had eluded the first but, as events since then confirm, that consensus was shallow, seemingly achieved not because political elites were convinced by the substance of the new constitution but because this time the perceived costs of not agreeing were too high socially, politically, and economically: Kenya in 2010 was very different from Kenya between 2002 and 2005 and this difference drove consensus and suppressed conflict. Among other things, the violence after the 2007 elections had revealed to Kenyans more starkly than ever before how high the costs of escalating disagreement could be. This recognition appears to have led prominent civil society actors and perhaps politicians to support compromises that they had rejected before.

Moreover, politicians were aware that the public was unlikely to be impressed if constitutional change was blocked yet again for reasons that were blatantly opportunistic. Further, as President Kibaki reached the end of his second (and final) term, calculations about future political prizes changed. Many said that Kibaki himself was eager to secure his legacy by promulgating a new constitution; for others, a new race for the presidency was to be won. All the main actors were also aware of the watchful eye of the international community. Kenya's economy had suffered a severe shock in the violence of 2007/2008 and its status as a leader in the region had been shaken. Promulgation of the new constitution would signal to the international community and, critically, investors, that Kenya was moving forward; failure to agree would signal the opposite.

More ominously, there was a sense in some parts of the commercial sector and perhaps elsewhere that not much would change under the new constitution: why would a new constitution change the way in which business was done or unsettle the arrangements that protected the interests of the elite (Ghai 2010)? In addition, despite the cross-ethnic support for the Constitution in the referendum, there was little to indicate that, generally, citizens' loyalty to the Constitution came anywhere near their loyalty to their tribal leaders. All of this suggests that the adoption of the Constitution neither was a "cathartic moment in which elites and society agree on a set of binding principles," nor marked "the beginning of a gradually consolidating consensus" (Wheatley 2013, 164).

III PUBLIC PARTICIPATION AND PEOPLE-DRIVEN CONSTITUTION MAKING

The programs of public participation in both Kenya's constitution-making processes have been rightly admired by constitution makers in other countries. Indeed, even before one takes account of the depth of engagement, the sheer scale of participation is astonishing. The CKRC collected over 35,000 submissions (Constitution of Kenya Review Commission 2002, 4) and, the CoE received 65,890 submissions (Committee of Experts 2009, 6; 2010, 41).[9]

The scale and depth of public participation in Kenya's two processes is largely attributable to the role civil society played over a long period of time and its insistence that the process should be inclusive (Mutunga 1999; Cottrell and Ghai 2004; Mutua 2008). For example, in 1999, lack of agreement between civil society and the government on the composition of the CKRC led to a parallel civil society initiative to review the constitution. In this initiative, a "People's Commission of Kenya," appointed along the same lines as set out for the CKRC in the Review Act, started to collect the public's views on constitutional reform. Clearly the CKRC could not conduct a legitimate process while it was regarded as an instrument of Moi's government and those in opposition were running their own process. The outcome was both revision of the composition of the CKRC and an understanding of the importance of including civil society.

Importantly, civil society activism was matched by the CKRC and CoE's commitment. So, a second reason for the extensive public participation programs was the energy that the constitution-making bodies put into it. The 1997 Review Act set out an elaborate framework for public participation requiring the CKRC to visit and set up forums in every one of the 210 electoral districts (section 18). The CKRC interpreted this mandate as one for "people-driven" constitution making and set about providing education on constitutional issues and then eliciting submissions. In doing this, in addition to the activities of its staff, members of the CKRC visited all electoral constituencies collecting views and received an overwhelming response (Cottrell and Ghai 2007). At the same time, it conducted a massive publicity

9 The higher number of submissions in the second process may be explained by the fact that the CoE counted oral submissions as well as written ones whereas the CKRC count may include written submissions only.

campaign through the media supported by civil society groups. As a result, during the life of the CKRC, constitutional reform was consistently a top media item. Its first draft constitution was accompanied by a "Short Report" explaining in simple terms what people had said, how it had responded, and why (Constitution of Kenya Review Commission 2002).

By the time of the referendum – the most inclusive element of public participation – people were well versed on the issues. Nonetheless, this process did not lead to a new constitution. Among others, Ghai, the chairperson of the CKRC, attributes this failure to the fact that the process was hijacked by politicians – the elite "interfered" (Abbiate, Böckenförde and Federico 2018; Macharia and Ghai 2018). However, as Negretto (see Chapter 5) and others argue, constitutional reform without elite support will either fail or, even if the constitution is changed, will not be implemented.

As already explained, the scale of public participation in the second process was intended to be more modest than that under the CKRC. However, as described above, to avoid alienating important and influential parts of civil society (including, importantly, the church), the CoE was to convene a "Reference Group" of representatives of thirty identified civil society groups to canvass views on the contentious issues and for assistance in breaking any deadlocks. This simply did not work except perhaps to allow the politicians to say that civil society had been given a fair chance. When disputes among politicians about membership of the Reference Group were resolved and it was convened, it was completely divided, reflecting well-known and deeply entrenched disagreements. The public consultations that the CoE itself did were more successful. Following the CKRC's example, it visited many parts of the country and accepted submissions. Constitutional issues were discussed on television shows both in the usual format of interviews and panels and through dramatized conversations that explained difficult concepts. As the process drew to an end, social media and, particularly, text messaging were used by the CoE to challenge a campaign of misinformation. Once again, for many months, constitutional issues dominated the media.

The bigger question is the impact of the inclusive process and ambitious public engagement programs. In particular, the civil society organizations that put huge energy into mobilizing public interest were neither united nor necessarily neutral. Moreover, as with other political groups in Kenya, civil society alliances were not stable. To some extent this complicates an attempt to distinguish between elites and the public. Although civil society actors claimed to speak for the common people, some representatives of civil society tried to straddle both elite interests and broader public interests and many were somewhere in between.[10]

The way in which the referenda campaigns were conducted and the fact that in both voting was largely along ethnic lines also may suggest that the energy and

---

[10] Matunga describes this situation in writing about the campaigns for a constitutional review process in the 1990s (1999).

resources expended on public participation was not justified. This needs further research. Saati's recent rigorous comparison of the Zimbabwean and Kenyan processes also suggests that, although the level of democratic engagement in Kenya increased over the period of constitutional review, we cannot simply conclude that the public participation process was the reason. But, as Saati notes, there are other ways in which a process of public engagement may enrich a society and strengthen constitutionalism: it may increase the legitimacy of the constitution; it may increase knowledge of constitutional rights; and it may contribute to reconciliation between previously antagonistic parties (Saati 2015, 279). As the conclusion to this chapter suggests, it is too early to assess this in the case of Kenya.

IV CONSTITUTIONAL CONTINUITY

As noted above, the independence constitution that governed the process of constitutional change required any alterations to be adopted by a 65 percent majority of all members of Parliament. The 1997 Review Act fleshed out this provision, setting out a process for developing new constitutional proposals but did not, and could not, change the requirement of parliamentary approval. Underpinned by the relatively common understanding across Commonwealth Africa that the authority to alter includes an authority to replace,[11] the legal framework signaled a commitment to legal continuity. However, as the process unfolded, the question of constitutional continuity became more complicated.

First, initially the 1997 Review Act captured the expectation of many Kenyans that the NCC would be the body that decided the content of the constitution and that the role of Parliament would be purely formal. Parliament was to approve the NCC's draft within seven days of receiving it with no amendment. In some ways, the NCC resembled the large national conferences that characterized constitutional reform in Francophone Africa in the early 1990s. However, those bodies generally declared themselves to be sovereign and to exercise constituent power – these were cases of constitutional rupture which the Kenyan process was not. Formally, the Kenyan approach was closer to the 1993 South African process where, to secure constitutional continuity, the draft Interim Constitution approved in multiparty negotiations was adopted by the apartheid Parliament with no changes. But, the political contexts in South Africa and Kenya could not have been more different.

The South African Interim Constitution was a political agreement, negotiated by political elites in a forum similar to the round tables of eastern Europe in the early 1990s, and then adopted in Parliament by the parties to that agreement that were then represented in Parliament. By contrast, the 2000 Kenyan process expected Parliament to accept a draft constitution agreed by a body in which elected

---

[11] Emphasis on public engagement over the past decades may be changing this assumption and see also Chapter 1 of this volume.

politicians could be overruled. When political differences over the NCC draft became acute, Parliament removed the provision in the Review Act that required it to approve the NCC draft without amendment. In doing this, the Kibaki camp was patently defending its political interests but its formal defense of the change relied on constitutional continuity. It said that, in removing Parliament's right to amend a draft, the Review Act was inconsistent with the Constitution.

Secondly, and more profoundly, the decision in *Njoya*, that the Constitution could not be replaced following the amendment procedure it set out, turned the generally accepted legal approach in Kenya on its head. Construed as an exercise of constituent power, the court said that the adoption of any totally new constitution was to be by referendum. The main judgment by Judge Ringera also asserts that the "basic structure" of the constitution, as understood in the Indian case Kesavananda Bharathi Sripandanagalavaru v State of Kerala (1973), can be changed only by the people. Although it was widely criticized, the *Njoya* decision was not appealed. Instead, provision for a referendum was added to the process.

Nonetheless, like the 2001 process, and despite *Njoya*, the 2008 process was built on an understanding that constitutional continuity was necessary. It was again set in motion by a Review Act that supplemented the process in the Constitution. However, as explained above, for both political reasons (the opposition wanted the agreed requirements to be set in stone) and legal reasons (legal clarity that amendment included replacement), on this occasion the Constitution itself was also amended to set out the parliamentary process more precisely and to confirm the requirement of a referendum.[12] In other words, in a marriage of constitutional continuity and constituent power, the Constitution was brought into line with the High Court's interpretation of the process for replacing it and the political agreement concerning a constitution adoption was constitutionalized.

V ROLE OF THE JUDICIARY

Kenya is famously litigious but the use of the courts is also informed by their reputation. It has been said that the aphorism "why hire a lawyer if you can buy a judge?" was coined in Kenya and, by the late 1990s, many Kenyans had little confidence in the judiciary both because it was perceived to act at the bidding of the executive and because many judges were notoriously corrupt. Nonetheless, or perhaps because of this, between 2001 and 2005, courts became involved in the review process as litigation was used persistently in attempts to derail it (Cottrell and Ghai 2004; Juma and Okpaluba 2012). *Njoya* was the most significant of these decisions. It changed the course of Kenyan constitutional history but, as Kenyans recognized, the litigation was also an attempt to block constitutional change.

---

[12] See Chapter 1 of this volume for other examples of legal continuity in democratic constitution making.

Perhaps ironically, in addition to adding the requirement of a referendum to the process, a requirement that may have seemed to strengthen the role of citizens, Njoya paved the way for elected politicians to change the draft approved at the NCC and replace it with their own.

Using the typology developed by Landau (see Chapter 4) of courts playing a "catalytic," "blocking," or "shaping" role in constitution-making processes, on the face of things Njoya is a case that shaped the process. However, along with a number of other cases, it contributed to a political strategy to block the process. It was blockage by degree, causing the process to stall and distracting the CKRC's attention from the substance of constitutional reform to defending itself and the process. What is different about the Kenyan litigation from the cases Landau discusses is that, in Kenya, like many common-law jurisdictions, there is no specialized and separate constitutional court; a single judge in a regular trial court could suspend the process or demand changes that would cause delay or even halt it entirely. The impact of the legal system on constitutional processes deserves further investigation.

The judiciary's prominent role in the first process, combined with the opposition's lack of confidence in the judiciary, presented a problem for the negotiators in the peace process in 2008. They all recognized that a judicial arbitrator was necessary but Odinga's side was not prepared to give that role to the existing judiciary. The solution, mentioned above, was to establish the Interim Independent Constitutional Dispute Resolution Court to "determine all ... matters arising from the Constitutional review process" (Constitution of Kenya 1963, Article 60A). Curiously, however, the foreign judges on the Dispute Resolution Court did not participate in any of the cases that came before the Court.

In the eighteen months it took to establish the Dispute Resolution Court, the High Court heard numerous cases challenging the process but, perhaps now sensitive to the changed (and volatile) political climate and recognizing that the process needed to proceed, every case was dismissed. The Dispute Resolution Court itself heard seven cases, many based on very technical matters. These included a case about prisoners' right to vote in the referendum, and various challenges to the way in which the CoE fulfilled its mandate (Mukuna and Mbao 2014). Of these cases Andrew Omtata Okoiti & 5 others v Attorney General and 2 others (2010) raised the widest range of issues, challenging virtually every aspect of the process and also alleging that the way in which the Independent Electoral Commission was conducting the referendum meant that it could not be free and fair. Some cases were brought late in the process, shortly before the referendum, and two came after the referendum in attempts to set it aside and prevent the promulgation of the new Constitution.

None of the challenges succeeded. Indeed, the Court seems to have interpreted its brief as being to keep the process of constitutional review going, which it did. In particular, the Court was emphatic that it had no say about the content of the

Constitution and was concerned with process alone (Alice Waithera Mwaura & 12 others v Committee of Experts & 2 others 2010).[13] So, to use Landau's typology again, although much of the litigation was patently politically driven and intended to derail the process, the Court neither blocked or shaped the process: it guarded it.

By way of example, the last case before the Dispute Resolution Court challenged the legality of the planned proclamation of the Constitution. Ever pragmatic, the Court decided that, although technically the case of the petitioners was sound (the Electoral Commission had not waited the stipulated time to allow petitions to be lodged before promulgating the results), it would not find in favor of them because they had not paid the deposit that was required to accompany a petition and the time limit for that payment was the very day on which the case was heard (Mary Arivisa Mwami & another v Interim Independent Electoral Commission & 3 others 2010).

The Dispute Resolution Court did not displace the regular courts entirely and the High Court judges' complicity in attempts to block the process was made apparent on one extraordinary occasion. In 2004, toward the end of the first process, twenty-six religious leaders brought a case before the High Court arguing that the inclusion of Kadhis' Courts in the then current "independence" Constitution was unconstitutional, although these courts had been included in that Constitution in 1963. The petitioners hoped that, if they won this case, they would be able to stop the 2004 draft constitution from going ahead as it too included provisions on Kadhis' Courts. No judgment was given until, completely unexpectedly six years later, in May 2010, near the end of the second process and at a time when the question of the recognition of Kadhis' Courts was being relied on aggressively by the referendum's "No" campaigners, the High Court dusted off the record and handed down a decision. With extraordinary reasoning, the judgment declares that, indeed, the inclusion of Kadhis' Courts in the 1963 Constitution was "unconstitutional" (Jesse Kamau & Others v Attorney General & Another 2004). Few believed that the judgment was impartial, a view that was strengthened when it was relied on (unsuccessfully) in challenges to the 2010 draft constitution before the Dispute Resolution Court (Joseph Kimani & 2 others v Attorney General & 2 others 2010). In the end, the case had no effect and the 2010 Constitution protects the Kadhis' courts.

VI CONCLUSION: KENYA AFTER CONSTITUTION MAKING

With the adoption of the Constitution, an item on the list of root causes of the conflict reflected in Agenda Item Four of the 2008 Accord could be ticked off. Moreover, the Constitution had been adopted with popular and elite support and it was seen to promise that government would address many of Kenya's social and

---

[13] The Court relied, inter alia, on the constitutional language that established it and that stated it was to be concerned with the "process" of constitutional review only (Article 60A).

economic problems. It is also more liberal than its predecessor, with stronger accountability mechanisms, and better protection of the independence of the judiciary and rights (Murray 2013). Moreover, the creation of a second tier of government has brought substantial change to the political arrangements. It has dispersed power considerably and has strong popular support despite the governing party's continuing aversion to it.

Now, the presidency is no longer the only political prize. Governors and hordes of politicians are elected in the forty-seven counties and engage both in local and central politics with a complicated new mix of interests and pressures. In addition, fulfilling a textbook description of one of the strengths of devolution (or federalism), in a significant number of cases, national losers have become local winners, presumably easing tensions somewhat. Moreover, fulfilling another textbook promise, some marginalized groups have been able to elect their own leaders and so, presumably, will be less alienated from the system more generally (Cheeseman, Lynch, and Willis 2014, 15). Of course, as is also common, the system has led to some political controversies being "devolved," that is, becoming county matters and driving county politics rather than dissipating entirely – sometimes considered a good thing, sometimes not. Cheeseman, Lynch, and Willis conclude in a thoughtful analysis of its impact, that "decentralization in Kenya has generated a political system with a more robust set of checks and balances, but at the expense of fostering economic inefficiency, corruption and a new set of local controversies that have the potential to exacerbate corruption and fuel local ethnic tensions in some parts of the country" (2016, 6).

However, the fundamental question is whether the constitution-making process and the new Constitution itself have really contributed to addressing the deep underlying malaise and tension in Kenyan society. As Negretto argues in Chapter 5, elite agreement is an essential ingredient of a successful democratic constitution-making process and, in Kenya, it was well integrated with relatively strong public participation, securing a constitution with considerable public legitimacy. However, as I have already suggested, using Wheatley's words, the process and the Constitution represented neither a moment of elite and public agreement on a new set of principles nor the start of a growing consensus that would gradually consolidate the kind of democracy that might be able to address the root causes of the conflict (2013, 164). Elite agreement and public participation in an open constitution-making process should have provided a good start, yet the persistence of ethnic politics and the "power of the elite to coalesce and protect its own interests ... prevents a genuine redistribution of wealth and opportunities" (Cheeseman 2018). The broader, immediate complex political context of constitution making including high levels of access to the use of violence by different factions and threatened prosecutions in the International Criminal Court together with the long-standing and deep structural problems in Kenya meant that constitutional change could do little on its own (Cheeseman and Murray 2017).

To outsiders and Kenyans alike, the troubling events around and after the 2017 elections provided stark evidence of the ongoing instability of the system. The first elections under the 2010 Constitution in 2013 were peaceful. However, then the focus was on avoiding conflict and, as Cheeseman, Lynch, and Willis suggest, their outcome in which, despite the hopes (and expectations) of the Orange Democratic Movement, Raila Odinga was again defeated, fed into mistrust of the system and a sense of political marginalization (Cheeseman, Lynch, and Willis 2014, 16). This prognosis was realized in the 2017 elections, which were preceded by a high level of violence, and of which the presidential election was found to be so flawed by the Supreme Court that it was set aside and a rerun held two months later (Raila Amolo Odinga & another v Independent Electoral and Boundaries Commission & 4 others & Attorney General & another 2017).[14]

The script was all too familiar. Presidential incumbent, Uhuru Kenyatta, once again, competed against Raila Odinga and, once again, was declared winner by the Electoral Commission. Odinga refused to stand in the court-ordered rerun and Kenyatta easily won. That too was contested but, despite widespread misgivings about the ability of the Electoral Commission to run a sound election, this time the Court upheld the results (Mwau & 2 others v Independent Electoral and Boundaries Commission & 3 others 2017). Angry, Odinga embarked on a campaign to have himself declared "the people's president" and was "sworn in" in January 2018 before a huge crown in a public park in Nairobi. The government reacted swiftly and harshly, closing down media and making arrests. In a move that puzzled all but seasoned observers of Kenyan politics, this elite standoff did not last long: in March 2018 and with much fanfare, Kenyatta and Odinga shook hands, marking, they said, the conclusion of an understanding. This dramatic gesture ended the many protests to the legitimacy of the government and switched the focus of politicians to the 2022 elections.

These events, including the now-famous handshake, received considerable international coverage. But there is little reason to believe that a corner has been turned. In addition to the corruption of the elections, there are many more examples of apparent government disregard for the Constitution that feed concerns about democratic backsliding in Kenya. For instance, despite clear provisions intended to secure probity in public finance, in July 2015, the Auditor-General reported that a quarter of the budget had not been properly accounted for and matters have deteriorated since then (Freedom House 2016; Ndi 2018); attempts by government to control NGOs continue despite clear constitutional provisions protecting them; and media freedom has been severely curtailed both through legislation and arbitrary state action (Committee to Protect Journalists 2013; Peralta 2018). The serious domestic security situation has also provided a rationalization for abuse of power by the security services. The handshake, observers fear, is simply a sign that politics is back on its

---

[14] This was the first time an African court set aside the results of a presidential election.

old track of deal-making among elites with little attention to the underlying problems that hold back development and render the state inherently unstable (Cheeseman et al. 2019).

This does not mean that the constitution-making process has had no impact. I have already referred to the partially destabilizing effect of devolution on longstanding patterns of the exercise of power. In addition, vigorous discussion about the Constitution continues now, ten years after it was adopted, and there is a constant stream of constitutional challenges to state action. In part, this is simply politics working itself out in the courts; in part, it reflects an active citizenry demanding that constitutional arrangements be honored. But the change is not what Kenyans concerned with reining in state power hoped for. This should not be surprising. A constitution cannot on its own resolve the entrenched structural problems in society. In seeking to understand why constitutionalism in Africa has failed, Yash Ghai points to the nature of the state, the economy, and society and their relationship to one another. These characteristics are similar in many African countries and, he argues, are rooted in the colonial experience: The state is coercive; the economy is largely (and corruptly) controlled by the state through an elite that may appear in opposition in politics but which shares enough to resist change; and society is weak, in part subjugated by the state and in part complicit in the protection of the existing economic and political practices that protect its (apparent) interests (Ghai 2010 and see Cheeseman 2018). Constitutional arrangements cannot on their own reform an entire system.

REFERENCES

Abbiate, Tania, Markus Böckenförde, and Veronica Federico. 2018. "Introduction" in *Public Participation in African Constitutionalism*. Tania Abbiate, Markus Böckenförde, and Veronica Federico (eds.) Oxford: Routledge, 1–10.
Andreassen, Bård Anders, and Arne Tostensen. 2006. "Of Oranges and Bananas: The 2005 Kenya Referendum on the Constitution" Chr Michelsen Institute Working Paper WP: 13. www.cmi.no/publications/publication/?2368=of-oranges-and-bananas.
Annan, Kofi, and Martin Griffiths. 2009. "The Prisoner of Peace – An Interview with Kofi A. Annan." Centre for Humanitarian Dialogue. https://reliefweb.int/sites/reliefweb.int/files/resources/6F9DC0AD3921DFA7C12575890033E862-Full_Report.pdf.
Cheeseman, Nic. 2008. "The Kenyan Elections of 2007: An Introduction." *Journal of Eastern African Studies* 2: 166–184.
  2018. "The Covert Reasons behind Kenyatta-Odinga Ceasefire." *The Nation*. March 18, 2018: Nairobi. www.nation.co.ke/oped/opinion/The-covert-reasons-behind-Uhuru-Odinga-ceasefire/440808-4345728-qwip9x/index.html.
Cheeseman, Nic, and Christina Murray. 2017. "Power-Sharing in Kenya: Between the Devil and the Deep Blue Sea" in *Power-Sharing: Empirical and Normative Challenges*. Allison McCulloch and John McGarry (eds.) London: Routledge, 36–62.
Cheeseman, Nic, Gabrielle Lynch, and Justin Willis. 2014. "Democracy and Its Discontents: Understanding Kenya's 2013 Elections." *Journal of Eastern African Studies* 8: 2–24.

2016. "Decentralisation in Kenya: The Governance of Governors." *Journal of Modern African Studies* 54: 1–35.

Cheeseman, Nic, Karuti Kanyinga, Gabrielle Lynch, Mutuma Ruteere, and Justin Willis. 2019. "Kenya's 2017 Elections: Winner-Takes-All Politics As Usual?" *Journal of Eastern African Studies* 13: 215–234.

Chege, Michael. 2008. "Kenya: Back from the Brink?" *Journal of Democracy* 19: 125–139.

Cohen, Roger. 2008. "How Kofi Annan Rescued Kenya." *New York Review of Books*. www.nybooks.com/articles/2008/08/14/how-kofi-annan-rescued-kenya/.

Committee to Protect Journalists. 2013. "Kenya Passes Draconian Media Laws." December 2, 2013. https://cpj.org/2013/12/kenya-parliament-passes-draconian-media-laws.php.

Cottrell, Jill, and Yash Pal Ghai. 2004. "The Role of Constitution-Building Processes in Democratization: Case Study Kenya." www.constitutionnet.org/vl/item/role-constitution-building-processes-democratization-case-studies.

2007. "Constitution Making and Democratization in Kenya (2000–2005)." *Democratization* 14: 1–25.

Freedom House. 2016. "Freedom in the World: Kenya." https://freedomhouse.org/report/freedom-world/2016/kenya.

Ghai, Yash Pal. 2010. "The Chimera of Constitutionalism: State, Economy and Society in Africa" in *Law and (in)Equality: Contemporary Perspectives*. Swati Deva (ed.) Lucknow: Eastern Book Co, 313–331.

Juma, Laurence, and Chuks Okpaluba. 2012. "Judicial Intervention in Kenya's Constitutional Review Process." *Washington University Global Studies Law Review* 11(2): 287–364.

Juma, Monica Kathina. 2009. "African Mediation of the Kenyan Post 2007 Election Crisis." *Journal of African Studies* 27(3): 407–430.

Kirkby, Coel, and Christina Murray. 2016. "Constitution-Making in Anglophone Africa: We the People?" in *Growing Democracy in Africa: Elections, Accountable Governance, and Political Economy*. Muna Ndulo and Mamoudou Gazibo (eds.) Newcastle upon Tyne: Cambridge Scholars Publishing, 86–113.

Lindenmayer, Elisabeth, and Josie Lianna Kay. 2009. *A Choice for Peace? The Story of Forty-One Days of Mediation in Kenya*. New York: International Peace Institute. https://peacemaker.un.org/sites/peacemaker.un.org/files/KenyaMediation_IPI2009.pdf.

Macharia, Rose W., and Yash Ghai. 2018. "The Role of Participation in the Two Kenyan Constitution-Building Processes of 2000–2005 and 2010: Lessons Learnt?" in *Public Participation in African Constitutionalism*. Tania Abbiate, Markus Böckenförde, and Veronica Federico (eds.) Oxford: Routledge, 86–99.

Mueller, Susanne D. 2008. "The Political Economy of Kenya's Crisis." *Journal of Eastern African Studies* 2: 185–210.

2011. "Dying to Win: Elections, Political Violence, and Institutional Decay in Kenya." *Journal of Contemporary African Studies* 29(1): 99–117.

Mukuna, John, and Melvin L. M. Mbao. 2014. "Constitution-Making Dispute Resolution Mechanisms: Lessons from Kenya." *Mediterranean Journal of Social Sciences* 5: 727–733.

Murray, Christina. 2013. "Kenya's 2010 Constitution." *Neue Folge Band Jahrbuch des offentlichen Rechts* 61: 747–788.

Mutua, Makau. 2008. *Kenya's Quest for Democracy: Taming Leviathan*. Boulder: Lynne Rienner Publishers.

Mutunga, Willy. 1999. *Constitution-Making from the Middle: Civil Society and Transition Politics in Kenya, 1992–1997*. Nairobi and Harare: Sareat/MWENGO.

Ndi, David. 2018. "Highway Robbery and Sex Toys: Plunder by the Numbers." *The East African Review*, March 31, 2018. https://theeastafricanreview.info/op-eds/2018/03/31/highway-robbery-and-sex-toys-plunder-by-the-numbers.

Odinga, Raila. 2013. "Speech at Promulgation of Constitution." Nairobi. www.capitalfm.co
.ke/news/2010/08/full-speech-by-kenya-pm/.

Office of the AU Panel of Eminent Personalities. 2014. "Back from the Brink: The 2008 Mediation Process and Reforms in Kenya." www.kofiannanfoundation.org/mediation-and-
crisis-resolution/back-from-the-brink-the-2008-mediation-process-and-reforms-in-kenya/.

Peralta, Eyder. 2018. "As Government Ignores Court Order, Kenya's Media Blackout Continues." National Public Radio. February 2, 2018. www.npr.org/sections/parallels/2018/02/
02/582649991/as-government-ignores-court-order-kenyas-media-blackout-goes-into-4th-day.

Saati, Abrak. 2015. *The Participation Myth: Outcomes of Participatory Constitution Building
Processes on Democracy*. Umea: Umea University.

Throup, David W. 2008. "The Count." *Journal of Eastern African Studies* 2: 290–304.

Wheatley, Jonathan. 2013. "Conclusion" in *Patterns of Constitutional Design: The Role of
Citizens and Elites in Constitution-Making*. Jonathan Wheatley and Fernando Mendez
(eds.) Farnham: Ashgate, 161–164.

Whitaker, Beth Elise, and Jason Giersch. 2009. "Voting on a Constitution: Implications for
Democracy in Kenya." *Journal of Contemporary African Studies* 27: 1–20.

Official Documents and Laws

1963 Constitution of Kenya. Nairobi: Government Printer.

Alice Waithera Mwaura & 12 others v Committee of Experts & 2 others. 2010. Interim
Independent Constitutional Dispute Resolution Court at K.I.C.C. Nairobi, Constitutional Petition No. 7 of 2010.

Andrew Omtata Okoiti & 5 others v Attorney General and 2 others. 2010. Interim Independent
Constitutional Dispute Resolution Court at K.I.C.C. Nairobi, Constitutional Petition
No. 3 of 2010.

Committee of Experts on Constitutional Review. 2009. "Harmonized Draft Constitution of
Kenya Published on 17th November, 2009 by the Committee of Experts on Constitutional Review Pursuant to Section 32(1)(a)(i) of the Constitution of Kenya Review Act,
2008." Nairobi, Kenya: Committee of Experts.

 2010. "Final Report of the Committee of Experts on Constitutional Review." Nairobi,
Kenya: Committee of Experts.

Constitution of Kenya Review Act, Act 13 of 1997, as amended by Act 6 of 1998, Act 5 of 2000
and Act 2 of 2001. (Review Act, 1997).

Constitution of Kenya Review Act, Act 9 of 2008, as amended by Act 6 of 2009 and Act 9 of
2009. (Review Act, 2008).

Constitution of Kenya Review Commission. 2002. The People's Choice: The Report of the
Constitution of Kenya Review Commission (Short Version). Nairobi, Kenya.

Jesse Kamau & Others v. The Attorney General & Another. 2004. Nairobi High Court Misc.
Application No. 890 of 2004.

Joseph Kimani & 2 others v Attorney General & 2 others. 2010. Interim Independent Constitutional Dispute Resolution Court at K.I.C.C. Nairobi, Constitutional Petition No. 3 of
2010.

Kenya National Dialogue and Reconciliation. 2008. Annotated Agenda and Timetable. Nairobi, Kenya. https://peacemaker.un.org/sites/peacemaker.un.org/files/KE_080101_Anno
tated%20Agenda%20for%20the%20Kenya%20Dialogue%20and%20Reconciliation.pdf.

Kesavananda Bharathi Sripandanagalavaru v State of Kerala [1973] Supp. India SCR 1.

Mary Arivisa Mwami & another v Interim Independent Electoral Commission & 3 others. 2010.
Interim Independent Constitutional Dispute Resolution Court at K.I.C.C. Nairobi,
Constitutional Petition No. 7 of 2010.

Mwau & 2 others v *Independent Electoral and Boundaries Commission & 3 others.* 2017. Supreme Court, Nairobi, Presidential Election Petition 2 & 4 of 2017: November 20, 2017.

Njoya and Others v *Attorney-General and others* [2004] LLR 4788 (HCK).

Njuguna Michael Kung'u, Gacuru wa Karenge & Nichasius Mugo v *The Republic, Attorney General and CKRC*, Kenya High Court Misc. Application No. 309 of 2004.

Raila Amolo Odinga & another v *Independent Electoral and Boundaries Commission & 4 others & Attorney General & another.* 2017. Supreme Court, Nairobi, Presidential Election Petition 1 of 2017: September 20, 2017.

Report of the Committee of Eminent Persons. 2006. Nairobi: Government Printer. (Kiplagat Report).

Report of the Commission of Inquiry into Post-Election Violence. 2008. Nairobi: Government Printer. (Waki Report).

Report of the Independent Review Commission on the General Elections Held in Kenya on 27 December, 2007. 2008. Nairobi: Nairobi: Government Printer. (Kriegler Report).

10

The Anatomy of Constitution Making

From Denmark in 1849 to Iceland in 2017

Thorvaldur Gylfason

In contrast to other case studies included in this volume, this chapter analyzes the making of a democratic constitution that, although drafted and ratified by citizens according to a procedure established in advance, is still not in force. It aims to present the politics underlying the constitution bill produced by Iceland's constituent assembly of 2011 and the outcome of this process in the light of its precedents, the 1944 Icelandic Constitution and the 1849 Danish Constitution. This comparative framework illustrates the inherent conflict between parliamentary elites and the people in Icelandic constitutionalism. This conflict, I argue, explains the recent failure to produce a new democratic constitution in Iceland.

The structure of the chapter is as follows. Section I traces the genealogy of Iceland's constitutionalism back to Denmark's 1849 constitution, tells the story of Iceland's constitution from 1874 to 1944 when Iceland declared full independence and became a republic, and then describes the semi-presidential-cum-parliamentary constitution from 1944 and the modest amendments made to it since then. Section II explains the factors that led to the decision to replace Iceland's 1944 constitution after the 2008 financial crash. Section III discusses procedural aspects of the revision and the reasons behind Parliament's refusal to ratify the new constitution despite its wide popular support. Section IV proposes some lessons to be learned from Iceland's experience thus far with the creation of a constitution within a preexisting democratic regime following a severe economic and political crisis. Section V concludes.

I HISTORICAL BACKGROUND

The common foundation of the constitutions of Denmark and Iceland was laid in 1849, after a spate of European revolutions the year before. The Danish monarch, King Fredrik VII, acceded to liberal demands for a new constitution to be drawn up by a constituent assembly elected in 1848. Effectively ending absolute monarchy, the new constitution outlined a constitutional monarchy in which the king would share power with a bicameral parliament where the lower house would be directly elected by the people and the upper house would include royal appointees. Denmark's 1849 constitution remains essentially unchanged to this day.

Two years later, in 1851, Iceland held its own National Assembly, which demanded increased political liberty as well as free external trade. Before it could conclude its proceedings, however, the representative of the king abruptly dissolved the assembly. When the Icelanders celebrated the 1,000th anniversary of the settlement of Iceland in 1874, King Christian IX of Denmark brought Iceland its first constitution, essentially an Icelandic translation of the Danish constitution from 1849. Iceland was still part of the Danish realm. The Icelandic Parliament had been unable to agree on a constitution and to agree with the Danish government, triggering the king's unilateral initiative to resolve the impasse in 1874.

In practical terms, the 1874 Constitution brought to Iceland by King Christian IX made no significant difference as it simply confirmed Iceland's position within the Danish constitutional monarchy, a less than crystal-clear arrangement due to the Danish constitution's somewhat murky provisions on the role of and relationship between the Parliament and the monarch. There was a desire for a democratic system of government characterized by a clear separation of powers along US and French lines, but this was not clearly spelled out in Denmark's 1849 constitution.

Home rule in 1904, granted to Iceland without constitutional change by the Danish Parliament in 1901, was arguably the most significant event in Iceland's political history. A new agreement (Act of Union) on a royal union between Denmark and Iceland in 1918 marked the beginning of Iceland as a sovereign state. The 1874 Constitution was amended accordingly in 1920 when the Supreme Court of Iceland was established.

In 1934, the constitution was amended a second time to increase the number of seats in Parliament to keep up with the population and a third time in 1942 to reduce the rural bias of the electoral provision of the constitution. The 1874 Constitution contained a detailed provision on elections to Parliament, laying out the division of the country into electoral districts in keeping with prevailing conditions. Unlike the Danish Constitution from 1849, the Icelandic 1874 Constitution did not proscribe an equal apportionment of parliamentary seats to ensure adherence to the principle of "one person, one vote."

In 1845, the number of seats in Parliament was 26, one for every 2,200 Icelanders, a figure that had decreased to 1,800 by 1874. The amendment of 1920 increased the number of seats to 42 to keep up with the increase in population. In 1934, again by constitutional amendment, the number of seats was increased further to 49, lifting the population-per-seat ratio slightly to 2,300. Then came the bitterly fought constitutional amendment of 1942, increasing the number of parliamentary seats to 52, 1 for every 2,400 Icelanders. At that time there were four parties in Parliament. The largest was the conservative Independence Party. The second largest was the

Progressive Party, which derived its support mainly from rural areas and was, therefore, overrepresented in Parliament. In 1931, for example, the Progressives had won a majority of seats in the Parliament with only 35 percent of the votes, a result they had almost achieved in 1927 when they won 45 percent of the seats with 30 percent of the votes. There were in the Parliament two smaller parties on the left, Social Democrats and Socialists, previously Communists.

In 1942, the Independence Party and the two left-wing parties united against the Progressives by changing the electoral provision in the constitution to make voting rights more equal, albeit far short of equal apportionment of parliamentary seats. Two elections were held in the spring and fall of 1942 as two consecutive Parliaments were needed to ratify the constitutional amendment. The Progressives became furious and were hardly on speaking terms with other parties for several years afterward. This episode was living proof that constitution making and consensus rarely go together. In the words of Elster (2012): "Contrary to a traditional view, constitutions are rarely written in calm and reflective moments. Rather, because they tend to be written in periods of social unrest, constituent moments induce strong emotions and, frequently, violence."

The 1918 Act of Union agreement included a provision stating that the agreement could be revised after twenty-five years should either country wish to do so. In 1943, at the height of the Second World War and with Icelandic politics in turmoil, the Icelandic Parliament decided to prepare a unilateral repeal of the Act of Union with Denmark which, occupied by Nazi Germany, was unable to fend for itself. The following year, 1944, the Icelanders decided in a referendum during May 20–23, to declare full independence and establish a republic. Turnout was 98 percent. Of the votes cast, 99.5 percent supported the separation from Denmark and 98.5 percent supported the new provisional constitution establishing the republic.

As is common when nations rise up to declare independence, a new constitution to replace the one from 1874 was originally intended to be an integral part of the establishment of the Republic of Iceland, or so it was hoped, but this was not to be. Rather than have a new constitution prepared as befitted a new republic, the parties in Parliament settled on modest changes to the 1874 constitution, the bare minimum required. Most importantly, the word "king" needed to be replaced by the word "president." The political parties in Parliament wanted the new president to be selected by Parliament and to be merely a ceremonial figure head, like a king, but Governor Sveinn Björnsson, soon to become Iceland's first president, was able to have his way, supported by Iceland's first scientific opinion poll that showed 70 percent of respondents in favor of a president elected directly by the people. This gave Iceland one of the first popularly elected presidents in Europe, after France in 1848 and Germany in 1919.

The replacement of a hereditary monarch by a popularly elected president was crucial as it implied that Iceland's new republic was fundamentally different from Denmark's parliamentary democracy under a constitutional monarchy. While there had been, since 1901, a consensus in Denmark that the royal veto of legislation was a thing of the past there was no presumption that the same would apply to a popularly elected president in Iceland. Herein lies a fundamental difference between the design of Iceland's semi-presidential parliamentary system of government (Duverger 1980; Kristjánsson 2012) and Denmark's purely parliamentary system.[1]

Some members of the political establishment in Iceland have taken the view of Iceland's 1944 constitution that its provisions on, for example, the authority of the President to veto legislation are dead letters like the corresponding provisions in the constitution of Denmark. The matter was settled once and for all in 2004 when the president exercised this authority for the first time. The key here is that a parliamentary republic with a popularly elected president differs fundamentally from a parliamentary constitutional monarchy, especially when the constitution makers are known to have been keen on the separation of power of the three branches of government with suitable checks and balances in place (Kristjánsson 2012). Those who insist on the powerlessness of the popularly elected president of Iceland usually do so as guardians of Iceland's political elites keen to preserve their executive as well as legislative powers and privileges, disregarding that Iceland's constitution was designed to empower a popularly elected president to exercise a certain independence vis-à-vis the Parliament to strengthen the foundation of Icelandic democracy.

A lack of clarity or, put bluntly, the apparent meaninglessness of several clauses concerning the role of the president of the Republic, is one reason why the 1944 constitution was described as "provisional" by representatives of all four political parties in Parliament at the time (Jóhannesson 2012). At first, they promised an overhaul of the new constitution no later than 1946. This is how they managed to convince 98.5 percent of the voters to support the new constitution in the 1944 referendum. In an address to the nation in 1949, President Sveinn Björnsson reminded the politicians of their failure to keep their promise of a new constitution: "we still have a mended garment, originally made for another country, with other concerns, a hundred years ago" (Björnsson 1949, my translation).

Since 1944, the constitution has been amended on several occasions. First, in 1959, the history from 1942 repeated itself when the Independence Party and the two left-wing parties in Parliament again united against the Progressives by changing the electoral provision in the constitution to make voting rights more equal, increasing the number of seats in Parliament to 60, giving a population-per-seat ratio of 2,800. At the same time, the last vestiges of the first-past-the-post electoral system gave way to proportional representation. A further change was made in 1984, effective in 1987, when the number of parliamentary seats was increased to its current level of 63,

---

[1] Today, in Europe, Austria, Bulgaria, Finland, France, Iceland, Ireland, Poland, Portugal, and Romania can be classified as countries with semi-presidential parliamentary systems of government even if the power of the President varies from country to country (Gylfason 2013).

giving a population-per-seat ratio of 3,900. Since 1987, population growth has increased the population-per-seat ratio to 5,200; a low figure compared with, for example, Denmark's 31,000. The constitutional changes of 1942, 1959, and 1984 were mainly intended to reduce the inequality of voting rights by moving parliamentary seats from rural areas with dwindling populations to the emerging towns, including Reykjavík. The last such corrective amendment, in 1999, sufficed temporarily to eliminate the systemic rural bias favoring the Progressive Party. This improvement did not last, however. The problem reappeared in 2013 when the Progressives won 30 percent of the seats in Parliament with 24 percent of the popular vote (Helgason 2014). Unlike the amendments of 1942 and 1959, the ones in 1984 and 1999 were accomplished without great mayhem in Parliament.

To this day, rural areas remain significantly overrepresented in Parliament. Following the constitutional amendment of 1999, Iceland has six electoral districts, three in and around Reykjavík where two-thirds of the population live plus three rural districts. The votes of some rural inhabitants weigh almost twice as heavily as do votes in urban districts, an improvement from earlier times when the ratio was first four and then three, but a ratio of nearly two is still far higher than, for example, in Norway, and has in recent years led external election monitors to state repeatedly in their reports on Iceland that unequal voting rights on such a scale constitute a violation of human rights.[2] By design, the electoral system has produced a disproportionate representation in Parliament of the one-third of the electorate living outside the Reykjavík area. The 2013 election granted 45 percent of the seats in Parliament to the three rural constituencies where 35 percent of the voters reside while 55 percent of the seats went to the three urban districts where 65 percent of the voters live. For another example, the 2016 election gave the Independence Party and the Progressive Party, in government together since 2013, 40 percent of the vote and 46 percent of the seats in Parliament, 29 seats out of 63.[3]

Other amendments to the constitution include a reduction of the minimum voting age to twenty years in 1968 and to eighteen years in 1984. Parliament was made unicameral in 1991 to streamline the work of Parliament. New but rather modest provisions on human rights were added in 1995. Since 1944, Parliament has rejected or not acted on 100 proposed constitutional amendments of various kinds.

Along the way, from 1944 onward, Parliament appointed one constitutional committee after another, most of them consisting of Members of Parliament or their representatives. The four electoral reforms of 1942, 1959, 1984, and 1999 grew out of such work, as did the other less significant changes described above. These committees could never agree on a general overhaul, however, solemn promises from 1944 onward notwithstanding (Jóhannesson 2012). One such committee threw

---

[2] See OSCE (Organization for Security and Co-operation in Europe). www.osce.org/odihr/elections/iceland.

[3] For more on the history and intricacies of Iceland's electoral laws, see Helgason (2014).

in the towel after the president invoked his constitutional right to veto legislation for the first time in 2004. The legislation concerned a media bill that outside observers and some members of the opposition saw as an explicit attempt to rein in media seen as insufficiently supportive of the government. This was four years before the crash of 2008. Business moguls were making their presence felt in the media market, some friendly to the government, others less so. The president exercised his veto. The atmosphere was tense.

Rather than hold a referendum on the bill as stipulated by the constitution, the governing majority in Parliament (Independence Party and Progressives) decided to withdraw the bill without an explicit constitutional authorization for such a course of action. What happened next was that the governing parties' representatives on the Parliament's constitutional committee tried to induce the committee to agree to the abolition of the president's constitutional right to veto legislation, a proposal that might have been passed in Parliament at the time but would probably not have enjoyed much support among the public. The attempt failed. The episode is instructive because it demonstrates a widespread attitude among Members of Parliament; to many of them, the constitution that they have sworn to uphold is a nuisance (Kristjánsson 2012). Their concept of parliamentary democracy is that Parliament is king. In what follows, we will encounter further examples of this attitude.

II THE DECISION TO ADOPT A NEW ICELANDIC CONSTITUTION[4]

When Iceland's financial system collapsed in the fall of 2008, ordinary people from all walks of life took to the streets, banging their pots and pans and demanding corrective action, including constitutional reform. The government of the Independence Party and the Social Democrats, in office from 2007, resigned in early 2009. The two left-wing parties in Parliament, the Social Democrats and the Socialists, now named the Left-Green Movement, formed a minority government with the support of the Progressives who promised to defend the government against a vote of no confidence in Parliament. The Progressives offered their support on the condition that the new minority government would launch a constitutional revision process in which directly elected representatives of the people rather than politicians and their lawyers would do the work. The parliamentary election in the spring of 2009 gave the two left-wing parties in the minority government a small majority in Parliament, making the support of the Progressives in Parliament no longer necessary. The new government faced two urgent tasks: to restore the economy to health with assistance from the IMF, the other Nordic countries, the Faroe Islands, and Poland and to move forward with the promised, long overdue constitutional reform.

---

[4] This section draws on Gylfason (2013; 2016a; 2016b; 2018) and Gylfason and Meuwese (2017). See also Landemore (2014) and Meuwese (2013).

It was considered helpful that the Prime Minister, Jóhanna Sigurðardóttir, had been a long-standing but lonely advocate of constitutional reform.

As already mentioned, Parliament promised immediate constitutional overhaul after enacting the 1944 constitution, openly acknowledging the provisional nature of the new charter. As it turned out, however, MPs proved unable to offer but modest improvements of the electoral provision to meet the migration of voters from rural to urban areas as well as a change from a bicameral to a unicameral legislature in addition to some marginal adjustments. There have been no significant disagreements on constitutional issues as such among the political parties, with four exceptions, two long-standing ones and two more recent. All four exceptions reflect political differences rather than jurisprudential ones. The first two are particularly important because they involve human rights.

First, as described before, the disagreement among political parties on the electoral system erupted twice, in 1942 and 1959. The Progressives benefited from the unequal weight of votes in rural and urban areas and thus resisted electoral reform while other parties that would benefit from less inequality favored reform, and the latter, led by the Independence Party, carried the day in both cases. As already mentioned, external observers have declared the unequal weight of votes in Iceland to constitute a violation of human rights because of the extent of inequality in the voting system involved.[5]

Second, from the 1980s onward, some felt that Iceland's natural resources and their ownership and management merited a provision in the constitution but the political parties and their representatives in one parliamentary committee after another proved unable to agree on a formulation. The Social Democrats wanted a declaration that Iceland's natural resources belong to the people while the rest (Independence Party, Progressives, and the Socialist forerunners of the Left-Green Movement) wanted language loose enough to preserve the status quo, which to this day grants vessel owners virtually free access to fishing in Icelandic waters. Specifically, in recent years, vessel owners have been granted about 90 percent of the fisheries rent, leaving about 10 percent for the people, the rightful owner of the resource by law if not yet by the constitution (Thorláksson 2015).

According to the Icelandic National Audit Office, fishing firms recently channeled 95 percent of their declared financial support for political parties to the Independence Party and the Progressives.[6] In 2007, the United Nations Committee on Human Rights issued a binding opinion stating that the discrimination involved in the allocation of fishing rights to vessel owners constituted a violation of human rights, and instructed the Icelandic government to rectify the situation by removing the discriminatory element from the fisheries management system and by paying

---

[5] Source: See n. 2.
[6] Source: Icelandic National Audit Office. http://rikisendurskodun.is/utgefid-efni/fjarmal-stjorn malasamtaka/.

damages to the two fishermen who brought the case against Iceland before the committee. The government responded by promising a new constitution that would define Iceland's natural resources as the common property of the people, a promise that the government has failed to keep.

Third, the transfer of sovereignty has recently emerged as a bone of contention among politicians. While it has long been understood that Iceland needs to amend the provision on the transfer of sovereignty in the 1944 constitution like Denmark did in 1953 and Norway in 1962 in anticipation of possible future membership in the European Union, it recently came to light that Icelandic MPs representing the Independence Party and the Progressives and some representing the Left-Greens do not want such a revision. Rather, they appear to prefer to keep open the possibility of contesting Icelandic accession to membership in the European Union on constitutional grounds, a situation that would, by denying the voters the right to vote in favor of EU membership in a national referendum, make Iceland unique in Europe.

Fourth, after the president of Iceland exercised for the first time his constitutional right to refer legislation from Parliament to a national referendum in 2004, a right that had laid dormant since 1944, the Parliament's constitutional committee at the time considered removing the provision on the president's veto right from the constitution but, once again, could not agree. At issue was not the principle firmly enshrined in the 1944 constitution anchoring the authority of the nationally elected president to hold Parliament accountable to the people under a semi-presidential form of government but rather the sheer frustration by politicians that they could not always do as they wished.

The new government in 2009 took several steps, initially in close collaboration with the Independence Party and the Progressives, together in opposition in Parliament for the first time in the history of the republic. First, Parliament appointed a seven-member constitutional committee chaired by Dr. Guðrún Pétursdóttir, a physiologist and director of the Institute for Sustainability Studies at the University of Iceland. The committee was to gather background information and offer analysis for the benefit of those who would be tasked with drafting a new constitution or revising the old one from 1944. The committee produced a 700-page dossier offering many ideas and options. Also, the committee organized a National Assembly (or National Forum) comprising 950 individuals drawn at random from the National Register.

The National Assembly met for a day in late 2010 under expert supervision well-versed in collective intelligence (Page 2008; Fishkin 2009; Landemore 2012), and concluded its proceedings by declaring (a) that a new constitution was needed and (b) that it should include provisions on equal voting rights and national ownership of natural resources, among other things. The random selection of the 950 participants and the methodical application of the principles of collective intelligence aimed to ensure that the conclusions of the National Assembly reflected the popular will because every Icelander 18 years or older had an equal chance of being invited to take a seat in the National Assembly. A year later, in late 2011, 25 Constitutional Assembly representatives were elected from a roster of 522 candidates by the Single Transferable Vote method, an advanced election method used in Australia, Ireland, and Scotland to minimize the number of dead votes (Balinski and Laraki 2010).

A little later, one of the Icelandic newspapers, *DV*, conducted a detailed poll on key constitutional issues reporting separately the answers of a sample drawn from the general public, a majority of the 522 candidates who put their names forward in the Constitutional Assembly election, and 23 of the 25 who were elected (two could not be reached). The poll demonstrated a remarkably broad consensus across the three groups, showing, for example, that 65 percent of respondents among the general public wanted to change the constitution while 17 percent were against (18 percent passed) and that 72 percent wanted equal voting rights while 17 percent did not (11 percent passed). This poll did not ask about national ownership of natural resources, but other polls had shown overwhelming support for national ownership, signaling strong and widespread opposition to Iceland's oligarchic management of its marine resources (Kristjánsson 2011). When the same newspaper asked 23 of the 25 representatives elected to the Constitutional Assembly, 20 expressed support for equal voting rights while two were against and 22 expressed support for national ownership of natural resources while one was against (Gylfason 2013).

The Constitutional Council was given four months to do its work, from early April until the end of July 2011.[7] The 2010 Act on a Constitutional Assembly gave the Council practically full autonomy without any restriction concerning, for example, the choice between amending and replacing the constitution. The Council decided during the first week of its work that the best way to reflect the broad consensus in favor of constitutional reform among Council members as well as among the general public as confirmed by opinion polls would be to draft a new constitution *ab initio* (from the beginning) rather than propose piecemeal changes to the 1944 constitution. Even so, the 1944 constitution provided the underpinning of the drafting process. Several articles from 1944 appear unchanged in the Council's bill.

III PROCESS AND OUTCOME

As Negretto notes in Chapter 1 of this volume, some constitutions enable the legislature to either amend or repeal an existing constitution. This was the case with Iceland's 1944 constitution. However, in view of the low esteem of political parties, Parliament, and other institutions after the crash of 2008, it was clear that

7 The Constitutional Council was so named after Parliament responded to the Supreme Court's invalidation of the Constitutional Assembly election in early 2011 by appointing the twenty-five individuals who had received the most votes to the Constitutional Council. The Supreme Court had thus enabled the opponents of constitutional reform to question the popular mandate of the elected representatives (Nordal 2011).

Parliament could not assume the role of drafting a new constitution. This is why a special convention was given the task of proposing constitutional reform even if the 1944 constitution authorizes Parliament "to amend or supplement" the constitution (article 79), a stipulation that is not considered to prevent Parliament from drafting a new constitution from scratch and approving it in two parliamentary sessions with a general election in between. Put differently, the words "to amend or supplement" have been taken to subsume radical revision or replacement. It was on this basis that the Constitutional Council felt free to draft a new constitution from scratch. In keeping with the 1944 constitution the 2010 Act on a Constitutional Assembly stipulated that Parliament had the right to accept or reject the bill produced by the Constitutional Council. Despite the low esteem of Parliament after the crash and in view of the conciliatory gestures made by both government and opposition at the outset, no objections to this procedure were raised at the time. Writing Parliament completely out of the manuscript would have required sidestepping the 1944 constitution, a step that was considered unnecessary and impractical at the time but which, in retrospect, might have helped to prevent Parliament from undermining the constitutional reform project that Parliament itself had launched.

The work of the Council went smoothly from beginning to end, which was not really hard in view of the broad consensus on the need for reform. The haggling that took place revolved around details. The work was well organized and high-tech to save time and to facilitate the participation of the public in the proceedings, as described in Gylfason and Meuwese (2017). Even if the Council did not see itself as being bound by the conclusions of the National Assembly in 2010, the bill proved fully consistent with the will of the National Assembly with the sole exception that the National Assembly had called for a reduction in the number of seats in Parliament whereas the bill stipulates an unchanged number of seats at sixty-three. This conclusion was reached on the grounds that a reduced number of parliamentary seats might have been seen to undermine the aim of the bill to strengthen Parliament and the courts against executive overreach.

In addition to key provisions concerning equal voting rights and national ownership of natural resources, the bill also features important new provisions on environmental protection, electoral reform, the right to information, increased use of national referenda, the right to share sovereignty with other nations, the appointment of public officials, including judicial appointments, and more. The bill also aims to eliminate the ambiguities inherited from Denmark's 1849 constitution, including those on the role of the president. Further, the bill aims to impose a US-inspired layer of checks and balances on the constitution while preserving its original character inherited from Norway and Denmark. At the end of the four-month-long proceedings, the Council adopted its bill with twenty-five votes against zero, no abstentions. Nearly all individual provisions were passed with an overwhelming majority of votes in the Council. Some members of

Parliament, their reputation in tatters and their trust among the public at an all-time low, were not amused.[8]

In late 2011, three years had passed from the financial crash of 2008. Under IMF tutelage, the national economy was growing again. Against the odds, unemployment had been kept from rising to double-digit levels. So, even if three or four foreclosures of people's homes and businesses took place every day, there was a growing feeling that the worst horrors caused by the crash were behind. This feeling of fading gloom gave the opposition parties, the Independence Party and the Progressives, the courage to revert to their old ways. The Progressives turned against the constitutional reform process that they had helped launch. The Independence Party also turned fiercely against reform.

Apart from the economic upturn, there were two main reasons for this development. First, it was one thing to advocate constitutional reform in the abstract following a financial crash that had humiliated the Independence Party, in particular, and quite another to be confronted by twenty-five directly elected Constitutional Assembly representatives in broad consensus as the National Assembly of 2010 had been about equal voting rights, national ownership of natural resources, and other democratic reforms. Equal voting rights and electoral reform would make several sitting members of Parliament unlikely to win reelection. National ownership of natural resources would sever the umbilical cord between Iceland's oligarchs – that is, the vessel owners – and their agents in Parliament. This is because national ownership entails that those who exploit the resources would be required by the constitution to pay full consideration – that is, market price – for their right of access to the resources, access that they have thus far been granted either free or, since 2002 when nominal fishing fees were legislated, practically free of charge.

Immediately after the Constitutional Assembly election, three persons with formal ties to the Independence Party filed technical complaints about the way the election was organized. Six Supreme Court justices, five of them Independence Party appointees, declared the election null and void even if no one had claimed that the alleged technical flaws could have influenced the outcome of the election as required by law for an election result to be invalidated. The relevant part of Article 15 of Act No. 90/2010[9] establishing the Constitutional Assembly states: "If a voter considers that a member of the Constitutional Assembly lacks eligibility, his candidacy has not fulfilled legal requirements or his election is unlawful for other reasons, he can file a complaint against his election with the Supreme Court which will rule on its validity." None of these conditions established by the law were met. This decision by the Supreme Court was visibly politically motivated, substantively

[8] For an external review of the bill, see Elkins, Ginsburg, and Melton (2012).
[9] See www.althingi.is/lagas/139a/2010090.html. Further, see the following open letter to the Supreme Court: https://notendur.hi.is/gylfason/SaNS%20-%20Gu%C3%Bobj%C3%B6rn%20J%C3%B3nsson,%20Opi%C3%Bo%20br%C3%A9f%20til%20H%C3%A6star%C3%A9ttar.pdf.

wrong, and unlawful to boot as argued by Axelsson (2011) and Gylfason (2013; 2016a).[10] The Independence Party and the Progressives that had seen their vote in parliamentary elections decline gradually from 80 percent of the total in 1931 to less than 40 percent in 2009 came to regard equal voting rights, the right of the nation to the rents from its natural resources, and other democratic reforms as a threat to their long-held privileges.

As Landau argues in this volume (Chapter 4), courts may play different roles in democratic constitution making. In the case of Iceland, however, it is not clear that the Supreme Court has any role to play, as it is not even mentioned in the 1944 constitution. The Constitutional Council bill has a new provision stating in article 101: "The Supreme Court of Iceland is the highest court of the State and it has the final power to resolve any cases brought before the courts of law." The appointment of judges has long been a source of controversy in Iceland because from 1926 to 2016 the Independence Party and the Progressives controlled the Ministry of Justice and thereby all judicial appointments for all but ten years (1944–1947, 1956–1958, 1979–1980, 1987–1988, and 2009–2013). To restrain ministerial power and increase public confidence in the courts,[11] the Constitutional Council bill stipulates that judicial appointments must be approved by the President or by a two-thirds majority in Parliament.

A second important event helps to understand the political environment at the time. Following the publication in 2010 of the nine-volume report of the Special Investigation Commission of Parliament where seven officials (including four from the Independence Party) were declared guilty of negligence in the sense of the law before the financial crash, Parliament voted to impeach only the pre-crash prime minister of the Independence Party (see Gylfason and Meuwese 2017). This made the Independence Party practically declare war on the government's weak and wavering majority in Parliament. Bent on thwarting basically all the government's efforts, including constitutional reform, the Independence Party managed to delay until October 2012 the national referendum on the new constitution that the government had wanted to coincide with the presidential election in June 2012 to secure a good turnout. Even so, turnout in the referendum October 20, 2016 was 49 percent, a respectable figure compared with earlier referenda except the special one in 1944, not least in view of the fact that the political parties, including the governing parties, did not encourage their supporters to go to the polls. The fierce opposition

---

[10] The Supreme Court justice leading the charge against the Constitutional Assembly election subsequently sued this author for libel even without being mentioned by name in the academic working paper in question and lost his case both in the District Court and the Supreme Court. He resigned from the bench before the expiry of his term and has since leveled serious criticism, perhaps better described as personal attacks, in Icelandic media against the chief justice of the Supreme Court and his wife, a law professor.

[11] In early 2016, Gallup reported that 32 percent of its respondents expressed trust in the Icelandic judicial system.

by the Independence Party and the Progressives in Parliament had sapped the energy and courage of the two government parties. Worse, several MPs representing the governing parties were known to be lukewarm in their support for the new constitution. As it turned out, 67 percent of the voters said yes to the new constitution as a whole as well as to equal voting rights per se, and 83 percent said yes to national ownership of natural resources (Gylfason 2016a). Many felt relieved that the people had scored a resounding victory against the political class.

Was this victory the first of its kind in Iceland? No, not quite. Iceland's first constitution in 1874 was a Danish product, true. Likewise, Iceland's home rule in 1904 was a Danish initiative that broke a decades-long deadlock in the Icelandic Parliament (Gíslason 1936). Again, the Act of Union between Denmark and Iceland in 1918 involved no direct popular participation. One might also be tempted to think that the 1944 constitution was a Danish product with minimal changes inserted by politicians without popular participation, but that is not the case. The first scientific opinion poll conducted and published in Iceland in 1943 showed 70 percent of respondents in favor of a popularly elected president. This poll helped the governor to reconcile politicians to the injection of a semi-presidential element into the 1944 constitution. Constitutional amendments, before and after 1944, including the fiercely contested ones of 1942 and 1959, were also made without popular participation. Does this mean that the people of Iceland feel unused to direct involvement in constitution making, encouraging political elites to take charge and resist reform? Hardly. The financial crash of 2008, sending shock waves through society, was a decisive moment in Iceland's modern history, equivalent to "constitution-making moments" in other countries. Icelanders took to the streets in 2008–2009, impelling the government to resign and call a new election. They did so again in 2016 when the prime minister's name appeared in the Panama Papers,[12] triggering his resignation within days. In the meantime, in large numbers, they contributed significantly to the drafting of the most widely crowd-sourced constitution in the history of constitution making in 2010–2011 (Landemore 2014) in an atmosphere of inclusion and ownership that probably helped secure the overwhelming support for the new constitution in the 2012 referendum.

After the referendum, opposition to the constitutional bill appeared to intensify. Several academics, including lawyers and political scientists, who had remained silent before the referendum held public meetings where they criticized aspects of the bill as if no referendum had taken place. Even the president of Iceland, uncharacteristically ambivalent up to that point, joined the chorus, claiming that constitutional reform required a consensus, thus pretending not to remember the discord produced by the constitutional amendments of 1942 and 1959 and not to understand that a constitution is a political declaration outlining rights and

---

[12] See Panama Papers, Politicians, Criminals and the Rogue Industry That Hides Their Cash. https://panamapapers.icij.org.

obligations some of which by their very nature provoke opposition (Elster 1995; 2012). After all, 33 percent of the voters had voted against the bill.

Despite these late-coming critical voices, the government, supported by a small opposition party, the Movement, a loyal supporter of the constitution, was not swayed. The Constitutional and Supervisory Committee (CSC) of the Parliament in charge of the bill had a six-to-three majority in favor of it – the same two-to-one ratio as the 67 percent to 33 percent ratio that emerged from the referendum. After the referendum, the CSC permitted only technical changes of wording and no substantive changes (Gylfason 2018). The bill was ready to be ratified by Parliament before it adjourned in preparation for the parliamentary election in the spring of 2013. However, the speaker of the Parliament failed to bring the bill to a vote, thus effectively deferring the bill to the next Parliament, which produced a new majority government by the Independence Party and the Progressives.[13] With them back in office (they had governed the country from 1995 to 2007), no progress has been made toward respecting the results of the constitutional referendum of 2012, exposing the weakness of Iceland's credentials as a democratic country.

Before adjourning in the spring of 2013, Parliament passed a temporary constitutional amendment seen by many as an attempt to make the barrier to constitutional reform even higher, and then confirmed the amendment after the 2013 election:

> Notwithstanding the provision of Paragraph 1, Article 79 it is permissible, until 30 April 2017, to amend the Constitution in the following manner: If Althing approves a legislative bill on an amendment to the Constitution with at least 2/3 of votes cast it shall be submitted to a vote of all eligible voters in the country for approval or rejection . . .. For the bill to be considered approved it needs to have received a majority of valid votes in the national referendum, though no less than 40% of all eligible voters, and it shall be confirmed by the President of the Republic and is then deemed to be valid constitutional law.

Here a simple majority in two consecutive Parliaments, the current arrangement, is replaced by a 67 percent majority in Parliament plus an implicit minimum required voter turnout of up to 80 percent in a tight election. Further, the 2013 amendment grants the president an outright veto rather than a right of appeal to the nation. By contrast, the Constitutional Council bill stipulates that the constitution can be changed by a simple majority in Parliament followed by a simple majority in a national referendum or, if only technical changes of wording are at issue, by a five-sixths majority in Parliament.

As described in Gylfason (2018), the new government appointed yet another constitutional committee consisting mostly of Members of Parliament. The committee picked out four of the 114 provisions of the bill to dilute enough to forge a

---

[13] In 2017, the former speaker was appointed chair of a new parliamentary ethics committee.

consensus within the committee. As it turned out, the committee could not agree on how to water down the provision granting Parliament the right to share sovereignty with other nations to forestall a legal or constitutional challenge to Iceland's application for EU membership pending since 2009 – and presumably still pending despite the foreign minister's attempt to withdraw it in 2015; it remains to be seen whether the European Commission accepts a minister's unilateral retraction of a membership application filed by Parliament. Here we have another example of many Icelandic parliamentarians' attitude toward democracy. They want the constitution to deprive the voters of the right to decide whether Iceland should join the EU or not. No other European constitution has ever precluded a nation's right to EU membership.

The formulation offered in the Constitutional Council bill to settle the issue is as follows (article 111):

> *Transfer of State powers.* International agreements involving a transfer of State powers to international organizations of which Iceland is a member in the interests of peace and economic co-operation are permitted. The transfer of State powers shall always be revocable. The meaning of transfer of State powers under an international agreement shall be further defined by law. If the Althing approves the ratification of an agreement that involves a transfer of State powers, the decision shall be subjected to a referendum for approval or rejection. The results of such a referendum are binding.

This article aims to make it clear that the constitution does not preclude shared sovereignty.

As to the other three provisions considered by the parliament's constitutional committee, all three are much weaker than the corresponding articles in the Constitutional Council bill (Gylfason 2018). A member of the committee, Ms. Valgerður Bjarnadóttir, who chaired the Parliament's Constitutional and Supervisory Committee in charge of the council bill during 2012–2013, stated the obvious: "The outcome [i.e., the constitutional committee's proposal] is what the reactionaries [i.e., opponents of constitutional reform] can accept."[14]

There were plans to hold a referendum on the constitutional committee's proposals but those plans did not materialize, as the committee proposal was dead on arrival. Apart from those plans it had been widely considered enough to hold the 2012 referendum and then have twofold ratification by Parliament in keeping with the 1944 constitution. A second referendum was considered unnecessary because Parliament was supposed to make only changes of wording, not of substance. Loose talk of a second referendum, like the failed proposals of the constitutional committee, came from those who were keen to thwart the results of the 2012 referendum, produce their own bill, and, perhaps, present that to a referendum. The opponents

---

[14] See http://herdubreid.is/um-stjornarskrartillogurnar/.

of constitutional reform who lost the 2012 referendum generally oppose restrictions on Parliament in any shape or form, including the president's right to refer legislation to the voters. In essence, they do not acknowledge the semi-presidential parliamentary setup of the 1944 constitution. Accordingly, if they thought they could get away with it, they might consider changing the constitution without holding a national referendum.

IV LESSONS FROM ICELAND'S EXPERIENCE THUS FAR

How could it happen that, in a country so deeply committed to liberal democracy, the Parliament has permitted itself to refuse to ratify a new constitution accepted by two-thirds of the voters in a national referendum called by Parliament itself?[15] Were there flaws inherent in the process that led to this outcome? No. Besides, the game is not over.

Some observers have asked: Was it a mistake not to involve politicians directly in the constitutional reform process? This question is often accompanied by a reference to Ireland's constitutional convention of 2012–2014 where 29 of the 100 members were Members of Parliament in Dublin, another 4 were appointed by political parties in Northern Ireland, and 66 were randomly selected citizens of Ireland in addition to a chairperson (Farrell 2014). For several reasons, such a formula was out of the question in Iceland. First, the law did not permit MPs to run for seats in the constituent assembly election in 2010 nor did the political parties field candidates in the election. Second, in keeping with the spirit of the law, the Constitutional Council avoided open consultation with MPs during its proceedings even if some Council members had informal private contacts with MPs. For example, a Council member advised some of her colleagues that the prime minister privately thought that a unanimous passage of the constitution bill in the Council would strengthen the hand of the government in getting the bill through Parliament. Third, their trust as measured by Gallup[16] had collapsed to 13 percent by early 2009; the political parties were so seriously discredited after the financial crash of 2008 that there was no interest anywhere, including in Parliament itself, in having parliamentary input into the process, not least in view of Parliament's sixty-five–year failure to accomplish a full-scale revision of the constitution as well as the government's declared intention of having a new or revised constitution drawn up by a directly elected constituent assembly.

---

[15] More precisely, the voters accepted the Constitutional Council bill as "the basis of a legislative bill for a new constitution," a formulation that the Constitutional and Supervisory Committee of Parliament in charge of the bill in 2011–2013 took to mean that Parliament could, after the referendum, adjust only the wording if needed but not the substance of the Constitutional Council bill. Opponents of the bill claim that Parliament can build whatever it pleases on the basis approved by two-thirds of the voters, an unreasonable interpretation because it assumes the right of Parliament to ignore the expressed will of the people.

[16] See www.gallup.is/nidurstodur/traust-til-stofnana/.

Possibly, even if that was not the case in Ireland, parliamentary obstruction would have been imported into the Constitutional Council proceedings rather than being reserved for the reception accorded the bill after it was delivered to Parliament. Further, it appears doubtful that a constitution bill with significant input from MPs would have garnered strong support in a national referendum, especially if the MPs had managed to weaken the key provisions of the bill on equal apportionment of seats in Parliament (one person, one vote) and national ownership of natural resources. Public support for those provisions – unlike, say, voter support for the emancipation of slaves in the United States in 1787 – was known to be strong so that diluting or discarding them was out of the question. Public confidence in the Constitutional Council was known to be high even if pollsters did not bother to report it. Public confidence in the Parliament, on the other hand, was reported to be at an all-time low (10 percent in early 2012; see Gallup 2016).

None of this means that the Constitutional Council adopted a confrontational attitude or tone toward Parliament, far from it. If the Council had had such in mind, it might have decided on a reduction of the number of seats in Parliament as advocated by the National Assembly, but the Council did not do so. This was the sole significant departure of the bill from the conclusions of the National Assembly. Further, based on sound logic and experience, the Council could have written Parliament out of the provision on constitutional revision, but it did not do so. Perhaps it was hoped that the requirement that future constitutional amendments be approved by a simple majority in Parliament as well as in a national referendum would expedite the Parliament's ratification of the bill, but that was not to be.

To quote Voltaire, did better prove to be the enemy of good? Would a less ambitious bill have been more likely to become the law of the land without delay? Again, the answer is No, because public opinion was clearly and strongly in favor of equal voting rights, public ownership of natural resources, and so on. A weaker bill might perhaps have stood a better chance of ratification by Parliament, but it would have been less likely to be accepted in the 2012 referendum. Those in Parliament who viewed the Council as encroaching on their turf would have resisted any bill proposed by the Constitutional Council. Ultimately, perhaps, the key issue was ownership. Too many MPs, especially those who still talk about the "so-called crash" and refuse to admit any political responsibility for it, did not respect the process by which Parliament put the drafting of a new constitution in other hands than theirs.

In retrospect, it is not possible to identify any flaws in the law regulating the revision process that could have reduced the likelihood of judicial or parliamentary sabotage of the project. After all, the National Assembly was convened in 2010 and did its job. The constituent assembly was also convened in 2011 despite the Supreme Court's attempt to thwart it and did its job within the time allotted to its work. A national referendum was held in 2012, even if a concerted effort was made by the opposition in Parliament to prevent it from taking place[17] and it produced an unambiguous result.

The sole problem with the process was judicial and parliamentary sabotage. Iceland is no different from other countries in that it is generally not possible, unless human rights are at stake, to protect the people against legal violations committed by the Supreme Court as occurred when the Court invalidated the constituent assembly election to undermine the project. Only if human rights are at stake can verdicts or, as in this case, administrative decisions of the Supreme Court be appealed to the European Court of Human Rights or the United Nations Human Rights Committee. In recent years, in fact, a number of Iceland's Supreme Court verdicts have been reversed by the European Court and, more-over, the Supreme Court's reversal in 2000, under visible political pressure, of its 1998 ruling that Iceland's fisheries management system is discriminatory and hence unconstitutional was declared null and void by the UNHRC, which instructed Iceland in 2007 to remove the discriminatory element from the system and award damages to the those whose rights had been violated and who had brought the case before the Court (Gylfason 2013). The government did not comply. These events help to explain why the Constitutional Council bill includes a provision that aims to strengthen judicial appointments.

In view of the 1944 constitution that requires two consecutive parliaments to ratify constitutional amendments, Parliament's sabotage of its own offspring could argu-ably only be averted by extra-constitutional means, which are rarely resorted to in democracies but not unheard of in Europe – the establishment of France's 5th republic in 1958 is a case in point (Elster 2018). In Iceland, for the new constitution to take effect, the 1944 constitution requires Parliament to ratify the new consti-tution, adjourn immediately thereafter, then hold a parliamentary election, and ratify the constitution a second time thereafter. In practice, this means holding one short parliamentary session solely to ratify the constitution in the first round as was done in 1942 and 1959. If, however, MPs prove unwilling to hold a short session, as some of them have declared, because they are eager to serve a full term even if that means jeopardizing the passage of the new constitution, they might instead consider passing a law to the effect that the constitution can be changed by Parliament's ratification followed by a national referendum and the president's signature (as stipulated by the Constitutional Council bill) and have the new constitution adopted that way. In this case, the MPs' eagerness not to risk losing their seats would require them to circumvent the 1944 constitution to ratify the new one. Indeed, this

---

[17] Some opponents of the constitution bill, on editorial pages as well as in Parliament, continue to refer to the referendum as an "irrelevant opinion poll." The President of Iceland, Mr. Ólafur R. Grímsson, did not mention the 2012 referendum in his addresses to the nation in 2013 or later. Instead, he repeated the arguments of the opponents, adding new ones that no one had raised before and Parliament, correctly, had not seen reason to ask the voters about in the referendum.

was the way the 1944 constitution was adopted extra-constitutionally. Other scenarios involving extra-constitutional passage of the new constitution can be envisaged.

An opportunity to salvage the constitution bill from the Parliament presented itself to the president of Iceland in April 2013 when Parliament adjourned without having held a vote on the bill, in violation of parliamentary procedure. When this happened President Ólafur R. Grímsson could, by the 1944 constitution, have reconvened Parliament, submitted the bill himself, and thus compelled Parliament to take a vote. A majority of MPs had declared in writing that they supported ratification so it would have been difficult for them to reverse course. Therefore, the bill would most likely have been passed. This course of action would have been extra-constitutional only in the sense that the president would, to secure ratification of the bill, have exercised authority granted him by the outgoing constitution but not by the incoming one. Thus, the President could have protected the people against the Parliament in this case as the semi-presidential character of the 1944 constitution authorizes him or her to do, but he chose not to. If Parliament persists in its refusal to ratify the will of the people, other forms of extra-constitutional ratification may have to be considered.

In view of all this, it is not fruitful to look for flaws in the constitutional reform process as an explanation for the current stalemate. A more plausible explanation is purely political. The constitution bill aims to reorganize rights and obligations by restricting the privileges of those who have long benefited from unequal voting rights, preferential access to Iceland's natural resources, and more. Those who are being asked to sit at the same table as everyone else persist in resisting those reforms even if two-thirds of the voters have accepted them. Their main instrument of obstruction is the 1944 constitution's requirement that two consecutive Parliaments must ratify the new constitution, an almost impossibly high barrier that makes constitutional reform conditional on the cooperation of those whom the reform aims to rein in.

Iceland's political culture that Parliament itself has declared wanting[18] lies at the heart of the problem. Consider the following three comparisons.

- Whereas 51 Danish names surfaced in the Panama Papers in 2016,[19] about 600 names of Icelanders came to light, including those of the prime minister, finance minister, minister of the Interior, and the wife of the president of Iceland. Denmark's population is fifteen times as large as that of Iceland.
- Whereas 15 percent of Danish respondents consider corruption to be widespread in government in Denmark, the corresponding figure for Iceland is 67 percent (Gallup 2013).

[18] Parliament resolved unanimously with all sixty-three votes cast in 2010 that "criticism of Iceland's political culture must be taken seriously and [Parliament] stresses the need for lessons to be learned from it."

[19] See n. 12.

- Whereas 88 percent of Danish respondents express confidence in the independence of Denmark's judicial system (Eurobarometer 2016), the proportion of Icelandic respondents declaring confidence in Iceland's court system is 32 percent (Gallup 2016).

In short, the evidence seems to suggest that the reason for the current constitutional impasse in Iceland can be found in Iceland's deficient political culture rather than in possible design flaws illuminated by constitutional theory and international experience. The new constitution aims in various ways to sanitize the country's political culture.

If Iceland's constitutional impasse continues it may have serious consequences for democracy in Iceland, at a time when democracy is under stress in Europe and the Americas to the point where Freedom House has recently demoted the United States from its long-held top rank.[20] The United States was practically the world's sole democracy until 1850 when Europe was swept by revolutions that led to the gradual emergence of democracy. Even so, in 1943, there were only five democracies in Europe: The United Kingdom, Ireland, Iceland, Sweden, and Switzerland. From 1945 to 2000 the number of democracies around the world rose to ninety, almost a half of all states, but thereafter the spread of democracy was halted again (Diamond 2015). Like Russia and Turkey, even Hungary and Poland, fully fledged members of the European Union, show new signs of dwindling respect for democracy and human rights.

Against this international background, the Icelandic Parliament's failure to ratify the new constitution comes at a particularly ill-chosen time, permitting politicians to hide behind political disarray abroad and to use the challenges confronting democracy elsewhere as an unspoken excuse for disrespecting democracy in Iceland. In view of their democratic tradition, the people of Iceland should be especially alert that now is not a good time to digress from the path of democracy. With democracy under stress, Parliament has a special responsibility to do the right thing by showing the rest of the world that when, after the crash of 2008, the people of Iceland produced perhaps the most democratic, most inclusive constitution ever made anywhere, they really meant what they did. Iceland needs to send the rest of the world an uplifting signal about democracy, a signal that would be welcomed by advocates of democracy and human rights everywhere. Parliament has neglected to send that message for almost six years now, thus inviting the rest of the world to wonder why.

Some of those who compile common indices of democracy such as the one from Freedom House as well as the Polity2 index from the Polity IV Project[21] have begun to lower Iceland's democracy scores, and they may lower them further if the impasse

[20] Source: Freedom House. https://freedomhouse.org/report/freedom-world/freedom-world-2016.
[21] See www.systemicpeace.org/polityproject.html.

persists. Or how would they have reacted if the British Parliament had decided to ignore the results of the Brexit referendum in 2016 on the grounds that it was only advisory? – a comparable case.

While democracy indicators have thus far deteriorated only slightly, measures of other aspects of social capital such as trust and the absence of corruption paint a much less flattering picture. According to the World Values Survey (Medrano 2015), Iceland's interpersonal trust scores are much lower than in other Nordic countries and were lower already before 2008, suggesting that low trust may have been a contributor to as well as a consequence of the crash (Gylfason 2015). Iceland's scores of trust in institutions (Parliament, judicial system, banks, etc.) are also lower than in the rest of the Nordic region and fell sharply after 2008. For example, according to Gallup, trust in Parliament fell from 42 percent in 2008 to 10 percent in 2012 and 17 percent in 2016 just before the outbreak of the Panama Papers scandal.[22] Gallup also reports that 67 percent of its Icelandic respondents in 2012 considered political corruption to be widespread in their government compared with 14 percent in Sweden and 15 percent in Denmark. There is a danger that the erosion of trust, amplified by the perception of political corruption, may further undermine democracy in Iceland. The Parliament's failure to enact the new constitution exacerbates such concerns. This failure was almost surely instrumental in reducing the number of parliamentary seats of the Social Democrats, who launched the constitutional reform project in 2009 only to leave it in a state of suspension in 2013, from twenty out of sixty-three in 2009 to three seats in 2016 and seven in 2017. This also helps explain the increase in the number of seats won by the Pirates, a new party that advocates the enactment of the new constitution, from three in 2013 to ten in 2016 and six in 2017.

V CONCLUDING REMARKS

In many ways, for reasons of history, Iceland stands on the shoulders of Denmark. Yet, for reasons that have a lot to do with the ways in which Iceland differs from Denmark, notably deep political dissent and dysfunction (but not necessarily small size; see Gylfason 2009), Iceland's declaration of independence in 1944 and the consequent adoption of a revised constitution set Iceland on a new path.

Denmark, like Norway and Sweden, is a constitutional hereditary monarchy under purely parliamentary democracy where the monarch almost exclusively performs a ceremonial role. Iceland, on the other hand, like Finland, by deciding to become "a Republic with a parliamentary government" (article 1) as well as to have a popularly elected president, adopted a semi-presidential form of parliamentary democracy. Iceland's president performs more than a merely ceremonial role. Iceland's first president, Mr. Sveinn Björnsson, in his preceding role as governor,

---

[22] Source: Gallup. www.gallup.is/nidurstodur/traust-til-stofnana/.

appointed an extra-parliamentary government in 1942 against the opposition of a dysfunctional Parliament. Iceland's fifth president, Mr. Ólafur R. Grímsson, invoked his right to withhold presidential assent on three occasions, in 2004, 2010, and 2011, triggering national referenda in 2010 and 2011.

Iceland's popularly elected President can also be seen to have constitutional authority to do the other things that the constitution from 1944 states that he or she can do without being bound by the accepted interpretation of corresponding clauses in Denmark's constitution. The difference is twofold. First, Iceland's president is elected by the people and is, therefore, unconstrained by the standard interpretation of the Danish constitution fit for a hereditary monarch. Second, the president of Iceland has already invoked some of the rights granted to him in Iceland's 1944 constitution. Even so, the lack of clarity in this regard, inherited from Denmark, is a demonstrable flaw in Iceland's 1944 constitution, a flaw that has not created any difficulties in Denmark to date and that the Constitutional Council bill from 2011, accepted in the national referendum of 2012, aims to fix among many others.

This flaw has played into the hands of parliamentary elites that have managed to exploit the Danish provision from 1849 requiring parliamentary consent, twice, to any constitutional change. To protect their own interests, Iceland's parliamentary elites use a Danish monarch's mid-nineteenth-century provision on the ratification of constitutional change as a shield against the people of Iceland who seek a new and better constitution fit for the modern age. Many Icelandic politicians still refuse to openly acknowledge the semi-presidential essence of Iceland's constitution because they view it, correctly, as an infringement of their position and power. Therefore, many of them feel that they must resist the people's right to modernize the constitution.

Will these flaws be fixed in due course? No democracy has ever before seen its Supreme Court nullify a national election, let alone illegally, or its Parliament disrespect the results of a constitutional referendum. If Parliament does not reverse course, Iceland will be in trouble, deep trouble, with its standing among democratic Nordic nations thrown into doubt.

REFERENCES

Axelsson, Reynir. 2011. "Comments on the Decision of the Supreme Court to Invalidate the Election to the Constitutional Assembly." http://stjornarskrarfelagid.is/wp-content/uploads/2011/07/Article_by_Reynir_Axelsson.pdf.
Balinski, Michel, and Rida Laraki. 2010. *Majority Judgment: Measuring, Ranking, and Electing.* Cambridge, MA: MIT Press.
Björnsson, Sveinn. 1949. "Nýársávarp til þjóðarinnar" (New Year's Address to the Nation).
Diamond, Larry. 2015. "Facing Up to the Democratic Recession." *Journal of Democracy* 26(7): 141–155.
Duverger, Maurice. 1980. "A New Political System Model: Semi-Presidential Government." *European Journal of Political Research* 8(2): 165–187.

Elkins, Zachary, Tom Ginsburg, and James Melton. 2012. "A Review of Iceland's Draft Constitution."

Elster, Jon. 1995. "Forces and Mechanisms in the Constitution-Making Process." *Duke Law Journal* 45(2): 364–396.

2012. "Constitution-Making and Violence." *Journal of Legal Analysis* 4(1): 7–39.

2018. "The Political Psychology of Constitution Making" in *Constituent Assemblies.* Jon Elster, Roberto Gargarella, Vatsal Naresh, and Bjørn Erik Rasch (eds.) Cambridge: Cambridge University Press.

Eurobarometer. 2016. "The 2016 EU Justice Scoreboard." Fig. 44: Perceived independence of courts and judges among the general public. http://ec.europa.eu/justice/effective-justice/files/justice_scoreboard_2016_selected_graphs_en.pdf.

Farrell, David. 2014. "The 2013 Irish Constitutional Convention: A Bold Step or a Damp Squib?" in *Comparative Reflections on 75 Years of the Irish Constitution.* John O'Dowd and Giuseppe Ferrari (eds.) Dublin: Clarus Press.

Fishkin, James. 2009. *When the People Speak: Deliberative Democracy and Public Consultation.* Oxford: Oxford University Press.

Gallup. 2013. "Government Corruption Viewed As Pervasive Worldwide" by Jan Sonnenschein and Julie Ray. www.gallup.com/poll/165476/government-corruption-viewed-pervasive-worldwide.aspx.

2016. Traust til stofnana (Trust in Institutions). www.gallup.is/traust.

Gíslason, Thorsteinn. 1936. *Þættir úr stjórnmálasögu Íslands 1896–1918* (Aspects of the Political History of Iceland 1896–1918). Reykjavík: Steindórsprent.

Gylfason, Thorvaldur. 2009. "Is Iceland Too Small?" *VoxEU,* August 19. http://voxeu.org/article/iceland-too-small.

2013. "From Collapse to Constitution: The Case of Iceland" in *Public Debt, Global Governance and Economic Dynamism.* Luigi Paganetto (ed.) Milan: Springer, 379–417.

2015. "Social Capital, Inequality, and Economic Crisis." *Challenge* 58(4): 326–342.

2016a. "Constitution on Ice" in *Iceland's Financial Crisis: The Politics of Blame, Protest, and Reconstruction.* Valur Ingimundarson, Philipe Urfalino, and Irma Erlingsdóttir (eds.) London: Routledge, 203–219.

2016b. "Iceland's New Constitution Is Not Solely a Local Concern." *Challenge* 59(6): 480–490.

2018. "Chain of Legitimacy: Constitution Making in Iceland" in *Constituent Assemblies.* Jon Elster, Roberto Gargarella, Vatsal Naresh, and Bjørn Erik Rasch (eds.) Cambridge: Cambridge University Press, 161–185.

Gylfason, Thorvaldur, and Anne Meuwese. 2017. "Digital Tools and the Derailment of Iceland's New Constitution" in *Digital Democracy in a Globalized World.* Corien Prins, Peter Lindseth, Monica Guisse, and Colette Cuijpers (eds.) London: Edward Elgar, 249–273.

Helgason, Thorkell. 2014. "Umbætur á ákvæðum um úthlutun þingsæta." (Improvements in the Apportionment of Parliamentary Seats in Iceland) *Stjórnmál og stjórnsýsla* (Icelandic Review of Politics and Administration) 10(2): 1–28.

Jóhannesson, Guðni Th. 2012. "Tjaldað til einnar nætur. Uppruni bráðabirgðastjórnarskrárinnar." (The Origins and Provisional Nature of Iceland's 1944 Constitution) *Stjórnmál og stjórnsýsla* (Icelandic Review of Politics and Administration) 7(1): 61–72.

Kristjánsson, Svanur. 2011. "Varð þjóðþingið að þjófþingi? Lýðræðið og kvótakerfið 1983." (Did Parliament Become Kleptocratic? Democracy and the Quota System 1983) *Skírnir, Journal of the Icelandic Literary Society* 2(Fall): 261–290.

2012. "Frá nýsköpun lýðræðis til óhefts flokkavalds: Fjórir forsetar Íslands 1944–1996." (From the Creation of Democracy to Unfettered Political Party Power: Four Presidents of Iceland, 1944–1996) *Skírnir, Journal of the Icelandic Literary Society* 1(Spring): 50–97.

Landemore, Hélène. 2012. *Democratic Reason: Politics, Collective Intelligence, and the Rule of the Many.* Princeton: Princeton University Press.

2014. "Inclusive Constitution-Making: The Icelandic Experiment." *Journal of Political Philosophy* 23(2): 166–191.

Medrano, Jaime Díez. 2015. "Interpersonal trust." World Values Survey. www.jdsurvey.net/jds/jdsurveyMaps.jsp?Idioma=I&SeccionTexto=0404&NOID=104.

Meuwese, Anne C. M. 2013. "Popular Constitution-Making. The Case of Iceland" in *The Social and Political Foundations of Constitutions.* Denis J. Galligan and Mila Versteeg (eds.) Cambridge: Cambridge University Press, 469–496.

Nordal, Salvör. 2011. "Umboð Stjórnlagaráðs." (The Mandate of the Constitutional Council) *Skírnir, Journal of the Icelandic Literary Society* Spring: 182–192.

Page, Scott E. 2008. *The Difference: How the Power of Diversity Creates Better Groups, Firms, Schools, and Societies.* New ed. Princeton: Princeton University Press.

Thorláksson, Indridi H. 2015. "Veiðigjöld 2015. Annar hluti" (Fishing Fees 2015. Part Two).

Index

Printed by Printforce, United Kingdom